Frank Arjava Petter

THIS IS
REIKI

TRANSFORMATION OF BODY, MIND AND SOUL
FROM THE ORIGINS TO THE PRACTICE

Translated by Frank Arjava Petter

T0170107

LOTUS PRESS
SHANGRI-LA

Important Note

The information presented in this book has been carefully researched and passed on to our best knowledge and conscience. Despite this fact, neither the author nor the publisher assume any type of liability for presumed or actual damages of any kind that might result from the direct or indirect application or use of the statements in this book.

The information in this book is solely intended for interested readers and educational purposes and should in no way be understood as diagnostic or therapeutic instructions in the medical sense. If you suspect the existence of an illness, we definitely recommend that you see a physician or healing practitioner and expressly discourage you from diagnosing and treating yourself.

1st English edition 2012
© by Lotus Press
Box 325, Twin Lakes, WI 53181, USA
www.lotuspress.com
lotuspress@lotuspress.com
The Shangri-La series is published in cooperation
with Windpferd Verlagsgesellschaft mbH, Germany
© 2009 by Windpferd Verlagsgesellschaft mbH, Oberstdorf, Germany
All rights reserved
Translated by Frank Arjava Petter
Edited by Karen Perry
Cover design: Peter Krafft, Designagentur, Bad Krozingen, Germany
The cover picture shows the family crest of the Usuis
Layout: Marx Grafik & ArtWork
ISBN: 978-0-9409-8501-8
Library of Congress Control Number: 2012932663
Printed in USA

Dedication

Dedicated to Chetna Mami Kobayashi who shared my life and path with
me for many years. Without you nothing would be as it is, and for this
I thank you, even though we go our separate ways now.

In the sacred memory of Tsutomu Oishi

What does Reiki mean to you?—Love.

—CHYOKO SENSEI—

Table of Contents

Credits

Countless people have worked on this book with me; some did this consciously while others did not. All my teachers and students, all my readers, and all of those who were not of my opinion have contributed to this work. I would like to take the opportunity to thank some of them in person, all the others I do thank in my heart.

I Thank:

My mother, Rosemarie Petter, who has been supporting me in everything I do from the day I was born. My father, Hans Georg Petter, who guides me from above. My spiritual teacher, Osho, for my spiritual birth. My brother, Raj Martin Petter, for igniting my interest in Reiki and many other good subjects. Chetna Mami Kobayashi, my ex-wife. Shizuko Akimoto, who wove the first contacts to the Usui Reiki Ryoho Gakkai. Tsutomu Oishi, for his trust, and the wonderful picture of Usui Sensei on page 64. Fumio Ogawa, for his generosity to share his precious time and knowledge with us. Jikiden Reiki Shihan Masaki Nishina, for presenting me with Gizo Tomabechi's out of print book. Walter Lübeck, who placed me on the Reiki map many years ago. William Lee Rand, for his support in the difficult early days. Ageh and Unmesha Popat-Guhl for thirty years of friendship and the Reiki Teacher's training in the Takata lineage. Chiyoko Yamaguchi for accepting me as her first non-Japanese student. Tadao Yamaguchi, for his trust and friendship, for the fruitful collaboration and his relentless effort researching the roots and practice of Reiki. Ikuko Hirota, Hideko Teranaka and Hiroko Arakawa for their dedicated efforts in the Jikiden Reiki Institute. Also a special thanks to Hiroko Arakawa for the wonderful handwritten kanji in this book. Mari Hall for her love and friendship and her encouragement with my writing. You were the first who sent me positive feedback when "Reiki Fire" was published.

Akiko Sato, for the translation of the original Japanese texts and the many hours of contemplating and researching their deepest meaning.

Silke Kleemann, for the creative input and the professional editing of the original German version of the book. Karen Perry, my editor for her friendship and her magic to make my German-English intelligible.

My German publisher, Monika and Wolfgang Jünemann, who have supported me over the years with all their heart, mind and action. The publisher's team for having given life to this dream-project.

Thank you to the Zorba the Buddha café in Eressos, Lesvos Island to be my temporary "office" during the writing process.

And most of all I thank my wife, Georgia Bhakti Mouriki, my daughter, Christina, and my son, Alexis, that they came into my life and that they endured me during the writing/production and translation of this book, when I had only one thing in mind …

Preface

Dear Reader,

This book is my love song to Reiki.

Reiki has changed my life and formed it anew. This new form is the formless that gives everyone and everything in existence its rightful place.

In my first books, I concentrated on research and questioning. I wanted to light up Reiki from all sides and bring it into correct cultural and contemporary light/view. A thorn in my heart continuously reminded me: you have to put the history right to get the misunderstandings out of the way and free Reiki of its excess baggage before it trips over itself.

Over the years, I have let go of more and more excess baggage and in the end only love remained. I hope that this love may shine in your heart in the following pages. In the different parts of this book I would like to share with you my experiences and insights from eighteen years of working with Reiki. In this time, my understanding of what Reiki is and how it works has changed considerably. During practice and the exchange with my fellow travelers and students it came to fruition and ripened.

During the introduction I would like to let you know my actual level of knowledge—Reiki as soul energy that is prevalent in everything and everyone and helps us on our path to simplicity and supports the miracle of seeing our true nature. Some of the key words of Japanese terms and concepts that we keep encountering in Reiki shall be described in detail.

The first part of the book is about Reiki history. All proven historical information about Reiki and its founding fathers are collected here for the first time in a single book. Besides that, you will read about Reiki practitioners with lifelong experiences—my beloved teacher, Chiyoko Yamaguchi, as well as the previous President of the Usui Reiki Ryoho Gakkai, Koyama sensei, Ogawa sensei, and Mr. Oishi. I am grateful for the fact that you, dear Reader, are now able to learn from their knowledge just as I have had the privilege of learning. For this reason, you will find the direct transcripts of my interviews with Chiyoko Yamaguchi, Ogawa sensei, as well as excerpts from Koyama sensei's teaching handbook appendix.

In the second part, I take you on a journey to the sacred Reiki sites in Japan, to Mt. Kurama in Kyoto, to the memorial of Usui sensei at the Saihoji temple in Tokyo, as well as to Usui sensei's birth village, Taniai …

The Buddhist background of Reiki and its subsequent development will be discussed in part three. Part four is dedicated to the practical aspects of

Reiki. In it you are introduced to the Japanese way of working with Reiki; special attention is given to the Byosen- the heart of Reiki and the key for a successful Reiki treatment.

And now I 'd like to say a word to you, dear reader. You are the one who carries the light of Reiki out into the world. You are Reiki. I hope that you will find inspiration in the following pages, and that you will be able to use some of what is written here with your family, your friends and your clients.

With love from Greece, your friend, Frank Arjava Petter

Introduction

Reiki will conquer the world, and heal not only its inhabitants but also the earth itself; thus it is written on Usui Sensei's memorial stone at the Saihoji cemetery in Tokyo. This prophecy is one of the very few prognoses for the future known to me that actually has come true. Reiki, in its different forms, is being practiced in millions of human hearts, in all countries of the world. The reason for this is due to a simple matter of fact. Usui Sensei explains: "Every Being that has had life breathed into (that God has bestowed a soul upon) can perform Reiki." I would like to examine this proposition a little further. In Usui's days, the Japanese word Reiki meant "soul energy". The Japanese assume that God provides every human with a soul on his path. This soul resides for the time of this incarnation within the head of the human.

After the death of the physical body, this soul is set free within 49 days and goes "home" then. After some time, this same soul reincarnates in a new body, up for the next ride on the merry-go-round.

This soul, or rather the soul energy, is being reactivated during a Reiki attunement, and the one being attuned to Reiki remembers his original nature, his essential Being. The knowledge of the soul does not belong to a specific religion or denomination, rather this notion is being found within all the cultures of the world. And this is why Reiki can be practiced by all and everyone.

Even though Reiki does not presume any specific philosophy or religion, it did grow out of the spirit of Japanese culture and language. In order to understand Reiki within this context, I would like to provide you with some insights into the most important principles of Reiki.

The Term Reiki

The Japanese word Reiki consists of two *kanji* (Chinese characters). These characters were introduced into Japan from China, via Korea, in the 4th century. In the Shinto cosmology,

Photo 1: The Reiki Kanji from the inscription on the Usui Memorial, Saihoji Temple, Tokyo

birds—the heralds of the Gods—are associated with the *kanji*. As legend has it, the birds left their tracks on the beach, and the humans copied these footprints that were regarded as messages from the Gods.

Japanese *kanji* may mean an idea, a concept, a thing, or a sound. Simple *kanji* are images derived from nature. The *kanji* for mountain or river, for example, depict what they mean precisely. With concepts, however, it becomes more complex. They are put together by combining several components, so that often the original images cannot be recognized anymore.

There are about 5000 Japanese *kanji* in comparison with almost 50,000 in Chinese writing. In order to get by in ordinary life, about 1500-2000 *kanji* will do.

The original meaning of the characters is an issue about which many scholars argue. Below I will present you with some of the interpretations that have appeared as the most obvious to my understanding.

The Character for Rei

The first character, Rei, can be divided into three parts. The first one means "ame", rain. Japan is a volcanic country. Volcanic ash combined with rain produce a fertile soil. Therefore, rain stands for fertility, on the one hand, and secondly, for the blessings coming from the cosmos down to earth. In the Shinto tradition, Japan's ancient religion, rain is connected to several deities. The most important being *Ame no Minakanushi no Mikito* and *Ame no Shihomimino Mikito*, who is the son of the highest goddess, *Amaterasu Omikami* (the Divine Mother, who illuminates the skies).

The character "ame" is written as follows:

The second dividable character means "utsuwa". The word *utsuwa* means container, or, metaphorically speaking, human body, the vessel for the soul.

When a complex concept is being written as a *kanji*, the characters it consists of may have to be simplified for better memorization. The simplified form of *utsuwa* that makes a part of the *kanji Rei*, looks like the following:

These three squares could be interpreted in a different way. One square stands for mouth, two of them for conversation/communication and three of them for prayer. In its original form *utsuwa* looks like this: 器

The third part stands for "miko" and means female medium, sorceress, or shaman (photo 2). A *miko* is a woman who understands the voice of the Gods. She is able to communicate with the souls of the dead, and in a state of trance she serves as a mediator between the gods and the humans. All Japanese Reiki sources talk about the aim for the practitioner to become like a *miko*. He/she is to rely on the sky and let himself be guided by the gods. Koyama Sensei from the Usui Reiki Ryoho Gakkai emphasized this again and again.

Within the character for *Rei* the character for *miko* is also simplified. The original form of *miko* looks like this: 巫女

Photo 2: Miko at the Sengen Shrine in Shizuoka City

The complete character for *Rei* looks like this and means soul (Jap. *tamashi*).

The Character for Ki

This character can also be divided into two components.

The first one is "kigamae" or "yuge". This word means steam or ether. In general, the ether is considered to be the vehicle for subtle matter.

The second character means "kome", rice. In Southeast Asia, rice is the staple food. The character for rice can be interpreted in different ways. Some linguists state that it has been derived from the image of boiling rice and the rising steam. Others suggest that it is a comprehensible image of a rice ear. And still others claim that it stands for the number 88, because it takes 88 days for a grain of rice to proceed from the seed to the dining table.

The complete kanji Ki looks like this and means energy:

On the following pages I will use the term Reiki solely, since Reiki energy would be a tautology: soul energy-energy. On page 15 you will find the extensive stroke order for Rei and Ki.

Exercise: Take half an hour. Write down the character for Reiki. I suggest that you follow the stroke order for best results. Begin with the character for Rei and do it 30-50 times. Then write down the character for Ki in the same way. After that, write down both characters one below the other.

In the beginning, it helps to write on lined paper, with a thick pen and not too big. This way the mistakes appear less noticeable! If you have a brush and ink available, and maybe even a teacher of calligraphy, it will work all the better.

In Usui Sensei`s day, the term Reiki meant soul energy or spirit energy. Within a different context though, it could mean atmosphere, whim, occult or spooky energy. In order to avoid this misunderstanding in Japan, Reiki was and is written today sometimes in Roman letters, or in Katakana (phonetic Japanese alphabet).

Nowadays, the word Rei is associated immediately with the meaning of ghost, and a short explanation is necessary if you want to go in the right direction in a conversation with someone from Japan who does not know Reiki.

Shin Shin Kaizen Usui Reiki Ryoho

心身改善臼井靈氣療法

Usui Sensei named the method he had given birth to Shin Shin Kaizen Usui Reiki Ryoho. This translates into: "For the improvement of body and

Photo 3: The characters for Rei and Ki to practice stroke by stroke

spirit/soul Usui soul energy healing system". And the society he founded was called Shin Shin Kaizen Usui Reiki Ryoho Gakkai. Since this name is a little long, it has been abridged over time in Japan as well as worldwide. First it became Usui Reiki Ryoho; today, most of us simply call it "Reiki".

As I mentioned before, our soul is a guest in the human body for the duration of this incarnation. In the printed interview with Usui Sensei (page 65 ff.), he answers the question "… is Reiki a psychic healing method?" He says: "Yes, you could call it one kind of psychic healing method, but you could also call it physical therapy. One may say as well, that Reiki was a physical healing method, because the whole body of the practitioner radiates light and energy." If we assume that past, present and future are being healed simultaneously through the soul aspect, this statement makes absolute sense. Therefore, Reiki is not designed to banish a little ailment, rather it is a spiritual path that heals the practitioner and his client holistically.

Gokai: The Five Reiki Principles

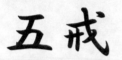 Now I would like to introduce you to the Principles of Reiki, which laid the foundation for the practice. These rules for life constitute the ethical basis for the work with Reiki, and at the same time they work as a kind of barometer for the practitioner. They are a kotodama (see page 24) and should be spoken in the original version.

All the versions of the Principles known to me (scrolls/documents), are headlined as follows:

Shoufuku no hihoo, manbyo no reiyaku

This headline explains to us the purpose of the Principles and what possible results you can expect, if you live by them! The words translate into "The mysterious art of inviting happiness, the spiritual medicine for all diseases."

If you practice Reiki wholeheartedly, if you follow the Principles and surrender to the will of the universe, you will become happy consequently. And, this happiness radiates from your heart into your environment. Thus, you will make yourself and others happy.

From Usui Sensei`s perspective all diseases of the body and the spirit, as well as karmic diseases, can be resolved with the help of Reiki. That does not necessarily mean that these diseases will be healed on the physical level in this lifetime, but rather that they will have fulfilled their sense and purpose

16

in this lifetime and will not be needed anymore when the soul takes incarnation the next time.

Therefore, the Principles are the path towards happiness on one hand, as well as a precise map of your own spiritual development. Whenever you take a look at the map, you will know exactly where you are. You will know what needs to be worked on, and you will see how you advance on the path. If you are searching for a teacher, look first in this direction. If he walks his talk, he will be able to teach you something of value.

Kyo dake wa: Today only
This reference to the here and now will make your daily life easier. Be present with everything you do and don't do, and carry it out with love in your heart. Whether in a bar or in a church, let yourself be guided by your heart and see the Divine in everyone and everything you meet on your way.

1. *Ikaru-na*: Do not be angry
Anger poisons body and soul and does no good for you, or to your environment, in most cases. The Japanese suffix –na, which is also part of the second precept, does by no means imply a moral judgment. It is being spoken from a meta-position and means that the one who offers the advice has a clearer perspective than yourself. He sees through the limitations, thus offering wise counsel to you: Don't be angry!

2. *Shinpai suna:* Do not worry
The second poison for body and spirit is worry. Again, we are advised to let go of worries. Because whatever happens does not depend on our worries. Whatever happens, happens. You might as well let go of your worries, rely on God and Reiki and let yourself be guided.

3. *Kansha shite*: Be grateful
Gratitude is the antidote for anger and worry. Whenever those two come visit you, remember gratitude. Now, in this very moment, while you are reading these lines, be grateful, and the heart becomes transformed. Transformation does not take time, transformation happens always here and now.

4. *Gyo o hage me*: Fulfill your duties (in the sense of: pursue your responsibilities, do the right thing).
The Japanese word Gyo could also be translated into karma or religious practice. In this case though, it carries a rather worldly meaning. Do what life asks of you—because everything that happens in your life is you.

5. *Hito ni shinsetsu ni*: Be good (kind, loving, compassionate) to your fellow men.

This is not only about helping the elderly cross the street, but also about ending the suffering of humanity. The historical Buddha is said to have declared that all life is suffering. That was not meant as a fatalistic statement. What he meant by that was that the human has distanced himself from his true nature, no longer knows who he is, and therefore, suffers.

With a Reiki treatment or attunement, you show him the way back home to his essence. That is the meaning of *shinsetsu*, true compassion that will show the way to the recipient in this and the following lifetimes. Once awake, the human will never go back to sleep again completely … Therefore, avoid doing harm to yourself and others from now on.

Usui Sensei also instructed us as to what to do with the written Principles:

Asa yuu gassho shite, kokoro ni nenji, kuchi ni tonaeyo:

Sit in the gassho-posture in the morning and in the evening and repeat these words aloud and in your heart.

Exercise: Recite the Principles aloud daily. Take five minutes of time and sit down comfortably. Fold your hands in the gassho-position in front of the heart. Pay attention to what happens with your hands while reciting. You are likely to feel Reiki in your hands, in your heart, or maybe also in your crown chakra, as soon as you begin to speak.

If you happen to have the gokai at hand in written form, hang them on the wall of your office. Hayashi Sensei and Chiyoko Yamaguchi would always do that (also see photo 41, Hayashi Sensei in Hawaii with gokai in the background).

It is recommended that the teacher or the practitioner sit with his back towards the gokai, thus letting him be supported energetically while working. The recipient is supposed to lay down with his head in the direction of the gokai, in order to be energized by them.

Photo 4: The author with Chiyoko Sensei sitting in front of Gokai Scroll

18

It is said that in the early days of his work, Usui Sensei was focused on healing physical diseases. But, since the soul resides within the body, it is possible to work more successfully when addressing the soul directly. The way to do that is with the help of the gokai. So let us recite the Principles together. The rest of the work is up to you. Integrate the gokai into your life, embody them. *Kyo dake wa …*

Japanese Keywords in Reiki

It is not necessarily possible to check upon Japanese words in the Japanese dictionary because they may change their meaning in their specific context. The following words have been explained to me by Ogawa Sensei, Koyama Sensei, Chiyoko Sensei, and Tadao Sensei. Still, dictionaries are a good resource, and while working I have the following dictionaries and encyclopedias:

1. My favorite source, Kenkyusha's New English Japanese dictionary.
2. English Japanese dictionary, Random House.
3. Kodansha Kanji Learner Dictionary
4. Tuttle Kanji Dictionary
5. Kenkyusha Romaji Doshi Kai
6. P.G. O'Neill Essential Kanji
7. English-Buddhist Japanese Dictionary
8. Bunshodo, A Glossary of Zen Terms
9. Dictionary of Chinese Buddhist Terms

Ki

The Japanese term Ki originates from China. Ki is an East Asian life-philosophy, and the description could fill books. For this reason, I would like to explain the term and its various forms in daily Japanese life to help you understand that this is not a far-out concept but something rooted in daily life.

Ki means energy. Even though this energy is subtle, it is common knowledge to every Japanese person and every one of us.

The Japanese word for happy, content and in good spirits is: Genki; Gen means original, original energy.

The word for sick or sickness is Byoki: Byo means sick, sick energy.

The word for negative energy is Jaki.

The word for mood is Kibun. If the mood is good, it is Kibun ga ii (good); if the mood is bad, you say Kibun ga warui (bad).

The word for skill or ability is Kishitsu; character is Kisho.

Motivation is Kiryoku.

To relax or to let go is Kiraku.

If someone is powerful we say about him that Ki ga aru or tsuyoi ki ga aru which says he has strong energy. If he is weak, you say Ki ga nai or yowai ki ga aru, meaning he has no or weak energy.

As you see, energy is tangible and in the fourth and practical part of the book I want to show you how you can feel or perceive and use this energy more effectively. Everything is energy, and, therefore, reacts positively to energy/Reiki; from the kidneys to your kids' toys.

Anjin Ryumei

Anjin Ryumei, anshin ritsumei or anjin ritsumyo is originally a Confucian concept that was adapted by Japanese Buddhist. It literally means to accept your own destiny/fate. In Zen Buddhism it means to have found absolute inner peace and to live in harmony with the ultimate reality. In Jodo Buddhism it means a mind that is content and has found peace. Anjin Ryumei is seen as Enlightenment in this tradition.

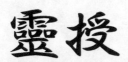

Reiju

Literally, granting the soul. Reiju is a ritual in which the student is reminded of his original state of being by his teacher (the oneness with the cosmos). From this moment on, the inherent soul energy is activated and flows through all the cells of the initiate, mainly through the hands, feet, breath and eyes. But it flows through all the cells. If you have already been initiated into Reiki, you can feel that now. Please close your eyes and take a few deep breaths, imagine that you breathe in the air and energy through all the cells of your body. While breathing out, feel how this process reverses. You and the Universe are One …

In principal, one Reiju would be sufficient to activate this soul power. However, we are too used to our sleepy state of mind. Therefore, this ritual is traditionally repeated again and again. Chiyoko sensei taught that one Reiju a month would be helpful. In the traditional schools, so-called Reiju Kai were held for those who were already initiated into Reiki. Koyama sensei suggested that the receiver should sit in the gassho position while they looked at their fingertips through their closed eyelids. The hands should be held in such a way that the out-breath touches the fingertips. The students were asked to concentrate all of their awareness to their fingertips. This devotional concentration helps to let go of the ego and transforms the receiver. So doing, he becomes aware of his soul and actually sees it in front of his inner eye. The soul moves and when you follow this movement, the body and mind become light and relaxed. To learn this you need practice.

For this reason, Reiju is received again and again. Reiki was born out of an Enlightenment experience and aims back at this. Usui sensei was ready to die for this experience and we too should work on ourselves with the same sincerity and devotion.

Maybe you doubt whether an initiation is really necessary. In theory, you are right. If you are consciously connected to the cosmic forces and are at one with the cosmos, you don't need initiation. But who could say that of himself in every moment of life.

療法 Ryoho (Healing Method)

As I will explain later in more detail, there were many alternative-healing methods like chiropractic, psychic healing, hypnotherapy, and so on in Usui's day, these were called Ryoho.

靈法 Reiho (Spiritual Method)

On the Usui Memorial in Tokyo, Reiki is described as the Rciho Method. But that does not mean that Reiki used to be called Reiho in the past. Reiho is an umbrella term.

Shoden, Okuden, Shinpiden (Shihan-Kaku, Shihan)

As everything that comes from Japan, Reiki is very well structured. The degrees are similar to those used in the Japanese martial arts and are being similarly used. Usui Sensei taught three degrees in Reiki. Ogawa Sensei told us that Usui Sensei used to ask his students to sit in front of him with their hands held in the gassho position. Then, he touched their hands to estimate their energy level. If their energy level was low, the student had to practice perception exercises before he was permitted to receive his reiju. This system has been discontinued and everyone is permitted to receive reiju right away.

初傳 Shoden

The word shoden is made up of two words. Sho means beginner and den means teaching or level. Shoden was again divided into teaching units. Each teaching unit took one day, but this division was only created for additional structure. Those teaching units were always taught as a package. Usui Sensei divided Shoden into roku to (6) go to (5) yon to (4) and san to (3). The lowest teaching unit was roku to, the sixth level. The Reiki workshops were called Reiju Kai (Initiation Meeting) and they took five days. It was expected that a student took part in several of these meetings if he wanted to advance to a higher level. The reason for the repetitions was not that one time was not enough, but that Reiki was and is seen as a way of life that takes dedication and a daily effort.

Later, in Hayashi Sensei's time, Shoden was divided into three teaching units; Chiyoko Sensei taught like her teacher.

奥傳 Okuden

Usui Sensei taught a student Okuden if he had brought good results with Shoden. Practically speaking this meant that one had to be able to feel the byosen, to understand it and to let it guide oneself throughout the treatment or the series of treatments. After you have read the chapter on byosen, you will understand that this process may take some time …

Okuden was divided into two parts, Okuden Zenki and Okuden Koki (first part and second part). Once again, this subdivision was meant as a teaching unit and each teaching unit was taught in one day.

Both Hayashi Sensei and Chiyoko Sensei taught Okuden in two days. However, they taught both Shoden and Okuden together in a five-day block. I was told that Hayashi Sensei did that when he taught outside of his Dojo (Training center) in Tokyo, so students who lived in far away places did not have to wait forever to learn the next level. He said that he could teach anyone the basics of the art of byosen in three days, and thus they were able to continue with Okuden right after that. As I said earlier, it was expected that students repeated the workshops time and again if they wanted to go on.

Okuden was the ending point for most of the Reiki practitioners in those days. Out of more than 2000 students that learned Reiki from Usui Sensei, as it is written on his memorial, only twenty were given permission to teach during Usui Sensei's lifetime.

神秘傳 Shinpiden

The word shinpiden means the mystical teaching. Shinpiden was once again divided into two parts: Shihan Kaku (師範格) and Shihan (師範). The word Shihan means teacher or instructor. It is a technical term that describes someone who has reached a certain degree of perfection in his art, which has been acknowledged by his teacher who has given him the permission to teach. The word Kaku means Assistant. The Shihan Kaku learned how to give Reiju, but was temporarily given only a limited permission to share his knowledge. During his training time, his inner development would be watched by his teacher and the other shihans in the school. If he became arrogant and the new position went to his head, he would be unlikely to advance much in the near future. But, if it was noticed that his heart was growing more and more loving and compassionate, the teacher would keep a special eye on him. In this case, he would be chosen to become a Shihan, providing he did not ask for it! It was seen to be a great honor to be given the Shihan title. Once this title was given it could not be reversed. Therefore, the Shihan status was given only after careful consideration. Ogawa Sensei told us in 1996 that from 500 members of the Usui Reiki Ryoho Gakkai only six were Shihans. Those Shihans were only permitted to teach within the association, and this is how it is until today.

As you see in the photo 34, all of the Shihans that were permitted to teach by Usui Sensei were men. The youngest was Hayashi Sensei, aged 47. After Usui Sensei's death, many women became Shihans as well.

先生 Sensei

The word sensei means teacher. Literally, it means the first-born. It is used in daily life to describe someone who is teaching his art to his students whether he is an artist, a doctor, a carpenter, a dancer or a lawyer. This title is conferred upon the teacher by his students out of love and respect for his skill and personality. The Japanese word for student is Seito—literally, the one who is following in life. The teacher does not call himself by his own title; in Reiki he would describe himself as a Shihan. Usually, you would address the teacher with his title plus his family name. Her students, however, called Chiyoko Yamaguchi, Chiyoko Sensei. This had a couple reasons: first, it showed the familiarity and closeness she entertained towards her students. We were like her grandchildren ... And, on the other hand it was done to differentiate her from her son, Tadao, who was referred to as Tadao Sensei.

Additional ways of addressing someone in Japanese are: Frank San, respected Frank, Petter san, respected Mr. Petter, Frank-chan-little Frankie, Frank Sama—his eminence Frank, or simply Frank. This last one can be both a sign of closeness and disrespect, it depends upon the context, the body language, the sound in the voice ...

23

Kanji, Shirushi, Kotodama, Jumon

In Reiki we deal with four different concepts that are governed by different sets of rules.

漢字

Kanji

Kanji are Chinese characters/pictographs. A kanji is a word that has one or several specific meanings, which may change depending on the context. All the Reiki Symbols have Japanese names, but their name is not necessarily written the same way the symbol is written. It simply points towards its usage as well as to its meaning.

印

Shirushi

The word shirushi means symbol. The first two Reiki symbols are shirushi. The power of a shirushi lies in its geometrical form. Therefore, it must be written to release its power. It is not necessary to visualize it while drawing it, and its name does not need to be chanted.

言霊

Kotodama

Kotodama is a Shinto term that appears in the Reiki teaching time and again. The word is made up of two kanji: the first one, koto, means word. The second one, dama or tama means soul. The kanji for tama/dam is the same that is used to describe the word Rei/soul in Reiki.

The meaning of the word kotodama is "the soul of a word" or "the spiritual power" of a word. What is meant is the mystical, spiritual power of a consciously uttered word. In Shinto, it is believed that the human being is the manifested word of the gods. In the old days, this was expressed in the polite way of addressing another as "mikoto". The bible too says: "In the beginning was the word ..."

The power of a kotodama lies in the pronunciation, the sound/frequency, and therefore, it must be spoken to reveal its power. Every word has spiritual power and it is our responsibility to find and use words and thoughts that are inherently positive.

In our Reiki practice we use several kotodama. The first and foremost is known

Photo 5: The Kanji for Rei-Tama, soul

24

as the five Reiki principles. They are to be recited in their original language, in Japanese, to release their power. Before each attunement they are to be recited by the teacher and his students to prepare, clear and transform the inner and the outer space for the attunement.

Chiyoko Sensei taught two more kotodama in her practice. One was used for the so-called Sei Heki Chiryo (page 236). The second one was taught only to the teachers to be used in the attunement process. Both kotodama are given to the student by his teacher in the appropriate context during the training and are not discussed here. But let it be said that they are wonderful tools for transformation and therefore, vital in every Reiki training. I suspect that they were introduced by Usui Sensei, but since I never took any formal training from the Usui Reiki Ryoho Gakkai I cannot say whether they are being used in their teaching today or not.

Jumon

The word Jumon means Mantra, or magical formula, but it can mean curse as well.

The distant healing symbol is a jumon and the power of a jumon lies in its geometrical form as well as in its sound/frequency. Therefore, it must be spoken and drawn at the same time.

Both words, Kotodama and Jumon have a positive as well as a negative meaning in the Japanese language and its culture. But in Reiki, all of our concepts are positive and geared towards purification and returning to our original state. Don't be afraid: Reiki is a one-way street and you can never set something negative in motion with a treatment or an attunement. You can never do wrong, just think of the word Reiki—Soul energy.

When you realize how Reiki purifies your mind, it will be easy for you to ban all negative patterns from entering your life. Be mindful of your thoughts and emotions. Be aware of what you say and respect every living being with your love and positive thoughts. *Kyo dake wa.*

Tanden

The Tanden (sometimes referred to as Hara, or Dantien, in Chinese) is thought to be our physical center of gravity. We differentiate between the upper, middle and the lower Tanden, and in Reiki we work with the lower Tanden—one of the most vital points in Chinese medicine and oriental healing/martial arts. It lies two or three fingers width below the navel and is not to be confused with the second chakra.

Takata Sensei writes in her diary that the Tanden is the home of Reiki in our body. For clarity's sake let me quote her diary entry from December 10, 1935, below. After Takata Sensei's death her daughter collected some Reiki related material and presented this in a small booklet to some of the elder students of Takata Sensei. Parts of it were some pages of her diary, as well as original photographs of Hayashi Sensei and Takata Sensei. Additionally, it featured the Hayashi Ryoho Shishin, the treatment plan laid out by Hayashi Sensei for his students that I have published earlier in the books "The Spirit of Reiki" and "The Hayashi Reiki Manual" (both with Lotus Press). Notice that Takata Sensei wrote the Word Reiki as "Leiki" which is the correct pronunciation.

Meaning of "Leiki" Energy within oneself, when concentrated and applied to patient will cure all ailments. It is nature's greatest cure, which requires no drugs. It helps in all respects, human and animal life. In order to concentrate, one must purify one's thoughts in words and in thoughts and to meditate to let the "energy" come out from within. It lies in the bottom of your stomach about 2 cm below the navel. Sit in a comfortable position, close your eyes, concentrate on your thoughts and relax, close your hands together, and wait for the sign. Kindly and gently apply the hands, starting from head downwards. The patient who is about to receive this treatment must purify one's thoughts, feel comfortable and (have) a desire to get well. One must not forget to feel grateful. Gratitude is a great cure for the mind. In all cases, the patient could be diagnosed just by the touch of the hand." (end of excerpt.)

合掌 Gassho

The word Gassho means "two hands coming together".

The correct way of doing gassho is to fold your hands with the palms and respective fingers touching each other. There is either no space or very little space in between the palms, and the hands are held at eye level, just below the nose. The out breath is felt on the fingertips. The elbows do not touch each other and there is enough space under the upper arm to place a fist or an egg. The back is held erect in a ninety-degree angle. This can effortlessly be achieved by shifting the pelvis back a little.

The belly, especially the lower abdomen, is relaxed and if tight clothing should prevent this it is loosened. Head, shoulders and neck are relaxed; you can imagine that your head is held upright by a helium-filled balloon. While sitting in this way, pay attention to what you perceive in your palms and fingers, especially in the middle finger. More detailed instructions for the gassho meditation will follow in the chapter on Japanese Reiki Techniques on page 237.

Kokoro

The word kokoro is often translated from Japanese texts as heart, but this is only half the truth. In our Western cultures we divide the human into three: body, mind and heart. The Japanese don't share this dichotomy with us. For them, heart and mind are one—fused in unity.

This unity is called kokoro. I sometimes wish that my thoughts and emotions were an integrated unity! This is a different way of perceiving self and the world, which has certain implications. If asked what a Japanese person thinks and feels about a certain issue, no specific answer may be forthcoming because there is no difference between thinking and feeling, they are united in Oneness.

Part One:
The Reiki History in Detail

*The human is the most evolved being in existence
and should live according to this.*

—Hayashi Sensei—

Usui Sensei and the Usui Reiki Ryoho Gakkai

臼井甕男 Mikao Usui may seem to you like a celestial being obscured by mystical fog, but first and foremost he was a human being like you and me: someone on the quest to find himself and to find peace and liberation. Unfortunately, we still don't know much about his personal life, but the more you understand the political, cultural and religious background of his times, the deeper your understanding of Reiki becomes. In front of your inner eye a fantastic image of healing and liberation appears, to be followed and replicated by your self. For this reason, I wrote this long and detailed chapter on Reiki history that has been carefully updated until today.

The following in-depth information about Usui Sensei's family and ancestors was passed on to me by Mr. Nakamura, the grandson of Usui Sensei's elder sister (see photo below). Concerning Reiki history, its philosophy and practice, I have relied entirely upon verifiable sources which are named as we go along.

Photo 6: Visiting Mr. Nakamura, one of Usui Sensei's relatives with Tadao Yamaguchi

Whatever has been written below cannot be the complete life story of Usui Sensei. Too much time has gone by after Usui Sensei's passing and those who have known him personally have all united with him in the beyond. You will find two first hand accounts of people who met him on page 63. Reiki has been used traditionally in Japan as a household remedy, and there must be thousands of families who still practice it in this way to this day. Because most of them practice Reiki in the privacy of their family, we don't know about them ... Every once in a while, however, one of those families appears on the Reiki heavens and enlightens our understanding of Reiki. One of those families is the Yamaguchi family about which we will hear again and again in the following pages.

Eighteen years of research consisting of countless phone calls, meetings and interviews with Mr. Oishi, Ogawa Sensei and Koyama Sensei set the ball rolling. The in-depth study of historical documents written by Usui Sensei, Tomabechi Sensei, Hayashi Sensei, Ogawa Sensei and Koyama Sensei supplied the necessary background information. And, finally, several years of studying under the kind guidance of my teacher, Chiyoko Sensei, presented me with the challenge to weave historical, philosophical and practical information in the context of their time into a never before published format. I hope that I have succeeded in this endeavor. Perhaps this chapter will be useful as a reference for your Reiki seminars when you teach your students where Reiki comes from and how it evolved so beautifully over the years. The many photos are meant to give you, your friends and students a taste of the lovely fragrance and character of Reiki, and may tickle your visual sense! All the following information can be verified by the respective sources.

Photo 7: The poetess Utako Shimoda

Ancestry

Mikao Usui was born on August 15, 1865, in the village of Taniai in the Miyama-Cho (district) of Gifu prefecture in southern Japan, near present day Nagoya. His father, Uzaemon, was the first son of his parents and he owned a wholesale and retail business for rice, grains, soy sauce (shouyu) red bean paste (miso), salt, construction wood and charcoal. He was one of the wealthiest citizens of Taniai, a so-called Shoya-San. He was a friend of the well-known Japanese poetess, Utako Shimoda, who, like Usui was born into an ancient samurai family. Some of her original tanka (poems) were on display in the Usuis' home. Shimoda received her artists name "Utako" (child of songs) from the Meiji Emperor to honor her unique talent.

Not much is known about Usui Sensei's mother, except that her maiden name was Sadako Kawai and that she lived until the age of 85. Her father's name was Shozaimon Kawai. The original house in which Usui Sensei grew up was destroyed, and the present property does not belong to the Usui family anymore.

Usui Sensei was the second child of his parents. His older sister, Shu, remained in Taniai while he went to Tokyo as a young man. Shu married a man named Jotaro Usui (in Taniai, confusingly, many people are named Usui for a reason that we will discuss later on) and they had a daughter called Tomiko (Mr. Nakamura's mother).

Unfortunately, the ancestral home of Usui Sensei burned down thrice over the generations and no documents or photos of the family members remained.

Usui Sensei's younger brother, Sanya, followed his elder brother to Tokyo and became a medical doctor. The fourth child of the Usuis, the youngest brother named Kunishi, remained in Taniai and took over his father's business. Nakamura-san told me about his uncle Kunishi, that he was not

Photo 9: The spiritual natural spring of Zendo Daishi in Taniai

32

Photo 8: The house on the property where Usui Sensei was brought up

wealthy in comparison to his siblings, and sold mostly Miso. An aunt of Nakamura-San told him that the relationship between Usui Sensei and his elder sister was not easy.

Usui Sensei's grandfather owned a sake brewery in Taniai, which changed ownership in 1887 (Meiji 20). The grandfather had signed as the guarantor for a friend and when the friend could not repay his debts, the Usuis lost the brewery. The brewery still exists but does not operate anymore (see photo 12). The founding of the brewery is documented on two memorial stones in Taniai, first, at the local Buddhist temple (photo 12) and, second, in the forest just outside the village (photo 9).

The Spring

In the year 1357, Chitsu Bosatsu, the founder of the local Buddhist Temple called Zendo Ji, spent one or more nights in the Soan (weekend house, retreat house for spiritual practice or Tea ceremony) of Kanemaki Usui, one of Usui sensei's ancestors. They had made an appointment to meet in the morning where the road in Taniai climbs up (saka michi). Walking, Chitsu Bosatsu told Usui that he had had a mystical dream the previous night. He had dreamed that he met Zendo Daishi (Japanese: Grandmaster Zendo,

33

Photo 10: The memorial stone at the spring in the forest in Taniai

613-681, one of the patriarchs of Jodo (Pure Land Buddhism) who told him that his body was buried in the forest just outside of the village.

To their surprise, Kanemaki had dreamed the same dream that night and they gathered some tools and made their way to the forest. They began digging at the appointed place and after a while found a stone Buddha Statue that later on found its home at the Zendo Ji Temple in Taniai. As they took the statue out of the ground, a natural spring gushed forth. Convinced that this was a sign from the higher powers, Kanemaki decided that he must brew rice wine from this water, thus beginning the long family history of brewing sake. The kanji used in Usui Sensei's first name Mikao, suggests that he was meant to continue this tradition, but life gave him a different elixir for humanity.

The sake was called Kei Sen Shu. Spring water that is found in a mysterious fashion is called Rei-Sui, (soul water) in Japanese.

The part of the road leading up the hill in Taniai is since then known as Yumei mi saka (dream seeing hill or uphill road).

Nakamura-San suspects that the Buddha statue might have been buried in ancient times in this place due to one of the many earthquake or mudslides so common in Japan.

Translation of the Inscription of the Memorial in the Forest (Photo 10)

The spiritual spring of Zendo Daishi. Chitsu Bosatsu, the founder of Zendo Ji (temple) dreamed of Zendo Daishi in the spring of 1357.

After the dream he found the statue of Zendo Daishi, as well as this spring here in the forest.

The water of this Rei-Sen (holy spring) is also known as Kei-Sui and flows ever since that day. It is worshipped as Rei-Sui (holy, soul water).

Translation of the Inscription of the Memorial at the Zendo Ji Temple (Photo 11)

Injyu-Zan Goshin-In Zendo-Ji

This temple was founded by Kou-Tokkou Chitsu Bosatsu in the fifth year of the Bunwa period (1357).

35

Chitsu Bosatsu was the Buddhist teacher of Kohen-In and Koshyomatsu-In (two aristocratic families) as well as of the Godai-go-tenno (Prince Takaharu, 1287-1339).

Due to the teaching of Chitsu Bosatsu, also Nijo Kanpaku Fujiwara Yoshiki Ko became a Buddhist.

He founded Nishi no Shyo Ryushyo-Ji (temple) in Gifu City.

Chitsu Bosatsu looked for a peaceful place in the fifth year of the Bunwa period (1357) and found Nishi no syo Kikkou Ike.

Chitsu Bosatsu stayed with Usui Shoji (Jiro Kanemaki Usui's nickname. He was the tenth generation of Usuis). In his dream appeared the great master Zendo Daishi of the Jodo Kyo (Kyo, Japanese for faith or church, also called Jodo Shu, Pure Land Buddhism).

(Another document tells us that not only Chitsu Bosatsu but also Usui had the vision of the Master.)

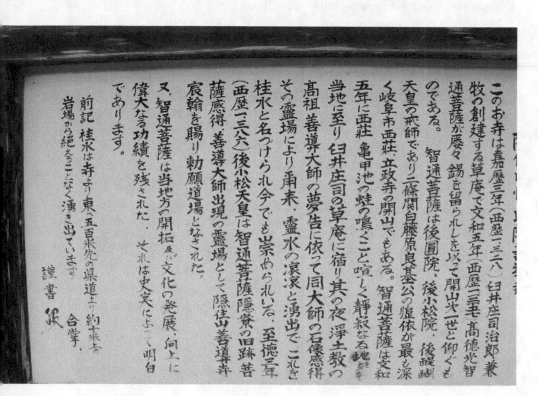

Photo 11: Memorial at the Zendo Ji Temple, Taniai

Photo 12: The Buddhist village temple Zendo Ji, Taniai

In his dream, Zendo Daishi prophesized where they would find a stone figure and a spring. The water of the spring is called Kei-Sui and is revered as holy water to this day.

The Emperor Gokomatsu who reigned during the third year of the Shitoku period (1386) proclaimed the place where Zendo Daishi had appeared as holy, sacred. He called this place Injyu-zan Zendo-Ji. He used this temple for his worship and prayers.

Chitsu Bosatsu worked on the development of agriculture and the development of culture in this area, and was very successful at this. The facts are proven by ancient documents. The holy/sacred water Kei Sui still flows from a rock ten meters off a national highway, which is located about 500 meters East of this place.

Translation of the Inscription of the Memorial in Front of the Springs at the Zendo Ji Temple (Photo 13)

Proclaimed as one of the 50 purest natural springs in Gifu Pre-fecture. The water of the springs flowed only after the founder of

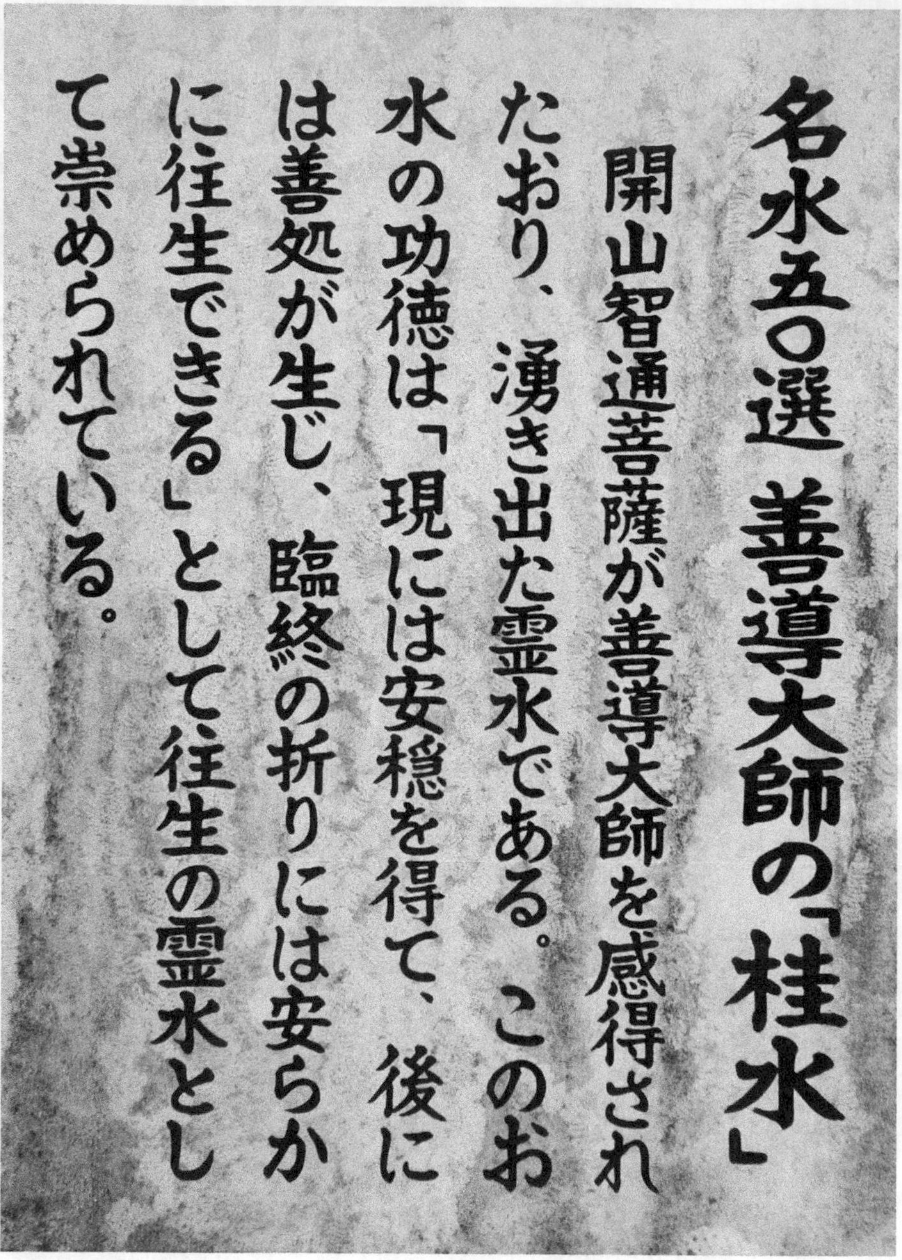

名水五〇選　善導大師の「桂水」

開山智通菩薩が善導大師を感得されたおり、湧き出た霊水である。このお水の功徳は「現には安穏を得て、後には善処が生じ、臨終の折りには安らかに往生できる」として往生の霊水として崇められている。

Photo 13: Memorial plate in front of spring, Zendo Ji Temple, Taniai

this temple, Chitsu Bosatsu, was inspired by Zendo Daishi in a dream.

Due to the power of this water, the one who drinks from it gains a quiet and peaceful soul. After that, he experiences appropriate happiness. While dying, one will be quiet and peaceful. Because of these (healing) properties, the spring is considered and respected as holy/sacred.

Usui Sensei's Birth Village

Taniai is a picturesque sleepy village nestled and hidden in the mountains of Gifu prefecture. It has been the residence of the Usui clan for about 800 years. The Usuis are originally from Chiba prefecture, north east of the Tokyo bay. As is written on Usui Sensei's memorial at the Saihoji Temple in Tokyo, the Usuis are part of an ancient warrior clan belonging to Tsunetane Chiba (Japanese folk hero, 1118-1201, was a general under emperor Go Shirakawa and the leader of the Chiba Clan from Shimosa, a province in the contemporary Kanto area between present day Chiba and Ibaraki). Tsunetane Chiba is well-known in history for the fact that he brought peace to the area around Kyoto in the year 1187.

In the thirteenth century, the Usui clan had to leave their homeland near Tokyo for political reasons. Under the leadership of the head of the family in the tenth Usui generation, Kanemaki Usui, they moved to Taniai, about 500 kilometers south of Tokyo. During the Kamakura period (1185-1333) the Usui clan owned a castle in the mountains of Taniai that unfortunately did not survive history.

In medieval Japan, wealthy families could be recognized and acknowledged by the title Daimyo (great name). At first, this title was given only to warriors, but later on it was conferred to wealthy merchants and landowners as well. These daimyos fought each other in order to expand their power and territory. The Usui Clan did not escape the common faith. During a conflict between two enemy forces in the area of Taniai, Kamisato Usui (in the eighteenth generation) allied his clan with a ruler called Tokiwada. One of his sons, called Kanedai, changed sides to the opponent Saito. This strategic move divided the family into two parts, and made sure that the family name would remain no matter who would take the upper hand in the conflict.

A later branch of the family, under the leadership of Mitsukane Usui and his five sons, regained their former strength in the twentieth Usui generation—about four hundred years ago. Mikao Usui is his direct descendent.

Around 1870, Taniai did not have an elementary school, and all the village children went to a temple school (Terakoya) for their education. This was common in rural Japan at that time, and it did not turn the little students into monks or nuns. However, they received a solid Buddhist education, which became vital in Usui Sensei's spiritual work later on. The local Terakoya in Taniai was in the Zendo Ji Temple (photo 12) that Usui Sensei's ancestors had renovated (with a generous donation) in the fourteenth century. As mentioned before, this temple belongs to Jodo Shu school, or Pure land Buddhism. Pure Land Buddhism was founded by the Chinese Master Eun (798-869) and is based on the sole devotion to the Amida Buddha. This

Buddha is represented by a Sanskrit seed syllable (Japanese: Bongo, photo 14) that we know and love in Reiki as the mental healing symbol (more about this in the chapter "The Roots of the Mental Healing Symbol"). One of the five patriarchs of this school is Zendo Daishi, who appeared to Kanemaki Usui, and the village temple in Taniai has the patriarch's name. The monk who takes care of the temple today is working there in the 41st generation since the foundation of the temple (Japanese temples and shrines are often inherited from father to son for many generations).

All of the Usui ancestors from Taniai are buried at the Zendo Ji's graveyard (photo 15), and all of them were followers of Jodo Shu Buddhism. Usui Sensei himself is buried at another Jodo

Photo 14: Detail of the Usui graveyard at the Zendo Ji temple, Taniai, depicting the symbol hrih-kiriku

Shu temple in Tokyo, about which we will talk later on. Therefore, Usui Sensei's membership of Jodo-Shu is testified and well documented.

With the exception of the Zendo Ji, most of the area in Taniai is Zen Buddhist. The familiarity of Usui Sensei with this school of Buddhism will play an important role in his later life. After completing elementary school in Taniai, Usui Sensei went to the next town for his higher education. Which school he enrolled in is yet unknown. It may have been in the birthplace of his later wife, Sadako Suzuki.

From this point on, the known facts in Usui Sensei's life become increasingly spare. It is known that he married Sadako Suzuki. The couple had two children; the son, Fuji (born 1908) and their daughter, Toshiko (born 1913). Fuji Usui died in 1946 at the age of 39. His sister, Toshiko, died even younger in 1935. Both children are buried at the Saihoji temple in Tokyo along with their parents.

Photo 15: Family graves of the Usui ancestors at the Zendo Ji Temple, Taniai

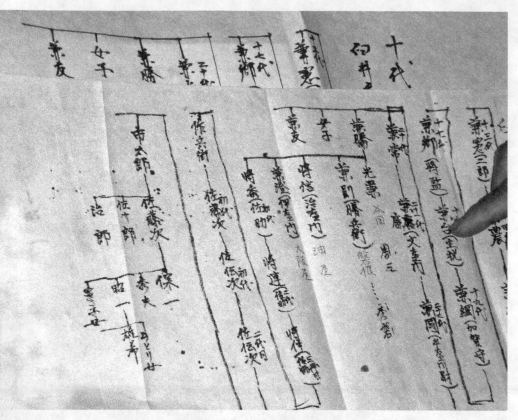

Photo 16: Family tree of the Usuis, Mr. Nakamura pointing to Mikao Usui.

Nothing is known about the life of Toshiko Usui and her family—if she was married already before her early death. In Japanese culture, the daughter leaves the house of her parents for good with her marriage, and becomes part of the family of her husband. In the nineties, I had Japanese friends from Southern Japan who told me that the wife had to ask her father-in-law permission to call her own dad! Fuji Usui married and had at least one son to whom I talked briefly in 2009. He told me that he did not know anything about his grandfather.

Career

According to Koyama Sensei, the previous president of the Usui Reiki Ryoho Gakkai, Usui Sensei worked in many unusual jobs during his career. For a while he was a journalist, but it is not known for which publication he worked. Later on, he worked as a prison counselor, a social worker, a company employee and as a Shinto missionary. Later on in his career he became a public servant.

Count Shinpei Goto

Koyama Sensei relates that Usui Sensei was the private secretary to Count Shinpei Goto, one of the most outstanding politicians in modern Japan. His title, Danshaku is the equivalent of the word "baron" in English. Goto was born on the 24th or 25th of July 1857, in Iwate prefecture, and died on the 13th of April 1929. He studied Medicine at Fukushima University and continued his studies in Heidelberg, Germany.

Later on he pursued a political career. He was employed in the health ministry for a while before becoming Minister of Health. In the year 1890, he became the chief of quarantine in the Imperial army during the Sino-Japanese war. In 1898, he was elected governor of Taiwan. In 1906, he became the chief of the Manchurian railway; after that he was awarded the posts of postal minister and minister for the interior. In 1908, be was chosen as minister of communications, and later became traffic minister. In 1918, he was elected foreign minister, before ending his career as the mayor of Tokyo. He is seen as the architect of modern Tokyo. After the great Kanto Earthquake that devastated the Tokyo Bay, he planned a grand and visionary re-construction of the Tokyo metropolis that, unfortunately, was not put into action due to the financial implications. Had his plans bccn followed back then, the human casualties during the bombardment of Tokyo in World War Two would have been greatly diminished.

Photo 17: Count Shinpei Goto

Goto was a visionary and first class statesman who founded many progressive institutes in his time. He gave birth to the Tokyo Seismographic Institute, the Tokyo Municipal Research Institute, as well as the Boy Scout Association of Japan. Goto was friends with Gishin Funakoshi, the founder of modern Karate, for whom he wrote a beautiful calligraphy that is published in his first book called "Karate Jutsu". The calligraphy reads: "Above all make your mind (kokoro) straight and true".

In Iwate prefecture, north of Tokyo, a museum in honor of Goto was inaugurated. Unfortunately, no information on Usui Sensei is available from the museum. Due to his long-term work with Goto, Usui Sensei had strong ties to high officials in the imperial army and navy, as well as in the government, which provcd vital when he began teaching Reiki later on. The fact that he was in public service with Goto also explains his many trips abroad that are mentioned on the memorial inscription at Saihoji Temple in Tokyo (see page 60 ff.). In his time, it was almost impossible for a Japanese citizen to travel abroad unless he was involved in politics. That means that Usui Sensei did not travel the world in the pursuit of his spiritual search, but as a public servant.

It is not clear what exactly Usui Sensei's responsibilities were in the entourage of Mr. Goto. Koyama Sensei says in her memoirs that he was a Kaban Mochi, private secretary/aide. Literally the word means "briefcase carrier".

Following his career in politics, Usui Sensei started his own business, of which we do not know what it was. All we know from Koyama Sensei is that he found himself in great financial difficulties and went bankrupt.

The Usui memorial inscription tells that Fuji Usui took over the family legacy, but that did not have to do with Reiki. If Usui Sensei operated another business, it is yet unknown, but we keep researching all possible leads.

Reiki—History

According to Koyama Sensei, Usui Sensei did not take the bankruptcy lightly and slid into an identity crisis. This led him to the fundamental questions of why we are here on Earth and what our divine purpose may be? In the pursuit of Anjin Ryumei, an inner state of peace and contentment (see the chapter on important terms in Reiki page 19) he went on a three-year meditation retreat at a Kyoto Zen Temple in 1919. The name of the temple is unknown and difficult to research. There are several hundred Zen Temples in Kyoto and Usui is a common name ... Traditionally many Japanese men spent a certain period of their life at a monastery. This period could last for three months, a year, three years or even more. Spending a certain period in a temple was possible without ordination as in Usui Sensei's case.

After his three-year retreat was up, he asked the abbot of the temple for advice. He had not found what he was looking for and the abbot told him that he saw only one single chance for Usui Sensei to reach enlightenment (Anjin Ryumei) after his three-year retreat had been in vain. He suggested to his student that he must die in order to find eternal peace. With this statement he did not mean the death of the ego, but the actual dying process of the physical body. When the physical body is dying and the etheric bodies begin to disintegrate it is likely that a sincere seeker may come home to his natural state. This seems to be a common understanding in all the Asian countries that I have travelled to: death is the final pathway to enlightenment.

Some Zen Buddhist schools proclaim that enlightenment is more likely to happen at certain times in one's life. These times are between 19-21, 27-29, 34-36 and 41-43. Please don't take this personally, but when these time periods are over one has to take grave methods to reach the Ultimate.

However, enlightenment cannot be forced, but it is possible to create a helpful environment for it. In any case, the apple falls when it is ripe, or not.

Some Buddhist schools speak of three pathways to enlightenment:

The First Variation

The first variation encompasses a period at a temple or, a solitary retreat. Temple life is not easy; it is no way out for someone who can't cope with daily life. The main objective of temple life is ego-destruction. This is implemented by sleep deprivation, long periods of meditation and the endless scrubbing of the already spotlessly clean temple buildings and grounds. Hard physical labor and abstinence from worldly pleasures along with a strict vegetarian diet are to keep body and mind grounded, and, prepared for the event of enlightenment. The rest of the day is spent with prayer, calligraphy, recitation and reading of sacred texts and other subtleties of spiritual practice.

Some schools add so-called Seishins, in which the participants sit in meditation for sixteen or eighteen hours a day in absolute silence. During the meditations at a Zen monastery, the master walks in slow motion in between the silent meditators, and when he feels that the student needs a wake up call, or if the student thinks it himself, the master will hit him with his Zen stick in between the shoulder blades (an experience not to be missed next time you visit Japan). All this and more had been experienced by Usui Sensei already, without bringing the desired result.

The Second Variation

The second variation is trauma. Trauma may consist of one of three aspects or of a mixture of them.

–Physical trauma: accident or illness.

–Emotional Trauma: A difficult fate like divorce from a partner or the death of a loved one.

–Mental trauma: financial difficulties, bankruptcy, unemployment etc. You may have experienced this in your personal life: when your identity is shaken by a difficult situation, suddenly you are taken into a transcendental state.

The Third Variation

The third variation is your own death. In the dying process, when the etheric bodies begin to dissolve, the meditator might experience truth and thus die liberated.

Only the first variation can be arranged quite easily. The second variation, trauma, is too risky and does not necessarily lead to enlightenment. Please don't try it at home!

But the third variation, physical death is a common path in many spiritual schools as a last resort (please forget that I said that and don't try this one at home either). In India, Japan and Thailand I have often seen Buddha Statues of individuals fasting unto death. The historical Buddha himself took this path. It is told that he spent many years with a group of ascetics, torturing body and mind in order to find himself. One day he realized that this was not the way, and he sat under the bodhi tree in Bodhgaya with the vow not to get up before enlightenment or death had taken him home.

In Jodo Shu, Usui Sensei's religion, it is said that one will be reborn in the Pure Land when he recites the name of the Amida Buddha. Then liberation is inevitable.

Like the historical Buddha, Usui Sensei decided to fast unto death on Mount Kurama, North of Kyoto, in March 1922. Whether he used a certain meditation technique during his fast is not known. He probably camped out in the wilderness, in order not to disturb other pilgrims and not be disturbed himself. In the late nineties, I had asked at the Kurama Temple

Photo 18: Mao Den Hall on Mount Kurama

if they offered three-week meditation retreats, but they said that they don't, they didn't and they won't!

Koyama Sensei speaks: "Usui Sensei sat for about twenty days on Mount Kurama in the gassho position in absolute emptiness, without a thought in his mind. On the last day of the journey to himself, the event that he was so longing for took place: Sitting in a small shrine (photo 18) on the mountain in the evening, something like a lightning bolt hit him in his forehead, and he became unconscious. His sense of time vanished and he did not know how long he remained in this state. When he gained consciousness again he felt his whole body vibrant with tremendous energy. Never before had he felt so deeply rested, and body and mind were filled with light and energy. This is how he experienced Reiki for the first time. Perhaps, he thought, this is what the abbot of the Zen Temple meant with Anjin Ryumei. This experience was to change his life completely."

After the Enlightenment

Usui Sensei broke off the fast in order to verify his experience with his teacher. Enlightenment may not be what one expects it to be. Therefore Eastern tradition suggests that the experience is verified by someone who has already reached his destiny. In India they say that it is best if three enlightened beings verify your state before you go on your way. As we all know, the mind is very tricky and imagines all sorts of things, even being enlightened and holier than thou!

Koyama Sensei tells further: "Usui Sensei climbed down Mount Kurama to drink water from a nearby creek. (*Comment Arjava*: probably in the village Kibune below Mount Kurama that is blessed by a deliciously clear and vital creek, see photo 19.) On the way down he ripped off one of his toenails, and intuitively paced his hands upon it. Mysteriously, the pain disappeared and the bleeding stopped. (*Comment Arjava*: Mount Kurama is inhabited by ancient cedar trees that grow air roots, see photo 20. Usui sensei was probably wearing so-called geta, [wooden clogs] like on the photo 32.)

When he reached the village he met a girl with a toothache and he healed her. This is how he encountered the healing power without having searched for it."

Later, Usui Sensei visited his teacher at the Zen Temple, who verified his enlightenment. He suggested that Usui Sensei should begin to teach what he had experienced. He also told him that the mysterious healing power he had experienced was a side effect of his enlightenment, and that it should be included in his teaching for the benefit of mankind. The historical Buddha

Photo 19: The creek in Kibune village

Photo 20: Cedar Roots on Mount Kurama

is reported to have said to his disciples: "Never forget compassion while you are meditating!"

The Usui Reiki Ryoho Gakkai

Usui Sensei entered the world once more and founded the Usui Reiki Ryoho Gakkai (臼井靈氣療法学会). As mentioned earlier, the original name of this association was "Shin shin kaizen Usui Reiki Ryoho Gakkai." This means "for the improvement of body and mind, Usui Reiki healing method Association." Koyama Sensei says again and again that this association is not a religious group, and that it is Usui Sensei's great achievement not to have turned Reiki into a sect or cult.

The aim of the association, Koyama Sensei explains, is to respect the great Reiki and to work on it, and oneself, with diligence daily. Reiki is seen as the spiritual power of the Universe. Even though the Universe is filled with

Photo 21: The Meiji Shrine, Tokyo, in the rain

Reiki, it is hard work to heal one self and others. Practicing Reiki Ryoho means to wish happiness, health and wellbeing to all beings. (Author's comment: see the Bodhisattva Vow on page 161.)

Koyama Sensei says about the members of the Usui Reiki Ryoho Gakkai: "Each member shall work upon himself to build his character and to purify his heart. In order to remain healthy, take care of yourself, eat and sleep well. Give yourself Reiki daily. Reiki helps all parts of the body; it stimulates the body's immune system. It activates the inner organs and helps with the regeneration of new cells, so you don't need to take medication and don't require surgery.

Usui Sensei began to teach Reiki one month after his experience on Mount Kurama. He opened his first Dojo (training center) in the Harajuku district of Tokyo in the vicinity of the wonderful Meiji Shrine (dedicated to the Meiji Emperor of Japan, in the heart of Tokyo, see photo 21). The headquarters of the Usui Reiki Ryoho Gakkai is supposed to have been on the grounds of the Togo-Jinja (Togo Shrine, photo 22).

The short time period between Usui Sensei's Anjin Ryumei and the inauguration of the Usui Reiki Ryoho Gakkai had previously aroused my suspicion. We thought that Usui Sensei had gone to Mount Kurama to meditate. The first time I heard of his three-year retreat at the Zen Temple was from Fumio Ogawa in 1994. Later on, Chiyoko Sensei and her son, Tadao Sensei, verified this. Someone who experiences enlightenment usually does not integrate this experience within a month. It takes time, time, more time and the support of an experienced master to help the student come to terms with his new situation. The individual self has exploded into a million pieces, and the puzzle has to find unity once more. When we found out that Usui Sensei had spent three years previous to the Kurama experience in pursuit of Anjin Ryumei, it made sense that he could integrate it so quickly. He was well prepared, and it can be taken for granted that this mystical experience was not the first of its kind on his long journey.

The Reiki Movement Grows and Expands

The Usui Reiki Ryoho Gakkai grew rapidly. Due to Usui Sensei's many foreign travels aboard imperial navy ships with Count Shinpei Goto (as mentioned on the memorial inscription), he was acquainted with high officials of the navy/army who soon became interested in his Reiki work.

Photo 22: The Shinto Shrine, Togo Jinja, Harajuku, Tokyo

The 1920's seemed to have been fertile ground for the development of spiritual groups worldwide. The same was true in Japan, and we will discuss some of these groups later on. During the Meiji period (1868-1912), the government, under the young Meiji emperor, installed Shintoism as the state religion for political reasons. The emperor himself was installed as an incarnation of the highest Shinto god, Amaterasu, to ascertain his power in worldly and spiritual aspects.

Buddhism and other religions were violently suppressed. Buddhist priests and nuns were forced to abdicate from Buddhism and their temples were desecrated. Murder and torture were common practice, and the Buddhist concepts that had entered Shintoism were almost successfully discarded. It was a time of great public unrest.

On the other hand, the Meiji Emperor (photo 23) and his government opened the country towards the West. This opening was not appreciated by all members of Japanese society. The farmers struggled with poverty and new land reforms, and many intellectual traditionalists hoped that Japan would once again remember its own cultural heritage.

In the Taisho area (1912-1926), the discrepancy grew further resulting in civil war-like revolts with the aim to end the monarchy. Afflicted with meningitis, the Taisho Tenno (emperor) was unable to lead his people and country with the same charisma that his father had had.

In Part three, I will give you an overview of the most powerful spiritual groups during Usui Sensei's time. Some of the most important groups were made illegal during the 1920's, and their leaders were imprisoned. The Omoto Kyo (see page 166 in the chapter "Spiritual Groups During Usui Sensei's Time"), for example, was wrongly charged with lèse-majesty, which was the worst offense in Japanese society back then. About 500 members of the Omoto Kyo held high army and navy posts, and they were threatened to loose their posts.

Perhaps this was one reason why Usui Sensei made the devotion to the Meiji emperor part of his teaching. He included 125 poems of the Meiji emperor in the Reiki manual he gave to his students, and he reportedly spoke very highly of his Emperor who had already passed on years before. During the Reiju (attunements), he and his Shihans used to recite a poem by the emperor. Hayashi Sensei continued this tradition later on. On his memorial, it is written that his followers ought to follow the legacy of the Meiji Emperor. Ogawa Sensei told me that the relationship between Usui Sensei and the emperor was like that between father (Emperor) and son.

The Japanese government outlawed hands-on-healing in the 1920's, and only those holding a medical license of some kind were permitted to "heal". To avoid legal conflict, many of the spiritual groups who practiced healing changed their direction and applied to be registered as a religious group. The Japanese constitution allowed those groups to perform spiritual healing, and thus, they avoided legal trouble.

Since the Usui Association was not against the monarchy, and some of its Shihans, as well as three of its later presidents, were high-ranking navy officials, the government left them in peace. The fact that the emperor was greatly respected in the teaching, and the group did not teach or practice a strange sectarian philosophy, was the single most important factor for its survival in such difficult times. Thus Reiki remained for future generations.

Photo 23: The Meiji Emperor

The Great Kanto Earthquake of 1923

On September 1, 1923, the greatest Earthquake in recorded history in Japan devastated the Tokyo Bay. Tokyo, Yokohama, Kamakura, Atami, Odawara, Ito, Hakone, Miyonoshita, Yokosuka and Soga were destroyed beyond belief. The official death toll was 140,000, with 180,000 injured and one and a half million people left homeless (photo 24). In Tokyo and Yokohama, 360,000 homes were destroyed; all together, 700,000 houses crumbled in the quake and burned in its subsequent fires.

Later on, the earthquake was called Kanto Dai Shinsai. Kanto is the region around Tokyo, and Dai Shinsai means "great, and by an earthquake-devastated area." The terrible thing about earthquakes in the past was the subsequent fires that razed everything to the ground that the quake had left standing. And then, perhaps, came the mudslides and tsunamis.

Most of the medical facilities in the greater Tokyo area burned to the ground, and the ones that were left operational could not handle the massive influx of the injured. In this situation, many of the injured had to seek help from unconventional sources.

It is a sad and strange fact that Usui Sensei and Reiki became known all over the country overnight due to this terrible catastrophe. But, life does not seem to think in terms of good and bad; it does not differentiate between life and death, everything is part and parcel of life as a whole. On one hand,

Photo 24: After the Great Kanto Earthquake 1923

thousands loose their lives, and on the other hand, millions are healed as a result, in the future …

As mentioned earlier, the fires that kept burning for a couple of days were even more devastating than the earthquake itself. On the property of the Army Clothing Depot in the district of Honjo, 40,000 people burned to death. The Asakusa Kannon Temple, in which 100,000 people sought shelter from the flames, was miraculously saved. The people whose lives were spared believe that it was their prayers to Kannon, the Buddha of Love and Compassion that ended the inferno.

Koyama Sensei says that the suffering was so great that Usui Sensei treated at least five people at once. He treated one person with one hand, and another person with the second hand. One more person was treated with his right foot, another one with his left, and one with his eyes. When, that too, was not sufficient anymore, he began treating whole groups of injured at once.

The second president of the Usui Reiki Ryoho Gakkai, Ushida Sensei (photo 25), helped him with this endeavor, along with seven other Shihans. According to Koyama Sensei, the Earthquake changed Reiki history completely. Until September 1923, Usui Sensei was the only one who was able to pass on Reiki to another person. He alone knew how to initiate others, and after the Earthquake he began sharing his art with humanity. He taught eight of his senior students how to initiate others. They spent many months walking through the area healing, treating and initiating the needy. Koyama Sensei speaks of several hundred thousand treatments!

Photo 25: Ushida Sensei

The Return to Taniai

The same year, Usui Sensei returned to Taniai to donate a Torii (Gate to a Shinto Shrine) made of natural stone to the local Amataka (heavenly eagle) Shrine out of gratitude. According to Nakamura San, Usui Sensei was a deeply religious person.

The Torii[1] (photo 26) has an inscription of its sponsors. We find Usui Sensei (photo 27) and both of his younger brothers, Sanya and Kunishi (photo 28).

---

[1] A Torii is a gate that heralds the entrance to a Shinto sanctuary. It tells the one passing through that he is entering holy territory. These gates are to be found all over Japan in various forms. Their shape is always more or less the same, but they can be manufactured out of stone, wood or metal. They stand either singly, in a row of a few, or many before a Shinto shrine, and a pious Japanese bows before he walks through one.

Photo 26: Entrance Torii Amataka Jinja, Taniai

The stone was manufactured by the stone smith, Isojiro Sugiura, and besides the names of the sponsors it gives Usui Sensei's address in Tokyo as such: Tokyo Shi (Tokyo City) Azabu Ku (Azabu ward), Morimoto Chu or Morimoto Matchi (the kanji has dual meaning, and I have not been able to find out which one is correct). The manufacture, transport and erection of this monument were estimated at about one million yen (the equivalent of 13,000 US$.) This was an incredible sum considering that one person could eat for one month with 20 yen! The reason why Nakamura San initially began researching Usui Sensei's life was this: he was wondering how his grand uncle was able to sponsor this monument at the local shrine, and how he made his living. In the area around Taniai there are no quarries, and Nakamura san suspects that the stone must have been cut and transported from Okazaki, north of Nagoya in Aichi prefecture. That alone was a feat of its own in those days. Nakamura San told me that in 1923 the villagers knew about Usui Sensei's work with Reiki.

After the 1923 Earthquake

After the earthquake, the political situation in Japan became even more tense and the openness that had previously taken place towards the West, shifted to the East. The Japanese people, deeply shocked, remembered their own roots and culture once more, and this was good for the development of Reiki. The mystic, Mokichi Okada, whom we will talk about on page 173, for example, writes in one of his books that the Kanto earthquake devastated him, and made him contemplate the meaning of life deeper than ever before. I am sure that many intelligent and compassionate people must have had similar sentiments.

The reconstruction of Tokyo took about seven years. Even after the 1995 Kobe Earthquake that you might remember, thousands of people lived in tents for months. The first time I heard about the fact that Usui Sensei worked on earthquake victims, the old fairy tale

Photo 27: Mikao Usui's name on the Torii at Amataka Jinja, Taniai

that was then widely circulated suddenly made sense. So Usui Sensei did not work in a beggar camp or slum for seven years as legend has it: he helped those who had lost everything in the Kanto Dai Shinsai. His memorial says that his heart became heavy with sorrow, and that the suffering people stood in a long queue in front of his dojo. Once, it is told, Usui Sensei treated a man who had just had a stroke. He was still unconscious as he suddenly began salivating during the treatment. A little while later he came to, got up and walked home.

The Move to Nakano

Usui Sensei's fame spread like a whirlwind through Tokyo and beyond, and in 1925 he moved his dojo (training-center) to a bigger place in Nakano, which was then an outskirt of Tokyo. Nowadays, it lies right in the middle of town, in the Suginami-Ku district. Every traditional Japanese house has

Photo 28: The names of Usui Sensei's brothers on the Torii at Amataka Jinja, Taniai

a mudroom (Japanese: genkan) before you enter the house, and this is where one leaves his shoes. Koyama Sensei tells us that the Usui's genkan was filled with shoes all day long.

Usui Sensei's relatives still live in this place. When I visited the area in 2007 to get a feeling for the place that he worked and lived in, I met Usui Sensei's grandson in front of the house. He asked me what I was looking for, but I left quickly in order not to disturb their peace. Later on, Tadao and I sent some traditional Kyoto sweets to him and his family to apologize for the disturbance. A little while later, Mr. Usui called Tadao to thank him for the sweets. He told us that he knew nothing about his grandfather, and that he did not know where his grave was. His relatives in Taniai also told us, that the Tokyo Usuis have no contact with them, and that they don't visit their ancestor's grave as is usual in Japan every summer during Obon Season (the ancestors festival). In 1994, I had talked to Mrs. Usui (the grandson's wife) who told us that her mother-in-law (Usui Sensei's daughter-in-law) had left a clause in her will that the name of Mikao Usui should never be mentioned in her house! We were not told why that had happened, but this is none of our business anyway. Mrs. Usui then asked me to leave them alone, and I stopped researching their story and concentrated upon what is important to us: Reiki!

Usui Sensei travelled throughout Japan to teach Reiki. On one of his tours, he had a cerebral hemorrhage after a stroke and died on March 9, 1926, in Fukuyama in the Hiroshima Prefecture in Southern Japan. According to Koyama Sensei, this happened during a Reiju Kai, an attunement session, while initiating a group of students. He had been able to cure himself of the after effects of two previous strokes. If you look at the photos of Usui Sensei in this book, you can see the effect of the strokes upon his face and body language.

He was buried at the Saihoji Temple in Tokyo in the Suginami-Ku (district). As his legacy, he left more than 2000 students and 40 branches of the Usui Reiki Ryoho Gakkai. The association permitted its Shihans to open their own branch, providing they had five students of their own. On the first anniversary of Usui Sensei's death, the association placed the memorial stone (photo 29) at his gravesite. The calligraphy of the memorial (photo 30) was done by his successor, Ushida Sensei, who was a gifted calligrapher. The headline to the memorial says: Memorial for the founder of the Reiho (spiritual method), Usui Sensei.

Below, a new translation of the inscription of the memorial by Akiko Sato and myself:

Photo 29: Usui Sensei's memorial, Saihoji Temple, Tokyo, with the memorial stone on the right

Memorial for Usui Sensei, the Founder of the Reiho (Spiritual Method).

Photo 30: The inscription of the memorial stone, Saihoji Temple, Tokyo

It is virtue that one finds as the result of diligent training of the mind and character.

It is success when one deepens the way of salvation for mankind, and thus doing gives some of the virtue to humanity and the environment.

Only after one has made both virtue and success great, one is called: A great Master.

One of these great masters was Usui Sensei.

Usui Sensei discovered a method that is based upon the Reiki of the Universe, which heals both body and mind.

He taught mankind the Reiki of the Universe.

Countless seekers came to him for healing and asked him to teach them the great way of Reiki.

His first name was Mikao, and his pen name was Gyohan (Comment Arjava: due to his work as a journalist). He was born in the village of Taniai in present day Yamagata City, the area of Yamagata in Gifu prefecture.

One of his ancestor's name is Tsunetane Chiba. His father's name was Uzaemon. His mother's family name was Kawai.

He was born in the first year of the Keio period (1865), called Keio Gunnen (the first year of the current period), on August 15th. He studied hard and had many amazing talents. As an adult, he traveled to several foreign countries, as well as to China. Abroad, he thought deeply about these countries (and their cultures).

Even though he was a wonderful person with great talents, he had to deal with many conflicts and challenges. But he did not give up and kept learning continuously.

One day he went to Mount Kurama on a meditation retreat and fasted more than twenty days.

On the last day, he felt the great Reiki energy in his head. He experienced enlightenment, and understood the dynamics of Reiki.

First he experimented with Reiki upon himself, and later, he tested it with his family. Because it worked well on various ailments, he decided to use it not only for his own good and that of his family members, but also to make it available for the world at large. He also wanted to practice his art with joy and honor, and to make it available to all in this way.

He opened a Dojo (training center) in Harajuku, Aoyama, Tokyo in April of the eleventh year of the Taisho Period (1922). He gave seminars and healing treatments to many clients. Countless people came to him from far and near. The clients had to cue up in front of his house for a treatment.

In September of the twelfth year of the Taisho period (1923), the devastating earthquake rocked Tokyo. Thousands were killed, injured and ill. Usui Sensei's heart was heavy with pain; and with this pain in his heart he went out and about to treat the earthquake victims throughout the city. Many injured that could not come to him (due to their injuries) were healed by him on one of his visits.

Soon, his dojo was too small, and in February of the fourteenth year of the Taisho period (1925) he moved to Nakano on the outskirts of town where he built a new dojo. The location of the new dojo was decided by prophecy or fortune telling.

His fame spread quickly throughout the whole country, and he was invited to come to many cities. Once, he travelled to Kure, another time to Hiroshima prefecture, then to Saga prefecture and Fukuyama.

He became ill and died, aged 62, on March 9th, in the fifteenth year of the Taisho period (1926) in Fukuyama.

The name of his wife was Sadako; her maiden name was Suzuki. They had a son and a daughter. The son, Fuji Usui, took over the family business after Dr. Usui's passing.

Usui Sensei was a very warm, simple and humble person. He was physically healthy and well-proportioned. He never showed off, and always had a smile on his face.

He solved challenges by being strong, honest, quiet and patient. He was a very cautious person. In many ways, he was a multi-talented soul.

He liked to read and had a vast knowledge of psychology, medicine, magic formulas (jap Jumon, see page 19), physiognomy, fortune telling and the world religions.

His life-long habit of studying and gathering information certainly helped pave the way to receive the Reiki enlightenment, and to be able to put it into action.

The main objective of Reiki is not only to heal illness, but it also amplifies innate abilities, balances the spirit, makes the body healthy, and thus helps achieve happiness.

To teach this to others, one should follow the legacy the Meiji Emperor, and integrate them deeply in one's heart.

1. Don't be angry today

2. Don't worry today

3. Be grateful today

4. Do your duties

5. Be kind to others

Following these great principles, one will achieve the quiet mind of the old sages.

The ultimate goal is to understand the ancient secret method for gaining happiness *(Reiki),* and thereby discover an all-purpose cure for many ailments.

To be able to share Reiki (with others), it is not necessary to begin with the far away places, but to start at home. Be silent and sit every morning and every evening in the gassho position. Have a balanced and quiet soul. Be just to your fellowman, as well as to yourself. This is possible for everyone.

Philosophical paradigms are changing the world round. If Reiki can be spread throughout the world, it will touch the human heart and will forever establish the right way of Oneness. It will be helpful for many people, and will not only heal disease, but also be a blessing for all beings.

Over 2,000 people learned Reiki from Usui Sensei.

More learned it from his senior disciples. In this way, Reiki spread to far away places.

It is a blessing to have received Reiki from Usui Sensei, to have experienced its grandeur, and to be able to pass it on to others.

Many of Usui Sensei's students convened to build this memorial at the graveyard of Saihoji Temple in the district of Toyotama. I was asked to write these words so his incredible work can continue.

I appreciate his work, in the depth of my heart, and want to let his students know that I am honored to have been chosen for this. I wish that many people will understand what service Usui Sensei has done for humanity for years to come.

End of the inscription

Epilogue: February in the second year of the Showa period (1927). Author of the inscription: Masayuki Okada, Jyu San I-Kun San To (doctor of literature).
   Calligraphy: Juzaburo Ushida Jyu Yon I-Dou San To, Kou Yon Kyu, (Admiral of the Imperial Navy) (*comment Arjava*: second president of the Usui Reiki Ryoho Gakkai, and Usui Sensei's direct successor).

Encounters with Usui Sensei

One of the two first-hand accounts of Usui Sensei's life and personality is from Harue Nagano Sensei:[2] "Usui Sensei healed many people. Because he could not do this on his own, he founded the association. In his day, there were about 40 branches. I met Usui Sensei for the first time at a Reiju Kai in Sagano, in May of the 1th year of the Taisho period (1925). He was a simple man (in the sense of not being narrow minded), he was humble and

---

[2] *This account is taken from Koyama Sensei's teaching manual, see appendices.*

humorous. He was an excellent speaker. During those five days (of the Reiju Kai), all the participants were highly concentrated and grateful to be able to be there. Reiki radiated from his whole body, and the participants gathered around him to touch his clothes to receive some of his energy. (Comment Arjava: traditionally you do not touch the Sensei's body). On March 9 in the 15th year of the Taisho period (1926), he died during Reiju from a cerebral hemorrhage, after he had been able to cure himself twice from the effect of two strokes. He passed away aged 62.

It is a pity to have lost such a spiritual person. Looking back at the 56 years since the inauguration of the association, I see the high and low points. During the war, the Usui Reiki Ryoho Gakkai was not active. The senior

Photo 32: Usui Sensei in Shizuoka

Shihans passed away one after another, and some of the branches had to close forever. But, thanks to the dedicated efforts of Koyama Sensei, the Association came back to life."

The second first-hand account that I am aware of comes from Gizo Tomabechi, a well-known politician who was the speaker of the House of Representatives. He was one of five Japanese statesmen to sign the international peace treaty between Japan and the world in San Francisco in 1951 (see photo 33).

Further interesting thoughts and tips about the Usui Reiki Ryoho, its practice and effectiveness are to be found in the appendices on page 254. They are taken from Tomabechi's book titled: "Kaiko Roku"—My Memoirs.

But now to his account:

"When I had just been introduced to Usui Reiki Ryoho, I heard about the wife of a colleague of mine, Mr. Amami, who had not been able to stand up due to a hip condition for a year. I asked Usui Sensei to give her a treat-

Photo 33. Signing the International Peace Treaty in San Francisco

ment. Usui Sensei gave her Reiki for 20-30 minutes upon which he told her to get up.

She had not even been able to turn in bed by herself, and standing was an absolute impossibility. Nevertheless, she tried to get up, and managed it. When standing, she screamed with joy. Usui Sensei looked at her and asked her to walk. She then began to walk in a small room with the help of her husband.

If there are miracles, I thought, this would be one, while Usui Sensei was watching the scene, smiling.

The two of them, and I, were speechless. After this experience, I wanted to learn Reiki Ryoho with great conviction, and received the Shihan certificate from Usui Sensei. I wanted to help humanity with Reiki. At that time, I was offered the job of Kansai (*comment Arjava*: area around Osaka) director of the Dai Nippon fertilizer company. After I moved to a new apartment without my family, I used the place for Reiki treatment. I gave Reiki treatments for free, along with some of my students.

After the great Kanto Earthquake in the 12th year of the Taisho period (1923), I spent a lot of time with Usui Sensei and watched him treat the injured. I saw that Reiki heals physical and mental/emotional ailments effectively. With total conviction, I studied Reiki and became a Shihan. I gave myself, and others, Reiki. Since then, my health has improved greatly, and I weighed more than 132 pounds (60 kg). For the first time since my childhood, I feel perfectly healthy."

The Usui Reiki Ryoho Hikkei

The Usui Reiki Ryoho Hikkei is the only written legacy of Usui Sensei himself. It is his teaching manual that he gave to his Reiki students. I was given a copy of this in 1997 by Ogawa Sensei, whose father had learned Reiki from one of Usui Sensei's senior Shihans. For this book, Akiko Sato and myself, have done a new translation of the manual.

The following questions about Reiki are answered by Usui Sensei in person. The exact date of the interview and the name of the interviewer are not known. Because the original text is about 90 years old, we have made minor changes to help you understand it better. Due to his many years as a journalist, Usui Sensei was able to embed great secrets in the text in simple language. Please read the text slowly and attentively, a few times. I occasionally read it again, and each time I find a new treasure … My comments are set in parenthesis.

Why I Am Teaching this Method Publicly
—Declaration of the Founder Usui Sensei—

Since ancient times, when someone finds an original secret law, they usually keep it for themselves or teach it only to their descendants. This secret is then used as the security of living for one's descendants. The secret is never allowed to be passed on to outsiders. But, this is an inherited habit of the past century. (The spiritual legacy of most of Usui Sensei's contemporary spiritual teachers was continued by their descendants. In most cases, however, the masters were unable to pass on the transcendental experience that they themselves had experienced, to their own students).

In times such as these, happiness is based upon cooperation of humankind, and the longing for the progress of society. That is why I will never allow anyone to own it (Reiki), at all. Our Reiki Ryoho is an absolutely original finding, and it is not comparable to any other (spiritual) path in the world; (therefore, Reiki has not been re-discovered, and did not originate in any other tradition). Therefore, I want to make this method (openly) available to the public for the welfare of humankind. Anyone has the potential to be showered upon by the divine, resulting in the oneness of body and soul. People in society at large will be able to receive the blessings of the divine. In the first place, our Reiki Ryoho is an original therapy based upon the spiritual power of the universe. Through it, the human being is first made healthy, then peace of mind and the joy of living are increased. Nowadays, we need improvement and reconstruction in our lives to be able to save our fellow men from disease and a suffering mind. That is why I dare to teach this method openly to the public.

Questions and Answers

Question: What is the Usui Reiki Ryoho?
Answer: We gratefully received and follow the legacy of the Meiji Tenno. To reach the right (spiritual) path of humanity, we must follow this legacy. That means that we have to improve our mind and body by (daily) practice (the original name for Reiki was Shin Shin Kaizen Usui Reiki Ryoho. Translated: for the improvement of body and mind, Usui Reiki healing method).

For that, we first heal the heart/mind. Second, we have to make our body healthy. When one's mind is on the healthy path of faithfulness and sincerity, the body becomes healthy by itself. Like this, mind and body become one, and one completes his life with peace and joy. You heal yourself, and the diseases of others, and increase your own happiness and that of others.

That is the mission of the Usui Reiki Ryoho.

Question: Is the Usui Reiki Ryoho the same as Hypnotherapy and Kiaijutsu (collecting the energy in the Tanden and letting out a scream when the energy is released through the hands) or Shinko Ryoho (religious therapy)? Is this a similar thing with a different name?
Answer: No, no. This is not a similar type as the above. At the end of many years of hard training, I found a spiritual secret. This is a method to heal body and mind.

Question: Does this mean that it (Reiki) is a Shinrei Ryoho (a psychic healing method)?
Answer: Yes, you could call it one kind of psychic healing method, but you could also call it physical therapy. Because energy and light radiate from all parts of the practitioner's body.

Mainly, energy and light appear from the eyes, the mouth, and the hands of the practitioner. Therefore, you either stare for two or three minutes at the sick body part, you blow at it or you rub it. Toothaches, headaches, stomach aches, swelling in the breast, nerve pains, bruises, cuts, burns and so on will go away just like that. (According to Chiyoko Sensei, Reiki works very well for injuries, if it is administered as quickly as possible after the injury occurs. If treated quickly, the wounds heal rapidly and often no scars remain.)

Chronic diseases cannot be treated so easily. But, even when treating chronic illness, a single treatment will have a positive and beneficial effect.

I am asking myself how I can explain this phenomenon with modern medical science, but reality is more amazing than fiction. If you witness the results, (that a Reiki treatment brings) you will agree to what I have just said. Even someone who wants to hide the truth cannot disregard reality.

Question: Is it necessary to believe in the Usui Reiki Ryoho for healing to occur?
Answer: No, because it is different from other kinds of psychic healing, psychotherapy or hypnotherapy.

Agreement or belief are not needed for it to work, because it doesn't work with suggestive techniques. However, it doesn't matter whether you suspect, deny or refuse to believe in it. For example, it works just as well on infants or seriously ill people who are unconscious.

Perhaps one in ten people who come for a session of this kind for the first time already come with trust. Usually, after having had one session, people feel the (positive) effects it has on them, and trust arises in them.

Question: What illnesses can be healed with the Usui Reiki Ryoho?
Answer: Any kind of disease, whether psychological or physical, can be healed with Usui Reiki Ryoho.

Question: Does Usui Reiki Ryoho heal diseases only?
Answer: No, it doesn't just heal the diseases of the physical body. It can correct bad habits like psychological illness, depression, weakness, fear, indecisiveness, nervousness, (see the chapter on Sei Heki Chiryo, the treatment of unwanted habits on pages 164 and 236).

With it (Reiki), the mind (of the practitioner) becomes God-like or Buddha-like, and it becomes your life-mission to help our fellowmen. Through this (Buddha-like nature), you make yourself and others happy. (Once you have integrated this, you have understood Reiki ...)

Question: How does the Usui Reiki Ryoho heal?
Answer: I haven't been initiated into this method by anyone in this universe. Neither did I make an effort to receive psychic powers at all. While I was fasting, I was touched by a great energy, and I was inspired in a mysterious way. By chance, I realized that the spiritual ability to heal had come to me.

That is why, even though I am the founder of this method, I have a hard time explaining it clearly. Physicians and scientists research this area passionately, but it has proven difficult to arrive at a scientific conclusion. There will come a time when Reiki and science will meet (if you are scientist, please get to work!).

Question: Does the Usui Reiki Ryoho use any kind of medication or instruments? And are there any side effects?
Answer: No, we use neither medication nor instruments.

It uses only staring, blowing, stroking, (light) patting and touching (of the afflicted areas). This is what cures the illness. (With all these techniques, Reiki is brought into the deeper tissue of the body, and as a result, the body heals itself. See the chapters on the Japanese Reiki Techniques on page 213 especially the following techniques: Gyoshi-Ho, Koki-Ho, Hanshin Koketsu-Ho and Ketsueki Kokan).

Question: Do you need any medical knowledge to use the Usui Reiki Ryoho?
Answer: Our Ryoho (healing method) is a spiritual method, which is beyond medical science, therefore, it is not based on medical science.

You will reach your goal by staring, blowing, touching and stroking the diseased body part. For instance, you touch the head when you want to treat the brain, the stomach when you want to treat the stomach and the eyes when you want to treat the eyes. You neither take bitter medicine, nor use hot moxibustion[3]), and will get well in a short period of time. This is why this Reiho (spiritual method) is our original creation.

Question: How do well-known, contemporary physicians view the Usui Reiki Ryoho?

Answer: It seems like the highly educated authorities are quite fair with their judgment (of the Usui Reiki Ryoho). These days, famous European medical doctors are very critical towards (a science that only prescribes) medication.

By the way, Dr. Sen Nagai, of the Teikoku Medical University says "We physicians know how to diagnose maladies, record it, and understand it, but, don't know how to treat it." (Another physician), Mr. Kondo says, "It is a great superstition that medical science made great progress, because contemporary medicine neglects the mental balance (of the patient). This is its biggest drawback." Professor Sakae Hara says, "It is quite insulting to treat the human being, who has spiritual wisdom, just like an animal."

I believe that the near future will see a great revolution in the world of health care. Professor Rokuro Kuga says, "The fact is, some people who are not medical doctors have (good) results with a number of techniques, like psychotherapy, that even medical science cannot claim for itself. This is so because these therapies take into account the character and the personal disease pattern of each individual patient. If you, as a physician, oppose those who are not attached to the medical faculty blindly, and would try to hinder them, it would be very narrow-minded. From: Nihon Iji Shinpo.[4]

For instance, medical doctors and pharmacists often acknowledge this fact and come to get initiated (into Reiki).

Question: What does the government think about it (Usui Reiki Ryoho)?

Answer: On February 6 of the 11th year of the Taisho period (1922), at the budget meeting of the assembly of the house of representatives of Japan, the representative Professor Dr. Keiji Matsushita asked "What is the government's opinion about individuals who recently treat patients (with psy-

---

[3]Moxibustion, an ancient healing art used in China, Tibet and Japan is based upon similar principles as acupuncture. Instead of inserting needles into the body, tiny balls of Mogusa (a variety of vermouth) are burned once or several times on certain acupuncture points.
[4]A medical journal with the title "Japan Medical News"

chotherapy and spiritual therapy like Usui Reiki Ryoho) without a medical license?"

Mr. Ushio from the government committee replied "Hypnotherapy and the likes, were thought of as superstitious over ten years ago, but these days it has been studied and researched well to be of use in psychiatric patients (treatment). It is difficult to solve everything concerning the human being by medication. Physicians follow certain pathways to cure diseases along the guidelines of medical science. Simply touching and using electro-therapy are not included in the healing methods of medical science." That's why our Usui Reiki Ryoho is not concerned with medical law and the laws that apply to acupuncture and moxibustion.

Question: The ability to perform spiritual healing must come only to individuals who were spiritually minded from birth? I don't think anybody can learn it, or can they? What do you think about this issue?
Answer: "No, no, all the beings who have received the breath of life, have been given the spiritual ability to heal as a gift (from nature, god, whatever you call it). Plants, animals, fish and insects—all the same. But human beings, who are the crown of creation, have the most power of all. The Usui Reiki Ryoho has appeared in the world to make it (the spiritual ability to heal inherent to all beings) practical, usable. (If you have learned Jikiden Reiki you will be reminded of the Kotodama in the Sei Heki Chiryo).

Question: Are you saying that anyone can receive initiation into Usui Reiki Ryoho?
Answer: Of course, men, women, old or young, physicians or uneducated people alike, who conform to social manners, can definitely learn to heal themselves and others in a short time period. Until this day, I have initiated more than a thousand people, and not even one person failed to have the desired result in the end. Everybody, even the people who have received only the Shoden level have clearly achieved the ability to heal disease. When you think about it, it is so strange to be able to learn the ability to heal disease, which is the most difficult thing for a human being to learn in such a short period of time. And, I, too, find this strange. That is the characteristic of our spiritual healing method that you can learn very easily to do such a difficult thing.

Question: With it (The Usui Reiki Ryoho), you are able to cure other people's disease but what about your own? Can you heal your own diseases as well?

Answer: If you cannot heal your own disease, how can you heal someone else's disease?

Question: What do you have to do to learn Okuden next?
Answer: Okuden is comprised of several healing methods: Hatsureiho, patting, stroking, and using pressure, distant healing, habit-healing and so on.

First of all, you learn Shoden. If you present (the teacher) good results, and you are well-mannered, honest, ethical and passionate (about the Usui Reiki Ryoho), you will get initiated into Okuden (the second degree).

Question: Is there more to the Usui Reiki Ryoho than Okuden?
Answer: There is 'Shinpiden'.

(End of the interview.)

After Usui Sensei's Death

Ushida Sensei took over the leadership of the Usui Reiki Ryoho Gakkai right after Usui Sensei's death. You will find him in the photograph on page 64 of all the Shihans of the Usui Reiki Ryoho Gakkai to the left of his teacher.

In the same photograph, taken in January 1926, you will find Chujiro Hayashi, the one person who will later on become instrumental in the spreading of Reiki all over the globe. Hayashi Sensei received his Shihan status in 1925. Before we continue talking about Hayashi Sensei, I would like to share some information on the other Shihans and the future presidents of the Usui Reiki Ryoho Gakkai with you. All of this information comes from Koyama Sensei.

Teachers (Shihans) of the Usui Reiki Ryoho Gakkai Who Had Their Own Students

(The sequence given comes from Koyama Sensei; the names are given in the Japanese tradition, with the family name given first.)

Hayashi Chujiro Sensei

Hayashi Sensei (photo 35) was one of the twenty Shihans who learned directly from Usui Sensei. He was very talented in giving treatments, and had a Dojo in

Photo 35:
Hayashi Sensei

72

同一者授霊法療気霊臼日善改身心
大正十五年一月十六日

Photo 34: Usui Sensei and his Shihans on January 16, 1926. Usui Sensei is seen in the middle. Ushida Sensei sits next to Usui on his right (from our point of view). In the first row, on the far left, you see Hayashi Sensei. In the back row, on the far left, we see Wanami Sensei. Taketomi Sensei is third from the left. Tomabechi Sensei was unable to attend and has for this reason been added later on, on the far right. The kanji under the photograph reads: All members who are permitted to give Reiju, January 16, 1926. This photograph is a clipping of the original. In the original, to be found at the Yamaguchi's home, we see the Gokai framed above the group.

Shinano Cho, Tokyo. At the Dojo, he had ten Reiki tables that were occupied by patients day in and day out. A student of Hayashi Sensei called Shou Matsui (1870-1933), wrote a book with the title "Kofuku na shakai o shuchi subeku" (How a Happy Society is Created. Unfortunately, long out of print).

Hayashi Sensei died during the war in Atami.

Shiki Sensei
Shiki Sensei had many, many students and died on July 20th in the 15th year of the Showa period (1940).

Imaizumi Tesutaro Sensei

Imaizumi Sensei (born on September 12, 1877) was the right hand of the third president, Taketomi Sensei, and taught in his stead when he was unavailable. Imaizumi Sensei was a high military official. His military service ended on September 12, 1940. He died on February 8, 1945, aged 67.

Isoda Shiro Sensei

Isoda Sensei learned first from Ushida Sensei, and then, later on, from Usui Sensei himself. He was the head of the three Usui Reiki Ryoho Gakkai branches in Hiroshima, Suma and Kyoto. He was a scientist by profession, and saw Reiki in a scientific way. His wife was well-known for her healing abilities.

Mine Ishie Sensei

Mine Ishie Sensei was a professional musician, and wrote a book with the title Michi Shirube (Reiki-) Signpost, as well as her autobiography titled: Kyuju Nen no Ayumi (Ninety Years of My Life Path), published on October 10, 1967). In this book, she talks about all the Shihans that were initiated by Usui Sensei, giving the dates and places, where and when, they received their training. She was the wife of Mine Umetaro Sensei, and led the branches at Kobe-Suma and Hyogo. She treated countless patients throughout her life and died at the age of 103.

Kaneko Shigeyo Sensei

Kaneko Shigeyo Sensei was a gifted speaker, and had the ability to capture and thrill his audiences and to convince them of his subject. He was a high official in the imperial army, and an outstanding personality. He gave seminars in Hiroshima and Kagoshima.

Tsuboi Sensei

Tsuboi Sensei was a master of Tea Ceremony. He died on November 20th of the 57th Showa period (1982) aged 99. Tsuboi Sensei studied Reiki with Taketomi Sensei in the 8th year of the Showa period (1933). In those days, the headquarters of the Usui Reiki Ryoho Gakkai was in Harajuku, Tokyo. Later on, during World War Two, the headquarters burned down. After the war, the Reiju Kai were held in Tsuboi Sensei's house in Higashi Nakano. Later on, Tsuboi Sensei moved and the meetings were held in Jiyugaoka (see photo 36) in the house of Tsuboi Sensei's son. In those days, only two or three people came to the meetings, and one of them was Koyama Sensei. Koyama Sensei and Watanabe Sensei (the fourth president of the Usui Reiki Ryoho Gakkai) were reunited there by fate. Both of them had become members of the association in Takaoka earlier. Watanabe Sensei was unable to propel Reiki much further in those days, but during Koyama Sensei's leadership the association grew strong again. Due to her efforts, the Usui Reiki Ryoho Gakkai flourished again after World War Two.

Morihaku Yoshiko Sensei

Morihaku Sensei learned from Taketomi Sensei. In the 9th year of the Showa period (1934), she healed the governor of the Oita Prefecture from gallstones, and, as a reward, received permission to give public treatments. She died in the 43rd year of the Showa period (1968).

Nagano Harue Sensei

Nagano Sensei learned directly from Usui Sensei, and worked at the Usui Reiki Ryoho Gakkai headquarters. Later on, when Wanami Sensei (the fifth president) became old, she helped him with his duties. She died in April of the 59th year of the Showa period (1984).

Photo 36: The Jiyugaoka dojo was somewhere in this block.

Further teachers were Mr. Harai, Mr. Harada, Mr. Haraguchi, Mr. Hida, Mr. Ichinose, Mr. Ichiraizaki, Mr. Isobe, Mr. Jo, Mr. Kobayashi, Mr. Kosone, Mr. Matsuo, Mrs. Nagano, Mrs. Nagamine, Mrs. Nakagawa, Mr. Nomura, Mr. F. Ogawa, Mr. Onizuka, Mr. Senju, Mr.Takayama, Mrs. Tamura, Mrs. Ushida, Mr. Usui and Mr. Yoshizaki.

Comment Arjava: Toshihiro Eguchi, who was well-known in spiritual circles in those days, and about whom many speculations abound on the internet, was only an Okuden student according to Koyama Sensei. Therefore, he does not appear in the list of the teachers.

The Presidents (Kaicho) of the Usui Reiki Ryoho Gakkai

The First President, Mikao Usui

Born on August 15, 1865, in present day Taniai village in the Gifu Prefecture. Died March 9, 1926, in Fukuyama in the Saga Prefecture. His pen name was Gyohan.[5] His wife's maiden name was Sadako Suzuki. His son, Fuji Usui, died on July 10, 1946, aged 39. His daughter, Toshiko, died in 1935, aged 22. Usui Sensei was a warm hearted, simple and humble man who always had a smile on his face. (*Comment Arjava*: More information on Usui Sensei's life is to be found on page 30 ff.)

The Second President, Juzaburo Ushida

Ushida Sensei was born in Kyoto on May 8, 1865. He attended the twelfth class of the Naval Academy.

1905, August 5, he became a Navy Captain and received Ko Yon (Award)

1905, August 5, he became Captain of the ship "Akitsu-Shu"

1905, December 29, Gunreibu, Sennin Fukukan, Navy Office Directive Senior

1908, February 20, "Okishima" Kancho, became captain of the ship "Okishima"

1908, April 7, Nisshin Kancho, became captain of the ship "Nisshin"

1908, November 20, Asahi Kancho, captain of the ship "Asahi"

1910, December 1, Gunreibu, Sennin Fukukan, Navy Conductive Office Senior

1911, December 1, Shosho, became Rear Admiral

1911, December 1, bu(mai) tchin sanbocho, the chief of the General Staff

[5]In Usui Sensei's time, it was common for someone to have three names. 1—the so-called Yobi na (the name by which you are called). 2—Jitsu mei (the real name by which you are registered), and possibly 3—Go (the artists pseudonym or pen name).

1912, December 1, Toku-Mei, On special mission

1913, May 31, Yobi, preliminary, reserve, spare

Ushida Sensei taught that the Reiki Ryoho is a spiritual practice and that illness can be healed primarily through work on ones character. He had many able students and was a gifted calligrapher. It was he who wrote the five principles (that appear in the top left corner of the photograph (photo 32) of Usui Sensei taken in Shizuoka City on page 64. He also wrote the beautiful characters for the inscription of the Usui Memorial (photo 37) at Saihoji Temple, Tokyo.

Ushida Sensei's military career ended on May 8th, 1926. He died on March 22nd, 1935 at the age of 69.

The Third President: Kanichi Taketomi:

Taketomi Sensei was born in Tokyo on December 28, 1878 . His military career was as follows:

1918, December 1, shosho, became Rear Admiral

1918, December 1, taisa, became captain

1918, December 1, ominato yokobu sanbotcho, the chief of the General Staff of Ominato harbor. Yokobu (main harbor). This is where he met Hayashi Sensei.

1919, December 2, Kure Ko Kensakan, Inspector of Kure town

1923, January 20, Setsu Kancho, Captain of the ship "Setsu"

1923, October 1, Setsu Tokumu Kancho, Captain of the ship "Setsu" on special duty

1923, December 10, Tokumei, on special mission

1924, February 25, yobi, reserve

Taketomi Sensei was very skilled in working with the Reiji-Ho technique (see the chapter on the Japanese Reiki Techniques page 213) and was able to diagnose effectively. During the training sessions he helped his students understand the Reiji-Ho technique, and was able to teach about 50 students at once. He asked his students to stand in a row, touching each other's shoul-

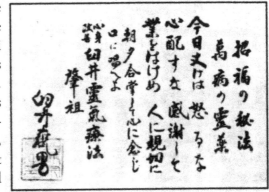

Photo 37: The gokai in Ushida Sensei's handwriting

77

ders. He himself stood as the last in line, and suddenly he said: "This is Reiki" (now you know where the title of this book comes from!) Upon saying this, he let the energy flow through his students with the help of his breath. He taught that it was vital that the Reiki students should increase their perception of energy.

Once, he treated a child with blood poisoning. He diagnosed that the cause of the illness was due to exhaustion, and he treated the child's spine, healing him/her. He taught his students the art of making an accurate diagnosis in order to be able to work effectively. (Chiyoko Sensei too worked in this way, see the chapter on Byosen, page 180).

In his professional work (as the chief of staff at Ominato Harbor, the largest naval harbor in Japan), he was occasionally asked to find and sentence criminals. Taketomi Sensei was known for the fact that he was able to identify a criminal from a number of suspects. He used the Reiji-Ho technique for this: he first wrote the names of all the suspects on several pieces of paper. He spread them on a table in front of him, and then let his hands run over them. Upon whose name his hand stopped was the guilty person. He used the same technique for answering positive questions. During the war, Taketomi Sensei lived in Kyoto. After the war, he went back to Tokyo, and continued his Reiki work at the Inogashira Dojo (Inogashira is a suburb of Tokyo). He died on December 6, 1960, aged 81. His military career ended on December 28, 1941.

The Fourth President, Yoshiharu Watanabe, Teacher

Watanabe Sensei (photo 38) taught at the Takaoka Koto Shogyo Gakko (Takaoka High school, meanwhile closed). Watanabe Sensei was employed there as an English teacher from March 25, 1929 (Showa 4), until the March 25, 1935 (Showa 10). His specialty was giving Reiki treatments. His wife worked with him in this. Once, he reanimated a drowning victim, and another time, he saved the child of a Reiki Ryoho Gakkai member, of dysentery, after the doctors had already given up. He

Photo 38: Watanabe Sensei

treated the child for half an hour with the Tanden Chiryo (see page 180). He led the association and the main branch after the war. He also died in December 1960.

The Fifth President: Hoichi (Toyokazu) Wanami

Wanami Sensei was born in Mie prefecture on November 2, 1883 (Showa 10). This is his military career :

1924, December 1, Sensuiko, Kyoto-Ken Dai Ichi, Ichisen Shirei, School for Diving-Submarine School, Vice President and Command of the first Ichsen team.

1925, December 1,Taisa, Captain (Kai Dai 15-Award)

1926, August 1, Kure Ko-Kenzo Sensui kann Gisso Incho, Town of Kure, director of the submarine construction factory

1926, December 1, Sensui ko kyotou, Vice president of submarine School

1927, November 15, Jingei Kancho, Captain of the boat "Jingei"

1928, December 10, Kan Honbuin, Navy boat, main Staff

1931, December 1, Kan Sui Dai go, butcho, Fifth Chief Director

Photo 39: Wanami Sensei

1931, December 1, Rear Admiral

1932, November 15, Dai Ni, Sensen, Shireikan, Second Submarine Combat Commander

1934, November 15, Sensui Kocho, president of submarine school

1935, November 15, Vice Admiral

1935, November 15, end of military career

1936, November 15, Shushi Showa 11, March 16, Tokumei, Special mission

1936, March 30, Yobi, reserve

Wanami Sensei was a warm-hearted man, who was always cheerful. He had many relations, as well as many friends. He taught many people Reiki. When he was old, he asked his successor, Koyama Sensei, to take care of his patients. He was very interested in all aspects of health, especially in the health of the elderly. He gave lectures, and was in the best physical condition. He climbed to the top of Mount Fuji when he was ninety years old! Wanami Sensei died on February 2, 1975, aged 91.

The text of the calligraphy in photograph 39 reads: "The answer of the true heart is the sacred light".

The Sixth President, Mrs. Kimiko Koyama

Koyama Sensei learned Reiki from Taketomi Sensei, in Takaoka in Toyama Prefecture, in the autumn of Showa 7 (1932). In the next three years, she took part in the local five day Reiju-Kai twice a year and learned much. Initially, she was drawn to Reiki to help her six children grow up healthily. It was then that she learned what Reiki is, and that Reiki is not only about healing illness. In 1935 (Showa 10), her husband was transferred, and consequently, she practiced Reiki on her own for the next 13 years. In 1948 (Showa 23), she commenced taking part in the Reiju-Kais of the Usui Reiki Ryoho Gakkai, and she learned from Watanabe Sensei, as well as from Wanami Sensei.

Koyama Sensei's husband served in Birma during World War Two. When her second son died, she first felt the powers of the heavens. During the war, she heard the voices of the gods at the Meiji Jingu (the Meiji shrine in Tokyo, see photo 21). Both of her elder sons were afflicted with dysentery, and she was unable to feel the byosen back then. She asked Wanami Sensei's expertise, who then treated the boys. After one hour of treatment, they passed black stool and were treated for the next three days with the Tanden Chiryo (see chapter Japanese Reiki Techniques 213).

Koyama Sensei says that she received Reiju from the Heavens and from the Earth daily (please don't try this at home, we need you HERE!). Meanwhile, all her teachers have passed away, and it is her turn to share her understanding with her own students.

In the year Showa 51 (1972), the headquarters of the Usui Reiki Ryoho Gakkai was situated in Jiyugaoka.

Koyama Sensei held weekly practice sessions at her house in the Meguro District of Tokyo. The main branch had about 250 members, and in total it was about 600. There were 13 branches (in the beginning of the 1990's). Koyama Sensei's daughter, Makino San, is the vice president of the association. Koyama Sensei died on December 3, 1999.

Koyama Sensei said about herself: "I work for the gods on a daily basis, as well as I can, and I take good care of myself. Reiki is not a religion, but

I have the impression that I am being led by a higher power. I always give the utmost, and sometimes I don't sleep at night because I send Reiki to my clients. When your heart is purified, the path is shown to you. If you are not egoistic, the heavens will light your path and they give you homework …"

In the appendices see page 251, Koyama Sensei's notes from her teaching manual are published for the first time. I received a copy of this document from Fumio Ogawa Sensei in 1997). I suggest that you read this chapter with intensity, because it is filled to the brim with Reiki treasures.

Here ends Koyama Sensei's account of the Shihans.

The Seventh President, Masayoshi Kondo, University Professor

Kondo Sensei took over the presidency of the Usui Reiki Ryoho Gakkai in 1998. He is a Professor at a prestigious Japanese University. Unfortunately, I have not been able to contact him in person over the years.

The information regarding the military careers of Ushida Sensei, Taketomi Sensei and Wanami Sensei stem from "Ricku Kaigun Shokan Jinji Soran (Kaigun Hen)", editor So or Misao Toyama or Sotoyama. Publisher: Fujou Shobo, published on the 56th year of the Showa period (1981). The complete Army/Navy Personnel Listing (Navy Section).[6]

The Usui Reiki Ryoho Gakkai after Usui Sensei's Death

As mentioned earlier, Usui Sensei taught twenty Shihans the art of initiating students and gave them official permission to teach. Tadao Yamaguchi Sensei always tells his students that Usui Sensei had taught that one must be well prepared for his own death. Usui Sensei followed his own advice, and prepared the future of Reiki for the time after his death by permitting his Shihans to teach.

It is not known how many of the twenty Shihans remained and taught in the Usui Reiki Ryoho Gakkai. Unfortunately, we also do not know who is who in photograph 34 of the teachers on page 73.

Koyama Sensei says that two of Usui Sensei's students later on started their own spiritual group. The names of the teachers are not known. It is likely that not all the Shihans remained in the association, and that some of them went their own ways after their teacher's passing. However, we suspect

---

[6] *The information on the Usui Reiki Ryoho Gakkai teachers and presidents comes from Koyama Sensei's teaching handbook.*

that many of the Shihans kept teaching, and some of them must have had many students.

Reiki spread rapidly throughout Japan, and there must be a large number of Reiki practitioners that have not been discovered by the public. I say this to make it clear that my account here is just the tip of the iceberg ...

Hayashi Sensei and the Hayashi Reiki Kenkyukai

林忠次郎 Now lets point our attention towards to our Reiki Father, Hayashi Sensei. The information about him comes from Chiyoko and Tadao Yamaguchi. Chujiro Hayashi was born on September 15, 1880, in Tokyo. He graduated as a medical doctor from the 30th class of the Japanese Naval Academy in 1902. After his graduation, he served in the Russo-Japanese war until 1906. In 1918, he became the commander of the defense section of the port of Ominato. The chief of staff at that time was Kanichi Taketomi, who later on became the third president of the Usui Reiki Ryoho Gakkai.

Hayashi Sensei was married to Chie Hayashi. They had two children, Tadayoshi (born in 1903) and Kiyoe (born in 1910). His wife, Chie was born in 1887. Nothing more is known about his children.

As we said earlier, Hayashi Sensei became a Shihan in 1925, about one year before Usui Sensei's death. Because of his professional training as a medical doctor, Usui Sensei asked his student to start his own institute or Dojo (training center). This fact saved Reiki from extinction. Most probably, the reason for Usui Sensei's advice had legal reasons. Already back then, it was legally permitted only for medical personnel, acupuncturists or massage therapists to treat patients officially and in public. Usui Sensei knew that Hayashi Sensei would become a perfect instrument to spread Reiki in Japan, and ... abroad. Perhaps, this too, was part of the greater plan.

Hayashi Sensei founded the Hayashi Reiki Kenkyukai (Institute) in the present day Shinjuku ward of Tokyo, one of the five large city centers of modern Tokyo. The institute was located at 28 Higashi Shinano Cho. Nowadays, this area has been completely transformed since it was heavily bombed during World War Two.

At this address, Hayashi Sensei built his Dojo, in which later on, Takata Sensei was healed. At the dojo, twenty Reiki practitioners worked on ten massage tables on their clients. The use of massage tables in Reiki was introduced by Hayashi Sensei.

The Hayashi Institute Flourishes

Due to Hayashi Sensei's status as a medical doctor, the Hayashi Institute grew rapidly. The fame of Hayashi Sensei, a charismatic gentleman, spread into all corners of the country, like the rising sun. Like his teacher before him, Hayashi Sensei began to travel extensively.

One of his students, Wasaburo Sugano, learned Shoden and Okuden (Reiki one and two) from him in Osaka in 1928.

Sugano had come to Osaka from Ishikawa Prefecture in western Japan, as a young man, to pursue his career. Financially, his desire had become reality: he was a hard-working man, and had become the manager of a large corporation that manufactured western paper. The costs and effort of manufacturing Japanese paper is very high, and therefore his company cornered the market in no time. He had become very wealthy, but as far as his private life was concerned, a dark shadow hung over his heart. Both of his children had died from tuberculosis. The first child died soon after birth, and the second one during adolescence.

In his desperation, he looked for a way to avoid this same fate for future generations. He began looking for an alternative treatment method that could heal what all the money in the world, combined with western medical science, could not manage.

When he was introduced to Hayashi Sensei and Reiki, he had found his teacher and a teaching that suited him. Soon after he had taken the initial Reiki Training, his wife came down with tuberculosis as well. Afraid that he would loose his beloved too, he asked Hayashi Sensei to work on her. Together they treated her intensively, and she went into complete remission. This convinced the Suganos of the power of Reiki, and they set out to spread it with their family and friends. Especially, Mrs. Sugano, had caught Reiki-fire.

Travelling was not an easy task in Japan in those days. Because of the geographic conditions, there were not many roads and railroad connections. The mountains were hard to conquer, the valleys, narrow. Traveling was time-consuming and expensive, making it possible exclusively for the wealthy. More and more of Sugano's friends were interested in Reiki and wanted to learn, but shunned the trip to Osaka.

One day Sugano asked Hayashi Sensei if it were possible for him to come to Ishikawa to teach. Hayashi Sensei's one condition for traveling to Ishikawa was that ten new students would be present for the workshop. This was soon arranged in the Sugano's hometown called Daishoji. Mrs. Chiyo Sugano was one of the new students as well as a handful of her relatives. It was back then as it is now: as soon as Reiki infects a family, sooner or later everyone practices it. Sugano practiced Reiki in his free time, and his wife, Chiyo soon practiced full time.

The First Workshop in Daishoji

This is how five years of fruitful collaboration took root in Ishikawa prefecture. In 1935, the first Shoden/Okuden workshop took place in the Suganos house; later on, the workshops became well-known as the Daishoji branch of the Hayashi Reiki Institute. Twice a year, Hayashi Sensei taught Shoden and Okuden workshops there, once in the spring and once in the autumn. When Hayashi Sensei taught at home in Tokyo, he taught Shoden and Okuden separately, but when traveling he taught them in a combined five-day group.

Photo 40: Chiyoko Yamaguchi (the fifth from the right) learned Shoden and Okuden from Hayashi Sensei in 1938

The Suganos loved Reiki so much that both of them were soon given the Shihan level by Hayashi Sensei. Most practitioners remained with Okuden, but the organizers of Hayashi Sensei all across Japan were likely to become teachers.

The Reiki Training was not cheap in Hayashi Sensei's time. Shoden and Okuden cost about double the salary that a young teacher earned per month. Therefore, most of the students came from the wealthy class of society. They practiced Reiki for their own transformation, as well as for helping alleviate the suffering of their fellow man. A Reiki treatment at that time was affordable for everyone. Either a minimal amount of money was charged, or something was bartered. The fisherman brought a fish, the farmer a bag full of rice. And when the recipient did not have anything to give, the treatments were given free of charge.

After a little while all the adult members of the extended Sugano family were introduced into Reiki, and they practiced avidly. In 1935, a niece of the Suganos, called Katsue, took part in the training. Chiyoko Yamaguchi, her sister, who was later to become my teacher, was still too young to participate. Chiyoko was born in 1921, and had been exposed to Reiki from childhood. After the Suganos had lost their children, they asked Chiyoko's parents who had many children if they would mind to let her grow up in the Suganos house. They happily agreed and Chiyoko spent her childhood with her relatives, and Reiki. Once, Chiyoko told me that she was very jealous of her sister, Katsue. After Katsue had taken part in the group in 1935, it was discovered that she was skilled at giving treatments. Ever so often, a car would pull up in front of the house and the driver would bring her to a client's house and drop her back at home afterwards. There were not many cars in Daishoji at that time, and Chiyoko told me that this is what she wanted for herself.

Her uncle and foster father, Wasaburo, kept stalling her when she asked to take part in the training. He told her that she had to finish her schooling first, and after the graduation he would sponsor her participation in one of Hayashi Sensei's workshops. The real reason was that all the young family members received Reiki Training, one after other, in sequence of their age. The faithful day finally came in 1938, and Chiyoko learned Reiki from Hayashi Sensei (see photo 40). Sugano had told her that Reiki was part of her dowry; with Reiki she could take care of her future family, her husband and herself.

When I first met Chiyoko Sensei, she was still in awe of Hayashi Sensei. He was so charismatic, so tall and good looking, and knew so much about

Reiki, she told me. After the workshop, Chiyoko began giving Reiki treatments at home and in her circle of friends. This circle spread farther and farther over the next 65 years until her death in 2003, but more of that later.

An Auspicious Meeting: Hawayo Takata Meets Hayashi Sensei

In 1935, Hawayo Takata, an American citizen born in Hawaii to Japanese parents came to Tokyo to undergo an operation. According to her own words, she heard an inner voice while already placed upon the operating table which told her that this operation was not necessary. She listened to her inner wisdom and the surgery was cancelled. She asked the surgeon if there was another possibility of healing for her, and he replied that he knew of one, but that this would require time. Takata Sensei decided that she wanted to give it a try and was introduced by the surgeon to Hayashi Sensei. After she was healed, she wanted to learn Reiki and moved into the Hayashi's private house as an in-house disciple. Thus, Reiki spread its wings across the ocean into a new territory. If this had not happened, Reiki might have gotten lost within a small secret association in Japan, but it was to be quite different.

On Takata Sensei's Shihan certificate dated from 1938 it is stated that she was one of 13 fully trained Shihans. You will find a copy of this document in the book, "The Spirit of Reiki," Lotus Press. Many more teachers were given the same status in the last two years of Hayashi Sensei's life.

Takata Sensei followed in the Reiki tradition that those who wanted to proceed on the association ladder were expected to invite the Sensei to their hometown to teach. She invited Hayashi Sensei to Hawaii where he taught and gave lectures in 1937 and 1938.

This fact probably saved Reiki from extinction, but may have cost Hayashi Sensei's life (see photo 41, notice the scroll with the Reiki principles hanging behind him. This tradition for the teacher to sit in front of the principles while teaching is continued by Chiyoko Sensei's Jikiden Reiki Institute.).

Photo 41: Hayashi Sensei teaching in Hawaii 1937

Hayashi Sensei's Death

Hayashi Sensei took his own life on May 11, 1940, and his wife, Chie, took over the presidency of the Institute. The reason why Hayashi Sensei killed himself is yet unknown. Takata Sensei said that he was a pacifist, and, therefore, ended his life, but this does not make much sense. Hayashi Sensei was sixty years old and Japan was not involved in World War II yet, until about 18 months after his death.

Tadao Yamaguchi suspects that the Japanese government may have asked him to spy on the US, due to the fact that he was a retired navy official, and, had been to Hawaii previously for a considerable time. Therefore he must have been aware of military installations etc. As a Japanese gentlemen of the old school and, a naval officer there was only one honorable way out. On one hand, he could not say yes to become a spy and therefore, helping to kill the very people he just taught Reiki to—and, on the other hand, he could not say no to his emperor and country. He could only end his own life. In Japanese culture this is not seen as a cop out, but as the only honorable way to deal with his predicament. If an old fashioned Japanese person heard this story, he would bow his head in respect and admiration …

Hayashi Sensei cut his wrists in the bathroom of his Atami villa with a surgical blade. His wife was instructed to keep the real reasons and the way he ended his life secret. This had cultural reasons: first, he wanted to protect his students from a similar fate, and second, the teacher is responsible for his students and should not leave them alone. Chie Hayashi took over the presidency of the Institute and moved to Ishikawa, thus strengthening the already strong bond she had with the Sugano/Yamaguchi families.

The Tide Turns

One and a half years after Hayashi Sensei's death, in December 1941, the Japanese air force attacked Pearl harbour and officially joined forces with Germany. After the surprise attack, the British declared war on Japan and things became difficult for Reiki in Japan. What had been a blessing since the 1920's became a curse. Before the war, the Japanese government had let the Reiki practitioners flourish due to the high positions of many of the teachers in the army and navy. Those two were the most respected agencies, and what was accepted in the armed forces was the law. Now the tide turned: The war was declared and all men of a certain age were drafted. The government made sure that there was no opposition to their course of action.

All spiritual and esoteric groups were (quite rightly) suspected to have links to the pacifist movement and had to go underground until August 1945. The Usui Reiki Ryoho Gakkai, as well as the Hayashi Reiki Kenkyu-kai, had to close their doors and stop practicing in public. The headquarters of the Usui Reiki Ryoho Gakkai in Tokyo was bombed out during a raid.

They had to move several times, and worked with Reiki only in their private lives. The Hayashi Institute must have had a similar fate: the area in Shinjuku where the institute was located was totally devastated during World War Two.

Still the interest in Reiki grew in the Yamaguchi family. Chiyoko Sensei's older brother, Yoshio Ushio, learned Reiki from Chie Hayashi on April 29, 1943. In Tadao Yamaguchi's delightful book with the title "Light on the origins of Reiki" you find a couple of photographs from those years depicting Chie Hayashi Sensei with her students, many of which were from the Yamaguchi family.

After 1945

After World War II, Reiki declined more and more. After the capitulation of the Showa Tenno (The Showa, Emperor, known as Hirohito in the West), the American Occupational Forces took over the rule in Japan. For Reiki, this was a disastrous event. The new rulers changed many laws, trying to rearrange Japanese society. They made some good changes, restructuring the Japanese agriculture for example, but also outlawed all the traditional Japanese healing arts. The American Pharmaceutical industry was given a huge market … and Reiki became illegal.

Reiki, Chinese medicine (called Kampo in Japanese), acupuncture and countless Hand Healing groups had to either discontinue their practice or change directions, as happened previously during the Taisho era. But Reiki always finds its way into the hearts of men to heal their body and mind and ultimately makes the world a better place to live in. After Reiki was outlawed in Japan it began to grow and develop through Takata Sensei in Hawaii!

Countless hand healing groups took on a religious cover, knowing that the Japanese constitution grants the freedom of religion, which may include faith healing … Luckily, neither the Usui Reiki Ryoho Gakkai nor the Hayashi Reiki Kenkyukai followed suit. Koyama Sensei says in her memoirs again and again that Usui Sensei's greatest achievement was that he did not turn Reiki into a sect.

Ogawa Sensei from the Usui Reiki Ryoho Gakkai told us that there were about one million Reiki practitioners in Japan before World War II. Chiyoko Sensei confirmed this. The Usui Association alone had 60 branches all over Japan back then. It is not known how many branches the Hayashi Institute had, but we guess that it must have been a similar number.

Chie Hayashi lead the Hayashi Institute until the mid-1950's. She did not possess the same charisma that her husband had had and times were hard. The Japanese infrastructure was destroyed and the capitol was in rubble; the civilians were demoralized, and due to the many deaths in the battlefield, there was not enough manpower to rebuild the country. To find a successor proved difficult for Chie Sensei, since Reiki was kind of illegal and you could not work with it in public. Who would want to take over an illegal group?

Tadao's uncle told him that Chie Sensei asked several Shihans of the Yamaguchi family if they were interested in taking over her position. They all declined for the above reasons; also they did not want to leave their home and move to Tokyo. Takata Sensei too was asked, but did not accept either. For this reason, the Hayashi Reiki Kenkyukai closed it's doors forever. But without a doubt, everyone who ever learned Reiki kept practicing it at home with his family, thus keeping the flame alive!

Precisely this is what happened in the Yamaguchi family. Tadao Sensei, who grew up with Reiki, tells us that he learned very quickly not to talk about Reiki at school. If you would like to know more about the Yamaguchi family and their involvement with Reiki, please read his book. I promise you that you will enjoy it.

Reiki in Japan—My Research

During the 1950's and 1960's, Reiki disappeared more and more from the public view. The elder Reiki generation died out one by one, and very few of Usui Sensei's original students were left. As mentioned above, the Shihans trained by Usui Sensei in person were all men who were born before 1875. You remember that Hayashi Sensei who was 47 at the time, was the youngest of the lot (he was born in 1880).

The Usui Reiki Ryoho Gakkai functioned like a lodge, or like the Lions Club. It was, theoretically, open to the public but in fact it was difficult to become a member. At first, one would have to know someone who was already a member. This person introduced one to the president of the Association first. If the president felt comfortable with the potential new member, he was introduced to the group and if all the group members agreed, the new member was welcomed. Membership is for life (therefore, the difficult first steps) and there are two types of membership. One can be a certified member, or, a so-called "friend of the association." A friend of the association is permitted to take part in activities, but is not certified.

Since Reiki has spread in the West and this movement reached Japan in the mid 1980's, one of the prerequisites to become a member is that one is not involved in Western Reiki. Foreigners have not been known to be accepted. An acquaintance of Tadao Sensei who is a member of the group, told us that in the past ten years only two new members were accepted. He calls himself "the last" … In 1997, I met a Japanese Reiki teacher from a splinter group that came out of the Usui Reiki Ryoho Gakkai who called them "The Dinosaur Club"!

The Japanese government makes life difficult for spiritual or religious groups that are not part of the main stream. As I mentioned earlier, there are thousands of groups that walk their own spiritual path. Some of these groups are obviously interested in their own spiritual development, while others seem to be interested in money and power. In Japanese society, there is no place for a subculture. Either you are in or you are out. The only possibility for a misfit is to be a part of a spiritual group—or a gangster!

The Usui Association was given two choices. Either they were to continue as before the war and be persecuted due to their conflict with the medical laws, or they were to found an association or a club that works exclusively with its own members. And this is the path that was chosen by the association. The sign post at the meeting place was dismantled, and there is no listing in the yellow pages. The group practices exclusively with their members, and, of course, within their families. Seen in this light, we can understand their reasoning.

When I first arrived in Japan in the summer of 1989, the only person teaching Reiki in public once or twice a year, was Mitsui Sensei, a student of Barbara Ray. At that time, I was not involved in Reiki yet, and worked as an English/German teacher with my ex-wife. Mitsui Sensei, we found out later, had been in contact with Ogawa Sensei (of whom we will speak a little later) as early as 1984. She taught Reiki One and Two exclusively, and many students were dying to continue their Reiki education.

I began my research of Reiki History, quite accidentally, in the spring of 1994, without much luck. No one that I talked to had any knowledge about Reiki, or of Usui Sensei. Those who had heard the word Reiki before in the healing context thought that this was something American …

The First Contact with Koyama Sensei

In the summer of 1994, I received a surprise phone call from one of my students from Yokohama, Toshitaka Mochizuki, who told me that he had the phone number of a lady who had been practicing Reiki for sixty years. He did not tell us who this lady was and I found out only after we had talked to her that it was Kimiko Koyama Sensei, who was then the president of the Usui Reiki Ryoho Gakkai—which I did not know existed! When Mo-chizuki Sensei gave me the number, he also made one condition: I should not tell Koyama Sensei from whom I had received her contact details. I did not understand this condition back then and a couple of weeks later the great moment arose. Later on, I understood that Japanese protocol demands that when contacting someone unknown, a proper introduction by a third person who knows the other is absolutely necessary.

My heart-beat was louder than the ring of the phone as an elderly lady an-swered the phone. Her first question was: "Where did you get this number" … I held my breath, and after a little while, she was willing to talk a little. Yet she asked again and again: "What do you want from me?" Chetna, my ex-wife, answered kindly, "We don't want to bother you. We are researching Usui Sensei's life for a book project". "I will not read that," she countered, "and I am not interested in Reiki that comes from the West." She also said that she was not ready to meet us. Previously, she had been asked by several foreigners to set up a meeting and had always declined. Later on, we found out that Phyllis Furumoto Sensei was one of those who were refused, too.

I was glad that I was not alone, but did not understand why she was upset and not open to a dialogue. I understood this only later on. In the course of the conversation, perhaps due to our composure and kindness, she answered some questions about Usui Sensei. She told us about his life and work with Reiki with great love and respect. She said that Usui Sensei possessed great charisma and radiated great energy. His students, she said, used to hold onto his kimono to receive some of his radiance (you are not to touch the Sensei's body but it is acceptable to hang onto his clothes …) She told us that he had had many amazing healing experiences: one time he treated a man who had had a stroke whose face and body were paralyzed. After the treatment, Usui Sensei told the man: "Now, you get up and walk home," which is precisely what he did!

Further on, she told us that Usui Sensei had a good sense of humor and made his students laugh; yet, he was serious and sincere when it was called for. He treated anyone who asked for it, and also taught Reiki to anyone who was interested in learning. During his lifetime, she said there were 40 Reiki Schools. Later on, we found out that these were the branches of the Usui Reiki Ryoho Gakkai. About 2000 seekers learned Reiki from him in person.

She also told us that Usui Sensei was buried at the Saihoji Temple in To-kyo. She said that Usui Sensei was originally from Gifu prefecture and that he died in Fukuyama. About Reiki she said, "Even the enlightened ones like

Buddha or Jesus understood that they themselves were but a small part of a greater divine presence. This divine presence is Reiki. Please don't misunderstand Reiki as a healing method for physical ailments. The basis of Reiki is love and we have to work upon this daily with all of our heart."

When she had said enough, she asked us not to call her again, and we promised. And a promise is a promise is a promise …

In the conversation with Koyama Sensei, she mentioned the Saihoji Temple as Usui Sensei's final resting place. I decided that this should be the next step on my journey and made preparation for the trip, 650 miles to the south of where I used to live. This trip was to be the first of countless visits to Usui Sensei's memorial. More of this in the chapter "Sacred Reiki Sights".

The First Contact with Tsutomu Oishi

I would like to begin this chapter from the back to the front. You probably read above that this book is dedicated to Chetna Mami Kobayashi, my ex-wife, without whom none of this research would have been possible. The other person the present work is dedicated to is Tsutomu Oishi. We never met in person and just talked on the telephone numerous times. Just before completing this book, I wanted to meet him in person to thank him for his kindness, because it is due to his efforts that Reiki history and practice had to be entirely reviewed. After we had lost track of each other for seven years, we arranged to meet on April 20, 2009, in Shizuoka City. When I arrived in Shizuoka City, it turned out that he had just passed away, and I found myself in his home, bowing to his ashes with the longing that my gratitude be received from above. Now, let's go back to the chronological order of events. At Saihoji Temple in Tokyo, I was surprised to find the memorial in honor of Usui Sensei's life and work (see the translation on page 60). The text states that Usui Sensei prepared to end his life on Mount Kurama, north of Kyoto. This place was to become the next stepping-stone on my journey, and this too is described in the chapter on the "Sacred Reiki Sites" (page 118).

Just before I was to travel to Kyoto in August of 1995, my Reiki telephone rang once more. This time, one of my friends and students, Shizuko Akimoto was on the line. (Shizuko, if you happen to read this, please contact me!). She was quite excited and told me that she had treated a Japanese gentleman with something other than Reiki the day before. During the treatment, this man had said to her: "You know, there used to be an amazing healing technique called Reiki!" "I am a Reiki Teacher," answered Shizuko, "and have learned it from a German teacher in Sapporo." The client, Tsutomu Oishi almost fell from the treatment table in surprise. His mother, he told Shizuko, had learned Reiki from one of Usui Sensei's direct students, when he was a child.

I was overwhelmed and decided to sleep on it for a night. It seemed that we had found someone who was ready to share his knowledge with us. The next day, I called Shizuko and faxed her a long sheet of questions to ask Oishi-San upon their next meeting.

On their next scheduled appointment, Oishi-San brought along the picture of Usui Sensei (photo 32) that had been given to his mother by Usui Sensei. He said, "Give this to your teacher." I was overwhelmed, and said that I would prefer just to have a copy, for a family treasure should remain with the family.

Shizuko asked Oishi-San about Reiki, but he told her that he did not know much, since his mother had not talked about Reiki to him. When he had asked her about it, she refused to talk about it (You understand this, remembering the way the Usui Association operated. Japanese society is structured into many small, coherent and exclusive groups. Outside of any group, its concerns are not talked about with "outsiders" even if they are your own children!).

One of the things that make Japanese culture tick is trust, and trust needs time to develop. I decided to take it easy and wait before bombarding Oishi san with more questions, even though this was a hard lesson.

When the two of them met again, Oishi-San told Shizuko about a Reiki Association with its headquarters in Tokyo that was in direct succession of Usui Sensei, The Usui Reiki Ryoho Gakkai. This was the first time that we heard about the existence of the association, and I was intrigued. Further on, Oishi-San told Shizuko that the association had several branches in other Japanese cities, and that he knew the leader of the branch in Shizuoka City personally. If she wanted to, he would introduce her to him and visit him together, proving that he agreed to meet her.

Photo 42:
Ogawa Sensei

A Shihan of the Usui Reiki Ryoho Gakkai—Fumio Ogawa Sensei

Now, the time had come. For the first time, so I thought, someone had succeeded in scheduling a meeting with a teacher from the original Usui Association. Later on, we found out that this was not the first time as mentioned above. Already in 1984, Mitsui Sensei had talked to Ogawa Sensei. A few weeks after their last meeting, Shizuko and Oishi-San travelled to the Shizuoka home of Fumio Ogawa Sensei together. He was a Shihan of the Usui Reiki Ryoho Gakkai, leading the branch in Shizuoka City. I faxed a long list of questions to Shizuko (see page 237 in the appendices) and waited impatiently at home for all the answers I was hoping to get. The first meeting with Ogawa Sensei happened on July 20, 1996. Ogawa Sensei had had a stroke in 1995, and according to Shizuko had recovered in an unbelievable way. There was no sign of the stroke left, and he was mentally, as well as physically, fit as a glove. At the same time, Ogawa Sensei was being visited by other Japanese Reiki practitioners and his family was trying to keep these visits to a minimum in order not to exhaust Ogawa Sensei.

He was 89 years old back then, and Shizuko was impressed with his character. After their first meeting, I was not sure if he really knew a lot. I had asked Shizuko to enquire about Takata Sensei and Hayashi Sensei, but Ogawa Sensei did not know them! Only later on did he remember Hayashi Sensei. This is due to the fact that Ogawa Sensei joined the Association after Hayashi Sensei's death.

Photo 43: Shoden and Okuden certificates that Ogawa Sensei issued for a student between September 18, 1942, and November 18, 1943

Further on, I had asked about the Reiki symbols of the second and third degrees and had asked Shizuko to show them to him. He was satisfied with the second-degree symbols, but had never seen the Master Symbol. But, he was a Shihan, a teacher, how could he not know the so-called Master Symbol? Did he forget it because of his advanced age? I remembered that my grandma could quote conversations she had held with her father 90 years earlier, but that she could not remember what we just talked about five minutes ago. Or else … a flagrant thought gripped me with a vengeance … perhaps the Master symbol did not exist in the original Reiki teaching. This doubt remained with me until I began the teacher's training with Chiyoko Sensei in 2002. It is true that the so-called Master Symbol is neither used in the Usui Reiki Ryoho Gakkai nor in the traditional Hayashi Lineage. How it entered the Western Reiki practice is unclear and can only be suspected.

Ogawa Sensei told us that the headquarters of the Usui Reiki Ryoho Gakkai was in Tokyo, and that the association had always had a president since the times of Usui Sensei. The first president was Usui Sensei himself. The second was Ushida Sensei. The third was Taketomi Sensei. The fourth was Watanabe Sensei. The fifth was Wanami Sensei. The sixth president was Koyama Sensei and this name sent goose pimples down my spine. This was the lady we had talked to on the telephone! Now, I knew why she had always asked us "What do you want from me?" She was the president of the Usui Reiki Ryoho Gakkai, and one year before her death, Kondo Sensei took over the presidency. This meeting rocked my Reiki-world greatly. Historical and practical "Reiki facts" had to be revised, and I found myself insecure and burdened with doubt.

In order to feel better, I asked Shizuko to give Ogawa Sensei a treatment upon their next meeting. He gladly accepted and was delighted by her healing touch. "It is beautiful what you do," he said to her, "but we do it quite differently …"

From their next meeting onwards, he began to teach her what he knew. She learned to work without a prescribed set of hand positions and discovered the art of Byosen, allowing the byosen to lead the way. During the next two years, they met occasionally as she learned more and more about his way of working. One of the first questions that I had asked her to ask him was whether or not Usui Sensei had given any written material to his students. I also wanted to know if there was any other written documentation about Reiki from his time. Already on their first meeting, Ogawa Sensei had said that Usui Sensei used to give a manual to his students, which was still passed on to the new students of the Association. Part of the manual was a treatment plan that was to aid inexperienced students to be able to work with their clients, before they had mastered the art of Byosen. (see "Original Reiki Handbook of Dr. Mikao Usui", Lotus Press).

In 1997 I met Shizuko in Tokyo at a coffee shop. She had told me that Ogawa Sensei had given her something for me. Shizuko handed me three documents: The first was a manuscript written by Ogawa Sensei titled "Everyone Can Do Reiki". After reading it, I asked him if he wanted it published, but he declined. The second was the previously mentioned Usui Reiki Ryoho Hikkei, Usui Sensei's handbook for his students. The third was a teaching handbook written by Koyama Sensei that was given to the teachers of the Usui Reiki Ryoho Gakkai on their 50th anniversary in 1972. Excerpts of this manual are published in this book for the first time. Some of the material is woven into the text, and is marked as coming from Koyama Sensei. The rest is included in the appendices.

In 1998, Fumio Ogawa passed away, and Oishi San told me on the telephone that his family had agreed to let me copy his legacy. This was a great honor, and I probably should have done it. But deep in my heart, a voice told me not to, it just didn't feel right. With Ogawa Sensei's death, the slightly open door to the Usui Association closed as quietly as it had opened.

In the beginning of January 1999, Koyama Sensei, too, passed away, and this left me with the feeling that now we had to go our own separate ways.

A Reiki Family, the Yamaguchis

Later that year, I heard repeatedly of a direct student of Hayashi Sensei, who was supposedly living in Kyoto. In the book "Light on the Origins of Reiki," Tadao Yamaguchi describes his family legacy in great detail, spiced with lots of rare photographs and practical Reiki information, an absolute must read!

I asked Toshitaka Mochizuki if he knew who it was, and he told me that it was Chiyoko Yamaguchi. But he did not have her address back then, and I called Hiroshi Doi, a member of the Usui Reiki Ryoho Gakkai, who gladly gave it to me.

Because of the difficulties I had encountered as a foreigner in the Japanese Reiki-World, again I asked my ex-wife to make the call. Tadao Yamaguchi answered the phone, and was open and relaxed from the beginning. We asked if Chiyoko Sensei was teaching publicly and Tadao told us that she was just beginning to do that. When questioned as to whether she would accept a foreigner as her student, he asked if I spoke Japanese. When he heard that I did, he said, "No problem, it does not matter that he is not Japanese." I was thrilled and could not believe my luck.

Tadao told us that his mother had learned directly from Hayashi Sensei and that she was going to teach us exactly what she had learned from her teacher. He also told me that it would be possible only to do Reiki One and Two with her. Hayashi Sensei, he mentioned, had taught Shoden and Okuden (Reiki One and Two) on five consecutive days and they were going to duplicate his format. Until the day we spoke on the telephone, she had not taught public workshops. For sixty years, she had given daily treatments and had initiated the people interested in private. Advertisement happened naturally, by word of mouth. The best way to teach someone Reiki, she had said, is this: "Someone is ill and he comes to you for healing. You treat him and he gets better and better, day-by-day. When he has recovered from his illness, he may want to learn Reiki himself, to share the blessings he himself has been showered upon. This way, you can be certain that he will understand the real value of Reiki, and he will continue using it for himself and his environment".

She said that she had met several Japanese Reiki practitioners, who had learned in the Western Reiki Lineage previously and that she was under the impression that it would be good for them, too, to begin from Shoden (Reiki One). This was not meant to mean disrespect for what we had previously learned. She said that the reason was that she wanted to teach exactly what Hayashi Sensei had taught, and that she wanted her students to have her knowledge—nothing less would do. She asked me not to mix what I would learn from her with what I already knew, out of love and respect for the teaching—and—the teacher. In traditional Japanese culture, one does not try to improve upon the teaching of one's own teacher. I was glad to have found a Japanese teacher who was ready to accept me as a student, and I gladly agreed to her conditions.

The next available Shoden/Okuden workshop took place in July 2000. It was challenging to sit up for so long, and I felt like a child waiting for Christmas: five more nights to sleep, four, three …

Reiki Training with Chiyoko Yamaguchi

Thus, my long-term dream of receiving Reiki Training in Japan came true in the autumn of 1999, ready for the new Millennium. Chiyoko Sensei had accepted me as her student, and I flew to Kyoto in the summer of 2000 for our first workshop. We spent five intensive days together, either from 9 am to 3 pm or from 1 pm to 7 pm. In the evening, after the workshop, I returned to the hotel, listening to the sounds of the ancient capitol. After having been a teacher for many years, I had become a student again, and felt how my heart opened up more and more. Remembering it now, a book by Shunryu Suzuki comes to mind titled "Zen Mind, Beginner's Mind". In his book, Suzuki Roshi talks about the attitude of not knowing, and living each moment with the mind of a beginner. What a blessing each moment is when you are just like a child …

Photo 44:
Chiyoko Yamaguchi

To experience this purification on a deeper level, each evening I sat quietly and reminisced about the day. Knowing that this training was a special occasion, I wrote a diary, and this is what I would like to share with you in the next chapter. It is my personal account of events, and I hope that it will inspire you, even though it is quite subjective. Purposely, everything that concerns

Photo 45:
Tadao Yamaguchi

the Reiki Symbols, their meaning and usage, as well as their names and mantras was left out. This is to be conveyed from the teacher to the student directly, and is, therefore, not for discussion in printed form.

The First Meeting

On July 24th at 9 am, I meet the Yamaguchis for the first time in person, and it is love at first sight. Later on, we find out that this love is mutual, and it is still as tender and all-inclusive today as it was back then. The training takes place in a 120-year-old traditional Kyoto townhouse, in which the Yamaguchis used to live.

For many years, the front part of the house has been used as a stationery store and office, the Yamaguchis family business. In the back of the house, we ascend a narrow and steep staircase to the previous living quarters in the upper floor. Years later, the house is completely renovated and becomes the tastefully designed home of the Jikiden Reiki Institute. Something seems to be wrong with my body: the long limbs, nose and neck are in the way while sitting, getting up, drinking tea, and even while visiting the restroom. The floor is laid out with traditional tatami (straw) mats as we sit at a low dining

Photo 46: Jikiden Reiki Institute, Kyoto, today

table that, later in the day, turns into a massage table with a cotton futon on top of it.

The interior is furnished in the traditional Japanese way. Antique Japanese drawers and wooden closets adorn the simple, but tasteful, room. The room is filled with emptiness and radiates Japanese culture. I feel like someone who has finally returned home from a long and arduous journey. Since childhood, a longing for the culture of Silence burns in my heart, and here I sit, right smack in the middle of it.

Original Reiki certificates radiate their energy from the walls onto the daily activities. Photographs of Usui and Hayashi Sensei and their unknown students give the room a sacred atmosphere. All of this culminates in a scroll, handwritten by Hayashi Sensei, that is placed behind Chiyoko Sensei's teaching seat. It shows the heart of the Reiki practice—the Five Reiki Principles (Gokai in Japanese). In the course of the day, we find out that this is a tradition going back to Usui and Hayashi Sensei: the teacher sits in front of the Gokai in the area of the room that has the most natural energy (the corner farthest away from the main entrance of the room) while he teaches. Have I been transported to Reiki heaven?

Besides Chetna and me, there are four other Japanese Reiki students present. They call Mrs. Yamaguchi, Chiyoko Sensei, and her son, Tadao Sensei. I do the same. It is lovely to be a student again, and not to think that I already know everything. Three of the others have had previous Reiki Training, while the fourth learns Reiki for the first time. I listen through her ears and see with her eyes.

Reiki is my passion, and therefore, I have many questions. Knowing that a Japanese student does not question his teacher, I enquire with Tadao in private if it is ok for me to quiz the two of them. He lets me know that I can ask to my heart's content. Asking the teacher a question is uncommon in Japanese culture for several reasons. First, a question challenges the teacher and doubts his authority. Second, the fact that something has been left unclear shows the teacher that he has not done his job well …

But I am not alone with the questions. One of the first things Chiyoko Sensei asks me is if I give treatments. "This," she confides in me, "is my standard question to those students already practicing Reiki." Telling her that I do give treatments, I add that I seem to attract clients with certain illnesses which I especially like treating. My all time favorite is asthma, but I also enjoy treating edema, back problems and psychological issues. She wants to know if I have ever witnessed any healing during my work. When I give her some examples, she smiles happily and says, "I am glad to hear that. When I ask this question to the Reiki teachers that come to me, many of them answer that they are so busy teaching, that there is no time for treatments left." "If you don't have any experience with healing," I ask them, "what on Earth do you teach your students?"

Chiyoko Sensei is a simple woman in the best sense. She is unpretentious and loving, and, in short, just as you would like your grandma to be: she is kindhearted and humble. She does not seem to mind much what others think of her, with the exception of her teacher, Hayashi Sensei. It seems that she feels a sense of duty towards him, a responsibility to continue his work, in his spirit. (If you remember the explanation of the 4th Reiki principle, you understand her Gyo, duty/responsibility towards the teacher and the teaching, and, the world as such). The feeling of having reached home permeates my kokoro (heart/mind-being) …

The First Day, Shoden Part One

After a few minutes dedicated to getting to know each other, Chiyoko Sensei commences with telling us all about her life story and the meetings with Hayashi Sensei. Since all of this is skillfully told in Tadao Sensei's book, I will not mention it here again. Chiyoko Sensei learned Reiki as a young woman, and continued the Reiki tradition after her marriage, within her own family. Her four sons grew up with Reiki: In the Yamaguchi household, there was no medicine cabinet. They did not have painkillers or antibiotic ointment. She says: "We are not medicine people!" The children, (Tadao and his brothers), and later, their own children and grandchildren are all receiving exclusively Reiki for their physical and emotional wellbeing. "In the old days, Reiki was used as a home remedy," Chiyoko Sensei tells us. "One worked with it at home and never advertised it in public."

The First Reiju (Attunement)

Tadao Sensei now gives us instructions regarding the first attunement that we are about to receive. The Japanese word for Attunement is Reiju (see page 20 key words) and he explains the word for me since the others are Japanese and need no further explanation. Reiju means giving/granting or activating the soul, and this is an activation process for Reiki. Reiki comes from the Universe, enters the top of the head, and goes down to the Tanden. From there, it comes up through both sides of the chest, travels down the arms until it comes out, primarily through the hands. We are asked to sit still on the floor with our eyes closed. The attention should be placed upon the Tanden and the in-breath should fill the Tanden with energy. In this ritual, we are helped to remember the soul energy that gives life to everything under the sun; we are to claim our birthright. Tadao turns off the light, and darkens the room further by hanging dark cloth in front of the windows. It is pitch dark, and we can hardly see our own hands that we were asked to hold in the gassho position, the fingertips in front of our third eye. From today on, we will receive a Reiju everyday given by Chiyoko Sensei and Tadao Sensei. Chiyoko Sensei now begins to chant the Gokai (The five Reiki principles). She chants in a firm voice: Kyo dake wa, and we chant: Ikaru na, shinpai suna, kansha shite, gyo o hage me, hito ni shinsetsu ni. This is repeated three times in the same way.

My hands feel like balloons filled with Reiki, as silence descends upon us. I don't pay attention to where and how I am being touched by the teachers, but focus my awareness to the inner process. In the inner room of the body/mind, Reiki becomes visible, all is Light, and the participants become one. Kansha shite, be grateful, is the only thought there is. Since the first contact with Japanese Reiki through Ogawa Sensei, I have been looking forward to this moment.

The Reiju takes about 25 minutes and I notice that the ritual is performed differently from what I have learned in the tradition of the Reiki Alliance. It is rather simple and without the fireworks. When we are asked to get up and sit in a circle so we can touch each other's shoulders, I cannot get up. It is not that the body cannot move, but there is no mental impulse. Everything is perfect as it is, no need to do anything. Later on, when I think about it, I am reminded of a Zen Buddhist term, shikan taza, which means: just sitting. A seemingly endless moment of peace and silence sets in; my hands and feet pulsate with energy and Reiki-Fire!

Tadao opens the curtains and turns on the light. Sitting in a circle we are asked to touch the shoulders of the person in front of us, while paying attention to the perception in our hands and the shoulders that are being touched from behind. This is done after the Reiju because it is now that our hands are most sensitive. This sensitivity is heightened every day, so we will be able to perceive what is going on in our client's bodies later on during future treatments. The art of perception is called Byosen, and tomorrow we are to learn more about that. After about ten minutes of this exercise, called Reiki Mawashi, each participant is asked what he or she felt.

After the Reiki Mawashi, the living room table transforms itself into a Massage table. A thick futon in placed upon it. We sit in front of the table, sometimes cross-legged, sometimes with the tired legs stretched out under the table. One of the participants receives Reiki from all of us. Chiyoko Sensei, as the most experienced of us, sits treating the client's head. The rest of us place our hands upon other strategically important parts of the client's body. (More about that in the chapter on Byosen).

During the treatment, she explains her way of working, using the case of a client who came to her with diabetes as an example.

"When the blood circulation is bad, due to the accumulation of toxins, this blood flows either to the liver or to the pancreas. If it flows to the liver, the blood gets cleansed there, and there is no problem. But if it flows to the pancreas, it creates an insulin shock. If insulin is then administered artificially, the pancreas stops the manufacture of insulin, and you become dependant upon medication. In this case, you treat the liver and the pancreas intensively. I have done this once before with a client for a month, on a daily basis, and he recovered completely. It also helps to eat Goya (bitter gourd) with yoghurt. Illness is a cleansing process. The inner organs oscillate, and in their vicinity toxic materials accumulate in the blood and lymph vessels. This toxicity interferes with the smooth mode of operation of the organs."

We are not emerged in "holy silence" while we are treating each other. Chiyoko Sensei gives instructions and comments on what she perceives while touching a certain area. Sometimes, she asks one of us to place a hand onto a certain position, and wants to know what we feel. Another time, she says, "hibitemasu-ne, it pulsates, doesn't it," and she takes someone's hand

and places it on the body part to feel what is going on. The atmosphere is relaxed, and sometimes day-to-day issues are discussed, like what sweets are good with a cup of tea, or which silk is useful to make a kimono.

She shares with us how Hayashi Sensei worked. He always had two practitioners work on one client, without using a set of premeditated hand positions. He suggested always treating the head, the soles of the feet, and the afflicted area. The more experienced practitioner of the group should treat the head, to determine the course of the treatment. A systematic treatment following a certain set of hand positions was not used, she says, because most of the time one worked with a team, and often the teacher was present who could be asked what to do next.

She tells us that there was no set time for a treatment and that you should do as much as you can. "If you have an hour, do an hour; if you have 2 hours, do two hours. But you should do at least 30 minutes. Less than that won't do. I am old and Reiki is my passion," she says. "I have no schedule, and during my many years of Reiki experience in which I did at least two treatments per day, I realized that it is best for me to work for about 90 minutes. But I never look at the clock, I listen to the Byosen." This last statement, I understand fully only the next day. Today, eleven years later, I realize that one needs much more time to learn the art of treating someone with Reiki than I anticipated back then.

She encourages us to schedule as much time as possible for each treatment, but remains pragmatic: "Use the time you have for your treatments. If you have an hour, the treatment takes one hour. If there are only forty-five minutes in your schedule, that's ok too. But what is important is that you work intensively. If your client is seriously ill, treat him every day for at least one month. After a month, you will have a good idea where the treatment is going, and then you can adjust the course of further treatment accordingly. Perhaps you cut down the number of treatments per week to two or three. The best thing to do is to initiate one of the client's family members (into Reiki) so they don't have to come to you so often."

She was quite clear about being comfortable when you work. We sat with our legs crossed under the table, and sometimes with our legs stretched out under the table, and sometimes with our legs falling asleep under the table! She told us that our physical comfort is the most important thing. "Don't put out your back while you are fixing someone else's. I suggest that you keep your body in the middle of your arms/hands and that you keep your wrists straight. This way you can sit comfortably for a long time, and keeping your wrists straight ensures that you are able to perceive the feedback from the body of the client that you are treating."

I feel comfortable in her presence, and my initial insecurity about my questioning mind diminishes. I ask her if she minds me asking her so many questions. She just smiles and says that she'd be glad to answer whatever is unclear to me.

The Second Day, Shoden Part Two

Today, we begin our morning with chanting the Reiki Principles and receiving the delightful Reiju. Chiyoko gives the Reiju together with Tadao, and it is lovely to see mother and son perform such a beautiful ritual together. I don't try to figure out whose hands are whose, and realize how suprapersonal Reiki is. The more the teacher is able to step back and leave his personality behind during the Reiju, the better it works. Then heaven and Earth become one …

Before we begin, she tells us that Hayashi Sensei used to chant The Meiji Emperor's poetry while he performed the Reiju.

Next, we practice the Reiki Mawashi again, and then we are taught the first symbol. We are told not to write the symbol down, but to memorize it by heart. This was an old tradition that goes back to Usui Sensei and Hayashi Sensei. Later on, when Chiyoko Sensei was continuously confronted with the inability of her foreign students to memorize the symbols (especially the distant healing symbol) instantly, she reluctantly changed her mind. She then allowed her non-Japanese students to copy the symbols, and she gave a printout of the distant symbol to them—but not to her Japanese students. "Hayashi Sensei will be upset with me," she confided with me then, obviously upset.

Tadao Sensei draws the first symbol on the whiteboard, and I nod my head in agreement. Chiyoko Sensei looks at me with a smirk, and says "Right—you use it in Western Reiki, too, don't you?" I agree, and she says with a mischievous smile, "and, you also repeat the name of it three times when you use it, right?" I agree again, thinking that, yes, we do it right! And she continues: "That is like picking up a spoon and saying three times 'Spoon, spoon, spoon!'" After we all enjoy a hearty laugh, she says, "The name of the symbol does not need to be spoken, it is the shape that counts." Thinking about this a while after the workshop, I realize that we work with four concepts in Reiki that all have different dynamics. We use Kanji, Shirushi, Kotodama and Jumon. For a deeper understanding of Reiki, these terms are described in detail on page 19.

The symbols that Chiyoko Sensei teaches us are written slightly different from what I have previously learned. Also, some of them have different names, and their meaning is deeply rooted in Japanese culture. All of the names of the symbols are originally written with Kanji, and providing that one knows the correct Kanji, their meaning can be checked in any concise Japanese dictionary.

After having recovered from the laughter, Chiyoko Sensei teaches us a delightful technique called Ketsueki Kokan that I have never come across before. In short, this is called Kekko (see chapter on Japanese Reiki techniques). Literally, Ketsueki Kokan means Blood exchange. This technique is used after each treatment in order to increase the blood circulation. It also brings the Reiki into the deeper tissue and helps the body eliminate accumulated toxins. With this technique, a healing crisis (when the toxins that have been dissolved enter the bodily fluids) can either be avoided all together or lessened. With the Ketsueki Kokan, the bodily fluids are exchanged, the toxins are eliminated and the client feels invigorated. If there is not enough time for a treatment, one could just do the Ketsueki Kokan instead, which takes a little under five minutes. In case of metabolic illnesses, it is suggested to perform the Ketsueki Kokan two or three times in a row. In the following days, we practice this technique every time after the treatments.

When I ask her about the meaning of the Five Reiki Principles she answers, "Incorporate the first four into your life.

1—Don't be angry
2—Don't worry
3—Be grateful
and
4—Do your duties fully.

After you have accomplished that, there is no inner work left to do. The only thing left to do is living the Fifth Reiki Principle:

5—Be kind to your fellow men. And that means: give them or teach them Reiki!"

Today we learn about the Byosen. In Chiyoko Sensei's opinion this is the central point of practical Reiki. Hayashi Sensei, she says, taught that the body deposits toxic waste materials in strategic places, to be able to eliminate them later. If the body lacks energy, the elimination process is disturbed, and more and more toxins accumulate. Then, you give the client Reiki. The process of Reiki energizing the body is like stirring up mud in a creek. You stir up the toxins and then the body eliminates them through the natural elimination avenues and the body fluids. Hayashi Sensei also said that giving Reiki works like peeling off thin layers of paper. You have to be patient. (More about this on page in the chapter on Byosen on page 180.)

"If you don't understand the Byosen in the body of your client," Chiyoko says insistently, "you will not be able to work effectively." As she makes this statement, I have an inner image of a man fishing in the dark. He brings up a fish from the bottom of the sea, but also old shoes and bicycle tires ... The art of Byosen seems to be the one issue in Reiki that she is not willing to compromise on at all. "Place your hand here," she says to me, "what do you feel"? It pulsates and tingles strongly in my hand ... Another question bubbles up in my mind, and I ask her what she feels when she is giving Reiki. "Love" she replies, and I feel that this is not a philosophical concept, but real hands on Love, the love of the grandma to her grandchildren.

Later, during the treatments, I ask Chiyoko Sensei what Reiki means to her. She answers, "You know, I always take the bus home in the evening after the workshops/treatments. When I see someone at the bus stop who is obviously suffering, I want to help."

One of the participants is treated while lying on the belly, and I am looking for another rule. I have become so accustomed to rules! I ask Chiyoko Sensei if there was a rule for treating someone laying on his or her back, or his or her belly. She answers with her typical pragmatism. "Whatever is most comfortable for the client and for you, is good. For example, when you are treating your own kidneys it may be uncomfortable to place your hands on them with the palms touching the body. If it is uncomfortable, turn the hands around so you give your kidneys Reiki with the back of the hands! That, too, works—make it easy for yourselves!"

Suddenly, she begins to stroke and massage the client's legs. "If you feel that a body area is blocked, you can open it up with a massage or a downward stroking movement. Sometimes, you can use pressure as in Shiatsu. But, after you have opened the area up, you should place your hands on it and give Reiki to it for a few minutes. In this way, the Reiki will go deeply into the body."

After a while, I ask her how much Reiki Training had cost in her childhood. She answers that the cost of Shoden/Okuden in the late thirties was 50 Yen, almost double the salary of a young professional. Only wealthy people were involved in Reiki then. She told us that Reiki was a way for the wealthy people to give something back to society, out of gratitude for the blessings they had received. Before I could ask, she said "The teaching was expensive, but the treatments were given either for little money, or a barter system was used. The farmer who received Reiki treatments brought a bag of rice, the fisherman brought fish …"

The Third Day, Shoden Part Three

Once more, we begin with the customary chanting of the Reiki Principles, and then the Reiju, followed by the Reiki Mawashi. Then, we spend a few hours with perception training, which we are asked to continue at home, whenever we have time. The best results, we learn, are obtained if this exercise is done on five consecutive days for about thirty minutes each time. The exercises, called Hatsurei-Ho, are meant to make the hands more sensitive so that the Byosen can be perceived. Chiyoko explains: "When your hands have become sensitive and you feel the Byosen, it leads you through the treatments. You will be able to (energetically) diagnose what is happening in the client's body. You will always know how long you must stay in each position, and how long the treatment or the series of treatments must be. Also, you will be able to watch the healing process of your clients. They always ask me how long and how often they must come, and one day, I tell them: that's it, no need to come anymore."

We begin by folding our hands in the Gassho position. Then we are asked to concentrate on the Tanden (see page 19 the key terms in Reiki). The importance of the Tanden is something I discovered in my adolescence in the writings of a German Zen Master, called Karfried von Dürkheim. Later on, my Tai Chi teacher Da Liu helped me understand it more deeply until I was reminded again by Ogawa Sensei. You will find a beautiful explanation of it by Takata Sensei on page 26.

While keeping our attention on the Tanden, we let our palms separate a few centimeters and feel the energy that builds up in between our hands. Then, we keep letting the palms of the hands come further and further apart—still feeling the energy. To end the exercise, we bring the hands in front of the Tanden, paying attention to the energy flow. Chiyoko Sensei suggests keeping the eyes open just a little during the exercise, to discourage the mind from wandering about. With a little bit of experience, she says, this exercise can be practiced with closed eyes as well.

After the first exercise, which is practiced alone, we now do a partner exercise. The receiver sits in a relaxed fashion while the other partner places one of his hands upon his own upper thigh, and the second hand on the shoulder of the partner. We are asked to feel the difference between the perception when treating a relaxed area void of toxic accumulation (the upper thigh) and an area that is tight and filled with toxins (the shoulder). The hand placed on my own thigh is warm and relaxed. I become aware of a light pulse. "This is Reiki" says Chiyoko Sensei, "you feel the Reiki coming out of your hands." My other hand pulsates and hurts a little. I have the sensation that something moves from the shoulder blade towards the cervical vertebrae of my partner. "This is the Byosen," comments Chiyoko Sensei.

After this exercise, we learn the Nentatsu-Ho, a technique for detoxification (see the description on page 232).

At the end of the day, we give each other Reiki again. Today, it is my turn. Chiyoko Sensei sits behind me, touching my temples. After a while, she starts massaging my shoulders lightly and lovingly. While she is massaging me she says, "Look, his skin looks much better already …" What a tender touch she has. I wish her hands would stay just there forever …

The Fourth Day, Okuden Part One

Again, we begin our day with chanting the Reiki Principles and receiving Reiju. During the Reiju, I am quite tired. Yet, I always feel both of them before they come around to me. I see them with closed eyes as beings of Light. The Reiju-Sha (Reju-giver) emits an amazing amount of heat, as well as a bright light. Electric shocks shake my body, and that makes me laugh. After the Reiju, my hands and feet are electrified, on fire.

After the Reiju, we practice the customary Reiki Mawashi, and then we continue with Reiki Okuri (another technique for increasing the perception and for maintaining health). We sit in a circle with our feet pointed towards the center of the circle and hold hands for about ten minutes. The left hand is facing with the palm up, and the right one is facing with the palm down. After a few moments, the current runs through the group quite spectacularly.

This morning is dedicated to learning the Mental Healing technique called "Sei Heki Chiryo." The word Sei Heki, Chiyoko explains to me, means "habit". In Usui Sensei's time, she says, sei heki meant the whole bandwidth of habits: physical, mental, emotional and soul-habits. Nowadays, the word Sei Heki is associated with sexual perversions … We are told that all habits could be treated with this miracle cure (In the years to come, I would witness amazing healings with this technique). Tadao writes down the second symbol on the board and explains its roots and meaning. This is in accordance with what I learned from a friend, Myoyuu–San, a Buddhist nun, a few years back. We will go into more detail about this on page 153, the roots of the Mental healing Symbol.

Now Chiyoko teaches us a powerful Kotodama, a mantra that is used in conjunction with the sei heki chiryo, the treatment of unwanted habits. Previously, I did not feel comfortable with this technique the way I learned it in the western tradition. But, now it is complete, and it puts Reiki into its correct light. Again, the symbol that we learn looks slightly different from what I learned previously, but the differences are minimal.

Chiyoko Sensei raves about the effectiveness of this technique and tells us a few success stories from her rich experience. The group is divided into pairs, and we are to decide what issue is to be treated. My partner in the exercise tells me that she does not want to drink any alcohol anymore. "You must be kidding," I answer, laughing. She smiles and says, "You got me, I just don't want to drink too much …" Later on, we switch over, and my issue is impatience. As I am writing this book, eleven years later, I begin to laugh. Whatever happened to impatience? I cannot even remember ever having been impatient. It works!

When we are done, I ask Chiyoko Sensei if she uses this symbol exclusively for mental/emotional issues, or if it can be used on the physical body as well. She declines with hesitation. I think to myself, oh dear, these awful, barbaric foreigners don't know how to behave, and ask her again. "Really, you don't use it on the body. I have experimented with it and have had good results." She tells us that she wants to teach us Jikiden Reiki, jikiden meaning what she has learned from Hayashi Sensei. Then she continues to tell us that she too has experimented and she proceeds to tell us how she has converted the original technique for working on the physical body. I get the feeling that she is not proud of teaching us something that she herself has devised, and feels rather shy about it. But behind this shyness shines the love and respect to her teacher, and I love the Japanese people for this.

Before we treat each other again today, Chiyoko shows us how to use Reiki for household emergencies or fresh injuries using the eyes and the breath.

In the course of the day, someone had asked her if we had to tune into Reiki before we give a treatment. We wanted to know if there is a special ritual or prayer that needs to be performed first. She laughs and puts one hand on the participant's shoulder saying "ON". She then takes her hand away and says "OFF." "We always say that we switch the Reiki on, just like you switch on the light."

Today, I noticed again that Chiyoko seems to be suffering from a backache; she stretches her back again and again, and changes her position quite often. Still unsure if I could cross the cultural borders, and knowing that the Japanese students would never dare to touch their Sensei, I asked Tadao if I could give her a back treatment (one of my favorites). Sometimes, it is good to be a foreigner who is not expected to know how to behave correctly. Tadao suggested that I should ask her. "You noticed that, didn't you," she said, with obvious pleasure and then happily accepted my offer.

In the evening, after the others had gone, I took care of her back. "Your hands are lovely," she says, while I am working on her aching back, "and I feel your love and experience. I feel like some huge energy is caressing me." I did not take that as personal gratification, but as an acknowledgement for all of us who practice Reiki in the West.

No matter where you have learned Reiki, from what lineage or school, the energy is one and the same—pure and uncontaminated love and light.

The Fifth Day, Okuden Part Two

Unfortunately today is the last day of our training. Time passes so quickly when you are having fun. We met at 3:30 pm and stayed together until the evening. In the morning, I reviewed the past few days, and noticed that because of the daily Reiju a new Reiki quality has come into being. I cannot quite put my finger on it and the best way to describe it is with an inner image: it is as if you walk through an ancient Shinto shrine at dawn, all by yourself. The wind blows through the onset of the new day, the fragrance of cedar trees caresses your skin, and a lonely crow awakens with its particular cry. Suddenly, everything is good enough as it is, and all my Reiki doubts that have been plaguing me for years have vanished.

As usual, we begin with the chanting of the Reiki Principles and receiving Reiju. Once again, my body is electrified during the Reiju, and I am expecting the system to short-circuit. But all the circuits seem to be strong and ready for this surge of energy. My hands and feet are purified in the Reiki-Fire! After the Reiju, we practice the Reiki Mawashi and Reiki Okuri for the last time.

Today, we are taught distant healing, called Enkaku Chiryo in Japanese. As expected by now, the distant healing symbol, too, is different from what we have learned in the West. So is the distant healing technique, and the philosophy behind it. As someone teaching in Japan to Japanese students, I know that it is impossible to teach misspelled Kanji. Imagine instructing your student to write an "A" and telling him that this is "B". Chiyoko Sensei tells me that she is often shown misspelled Kanji in the distant healing symbol by her Japanese students who had previously learned Reiki elsewhere. She tells them, "You are Japanese, how dare you write like this?" "I learned it like this from my teacher," they reply ruefully … "The distant healing symbol is a Jumon, a magic formula (see page 25, key words), says Chiyoko Sensei, "but, if it has been completely distorted …"

Looking back at the teaching that I have received, I see a complete image of transformation. The meaning of the Reiki Kanji, the Habit Healing Technique with its Kotodama, as well as the distant healing Jumon all point in the same direction. We are to remember our original state, and are asked to come home. Again and again, it is suggested that we leave our suffering behind, and celebrate our true nature in oneness with the Universe. Now, Reiki makes sense to me, for the first time, beyond doubt and the confinement of the ego. I have come home.

I ask Chiyoko Sensei how long a distant healing treatment should take. She answers that a physical treatment, a Mental/Emotional treatment, as well as a distant treatment should be done as long as possible, but at least 30 minutes. I tell her that I am not able to concentrate for an hour when giving distant Reiki. "That does not matter at all," she replies. "You drift off at times, and when you remember what you are doing, your attention returns. Even when giving a physical treatment, you may daydream in between. Reiki has nothing to do with your personality and mental activity. Even when you are not present for a while, the energy keeps flowing. I am not saying that you should be absent-minded …"

After the distant healing technique was explained, and all questions answered, the group was divided into pairs. The group of "senders" remained in the classroom, while the "receivers" went downstairs. Thus, a virtual distance was created. The result of the distant healing was surprising: I never felt such a clear feedback from my client before, in all my years of working. The Byosen of the client was easily felt, and all I could do is smile. After a short feedback round, we are given our certificates. This certificate will find its place in my treatment room …

It has been such a pleasure to be in Chiyoko Sensei's presence. I notice that I am more perceptive in her presence than when I work by myself. Years later, the same is noticed by my students. The energy level of the student adjusts to that of his teacher temporarily, and learning happens effortlessly.

For years, I have been wondering what happens to a person who is exposed to Reiki for a long time. Chiyoko Sensei displays this transformation in her simple manner. In her presence, my questions are erased, and her vast experience is impressive. I am convinced that I will walk this path with all my love and energy. But, what impresses me most is her character, her humbleness and clarity. Her refreshing simplicity, and the ease and conviction with which she works, is a real eye opener. She knows, while we are yet in doubt. She lives the Reiki-Principles in her day-to-day activities, as well as, in the classroom. All her skills and character traits mingle in her heart to create a delicious Reiki Cocktail that I so readily savor. A new treasure shines in my heart, and I look forward to sharing this with others.

In her presence, I feel like a child, and tell her upon leaving: "I am grateful to have met a Reiki adult, and I sincerely hope that many of us will come to quench their thirst." In the evening, we go out to dinner together for a lovely vegetarian feast and a couple of glasses of beer. Before we say goodbye on that evening, I ask Tadao if he would like to publish a book with me, and the rest is history … and, the beginning of a fruitful collaboration.

Before Chiyoko, After Chiyoko

Back in Sapporo, I told all of my Reiki friends of Chiyoko Sensei, and some of them answered the call. While having dinner with Chiyoko and Tadao on that last evening, I had asked her if she was willing to come to Germany to teach. Later, after her death, Tadao kept telling me that she had said "I am not interested to go anywhere anymore, but I want to go to Germany, to Frank-San."

Almost exactly a year later, I invited Walter Lübeck, Heinz Schoel, and some other friends of Walter's to come for a workshop with Chiyoko and Tadao Sensei. They arrived in Tokyo, where we met and visited Usui Sensei's memorial. The next day, we travelled to Kyoto together. The workshop was to take place at her apartment—a great honor for us. It was the first time that she taught a group of non-Japanese.

Unfortunately, I did not keep a diary during this workshop, but one funny occasion remained etched in my memory. On one of the workshop days, we could not go to Chiyoko Sensei's house, and, instead, held the workshop at a Christian Seminar Center in the mountains north of Kyoto. We were asked to keep the windows closed, to keep a tribe of mischievous monkeys out.

When the symbol used with Byosen was explained, Walter asked Chiyoko Sensei whether this was used for clearing a space, as it is done in our western Reiki Tradition. Chiyoko looked puzzled, and when Walter explained exactly what he meant, he asked her if he could show the technique to her. She agreed, and Walter proceeded in his dynamic way to the middle of the room, where he drew a symbol before whizzing into all the corners of the room, where he drew another symbol in each. Chiyoko Sensei was sitting in her chair, sweating. After Walter was done, she rushed to the window,

Photo 48: At Mount Kurama with Tadao Yamaguchi

and upon opening it exclaimed, "Too much energy in here, must open the window!" We laughed heartily, and afterwards, she said that the only way a room is cleared in her tradition is by either hanging the gokai in it, or else reciting them three times out loud.

I was asked to be present as the translator, and when the group was instructed to receive their first Reiju, I was also asked to sit down and receive the blessings. Surprised and immensely happy, I thought that I was in heaven; I was to receive another five Reiju from Chiyoko and Tadao Sensei.

In the course of the workshop, many questions came up. I had warned the Senseis about this previously, telling them about the inquisitiveness of the Western mind. Sometimes, there was no answer to a question, and in those cases, Tadao would say, "It is like this because Hayashi Sensei said so." Over the years, this has become a standard joke during the workshops.

Often, Chiyoko Sensei replied to a question: "You guys think too much." This was not meant to be criticism, but a simple fact. "Reiki is the most simple thing in the world," she used to say. Sometimes, she did not understand the complexities of our thought, and some questions that I was to translate were quite embarrassing to me.

During this workshop, Chiyoko Sensei remembered a ritual called Reiki Kokan that Hayashi Sensei had performed when visiting Daishoji. Nowadays, it has become a part of the Jikiden Reiki Teaching that is loved and cherished by the students. As I had previously heard from Ogawa Sensei, Usui Sensei had also attuned Quartz Crystals with Reiki that were given to his clients who could not always come to him for healing. They were to place them on the ailing body part (in place of the practitioner's hands). Heinz Schoel was given a lovely specimen by Chiyoko Sensei …

Upon leaving, Chiyoko Sensei told me that I could begin with the teacher's training in a year's time, if I wanted to. This came entirely unexpected, and I was moved to tears.

Teaching Jikiden Reiki

On July 18, 2002, I completed the Shihan Kaku training with Chiyoko Sensei at her apartment (photo 47). She taught me how to perform the Reiju, and, thus, to attune others into Reiki. Upon returning home, Chiyoko Sensei told me that I could finish my training with her in the summer of 2003. Right after the workshop, my personal life took an unexpected turn: I left Japan and my wife, and started over again in Germany.

During the night of August 19, 2003, I had a strange dream. I dreamed that a nun was dying, and several monks were sitting around her, praying and chanting mantras. I was one of the monks. Puzzled upon awakening, I had no idea what this dream was trying to tell me. That evening, I received word from Japan that Chiyoko Sensei had passed away. Unfortunately, I was unable to attend to her funeral.

In the summer of 2004, Tadao Sensei came to Germany upon my invitation to fulfill his mother's dream. This was the first time that Jikiden Reiki was taught outside of Japan.

On July 28, 2004, I received the Shihan status from Tadao Sensei, and on October 22, 2007, I was given the title of Dai Shihan. On May 18, 2009, on one of my journeys to Kyoto, I was, surprisingly, installed as the Daihyo Daiko, the Vice Representative of the Jikiden Reiki Institute, giving me the permission to teach Teachers and to take on other resposibilities as Tadao's right hand.

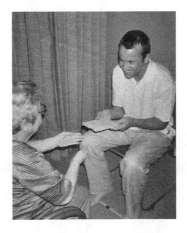

Photo 47: Receiving the Shihan-Kaku certificate from Chiyoko Sensei.

Tadao Sensei has taken over the role of his mother with great love, devotion and diligence. He teaches in Chiyoko Sensei's spirit, worldwide, and if you want to be kind to yourself, please join one of his workshops.

You will find his schedule at
www.Jikiden-Reiki.com
and mine at
www.ReikiDharma.com.

Part Two:
The Sacred Reiki Sites

Gratitude is a great cure for the mind

—TAKATA SENSEI—

Experiencing Japan

If you ask me, a trip to Japan is a must for any serious Reiki practitioner, just like it is a must for any US-visitor to see the Grand Canyon. Japan must be the safest travel destination on Earth, and especially Kyoto, is easy-going for someone who does not speak Japanese.

Reiki is pure Japanese spirituality, and is best understood from the inside, in its original surroundings. If you would like to smell the fragrance of Japan before you travel, or you'd rather stay home today, you will find a little taste of the sacred Reiki sites in Japan below.

Photo 49: View from Mount Kurama

Mount Kurama

鞍馬寺 First I would like to take you to the Kurama Temple, situated about ten miles north of downtown Kyoto. To me, Kyoto is one of the most beautiful cities in the world. There, 1650 Buddhist temples and 400 Shinto Shrines are bound to take your breath away. For a Reiki-Lover, the Kurama temple takes first place.

Kurama village lies idyllically nestled beneath Kurama Mountain, which is the home of the Kurama Dera (temple) that has played an important role in Japanese History over the centuries. The Kurama Temple is a breathtaking center of Japanese spirituality, and is seen by some as one of the very few temples in Japan that is not a tourist attraction in the first place, but a place for transformation and introspection.

Surrounded by ancient cedar trees, that give the air an amazing fragrance, Mount Kurama is the birthplace of Reiki. The imposing Kurama temple was founded in the year 770 by the monk Gantei, a disciple of Ganjin, the founder of the great Toshodaiji Temple in Nara, after he had had a deep spiritual experience

Photo 50: Kurama written in Kanji

on the mountain. Until 1949, the Kurama Temple was a part of Tendai Buddhism, which will be discussed in more detail in the on page 155. Since then, it is the headquarters of the Kurama-Kokyo sect. The term sect is used here in the original sense of the word, meaning a splinter group of a larger school. Tendai Buddhism is one of the two schools of Japanese esoteric Buddhism. Esoteric, or tantric Buddhism, arrived in Japan in the ninth century with two Japanese monks who studied in China. One was called Saicho, or Dengyo Daishi 767-822, the founder of Tendai Buddhism. The other was Kukai, or Kobo Daishi 774-835 who founded Shingon Buddhism.

In its 1200-year history, the Kurama Temple burned down eight times due to earthquakes, and was once destroyed by a mudslide after a quake. In 1974, a giant water tank was erected to avoid further damage. The main Hall of the Temple called Honden was rebuilt with fire resistant concrete.

The Kurama Temple is home to several pieces of art that are part of the Japanese National Treasure, the most important one being a statue of Bishamonten. This statue was luckily saved when the temple burned down completely in 1238. You will find it in the Kurama Dera Museum, which is worth a visit. Also, an impressive statue of Senju Kannon is displayed there; for me this is the most beautiful Buddha Statue I have ever seen. Sitting in front of it you will understand the fifth Reiki Principle—promise!

Noble and powerful figures of Japanese History took spiritual refuge at Mount Kurama over the centuries. Several Japanese emperors visited the temple to worship there. They ordered the temple authorities to take good care of the mountain and to leave it in its original splendor. You do not find a single garbage bin at Mount Kurama; every visitor is asked to take the refuse back and dispose it elsewhere in a proper place. Mount Kurama is perhaps the cleanest, ecologically healthy mountain I have ever come across. The mountain, in itself, is the spiritual symbol of the Temple.

Photo 51: The spiritual Symbols of the Kurama Temple

The temple grounds are vast. Upon my first visit, I came across a small shrine behind which three plates hang behind an altar, depicting three symbols (photo 51). Later on, I found out that the Kurama philosophy is quite similar to Reiki philosophy. The word Reiki, for example, was used to describe the all-pervading energy in the Universe. But, in actual fact, it is rather the other way around. In the autumn of 2008, I interviewed the abbess of the Kurama temple on another subject, and her condition to agree to the interview was that it was not about Reiki. The authorities do not want us to equate Reiki with the Kurama Temple. It has its own sacred history and philosophy, and Usui Sensei is seen as only one of many finding liberation there.

Kurama Philosophy

The basic principle of the Kurama philosophy is called "Sonten" and means Universal Life Energy. This energy is thought to be the Source of Existence. It is the absolute truth and transcends the differences between religions. Sonten permeates the Universe, and thus humanity. Sonten manifests on Earth in three transcendental qualities: Love, light and power. Sonten is

120

comprised of this trinity, but each component contains in itself, the Whole. The love principle corresponds to the moon, and is represented by the Buddha of Love/Compassion, Senju Kannon, called Avalokiteshvara in India. The light principle corresponds to the sun and is represented by Bishamonten or Tamonten, called Vaishravana in India. The power principle corresponds to the earth and is represented by Gohomaoson, a Kurama specific deity that is supposed to have descended on Mount Kurama from Venus about 6.5 million years ago.

Together this trinity forms Sonten. The word Sonten can also be pronounced and written the same way as the so-called Reiki Master symbol. The Kurama philosophy tells us that when we live in harmony with love, light and power, happiness happens on its own accord. We understand that the Universe cares about each human like a mother tending to her child. Find harmony and love in yourself, and learn to honor and respect the universal life force in everything.

The Kurama philosophy teaches us three principles that concern the outer, as well as, the inner world.

> 1–Don't say anything bad; don't do anything bad, and work upon yourself. This includes not to do harm to your own body, mind and heart.

> 2–Be honest and work on the betterment of human kind.

> 3–Immerse yourself deeply in the Universal Life Energy and trust this source unconditionally.

The more people follow these principles, the more light permeates this planet. Since ancient times, there are two options to experience this philosophy of the Universal Life Energy at the Kurama Dera. One option is to take part in one of the spiritual ceremonies held at Mount Kurama, and the other is to be initiated by the abbess of the temple. The possibility of initiation is open for anyone, regardless of nationality, creed or religion—providing that one is ready to dedicate all his energy towards his spiritual growth. It is not necessary to convert and let go of ones birth religion. The Universal Life Energy will give you strength, awareness and light whatever way you may be traveling upon.

Below, you will find the Kurama prayer to Sonten for happiness

The Trinity of Sonten of the Kurama Mountain
1. The spirit of the moon—Love
2. The spirit of the sun—Light
3. The spirit of the earth—Power

O Sonten
Beautiful as the moon
Warm as the sun
Strong as the earth
Bestow upon us your blessings to raise humanity and to increase our wealth and honor.
At this holy place ensure that peace will conquer discord, selflessness will conquer greed, true words will conquer lies, and respect will conquer insult.
Fill our hearts with joy, raise our spirit and fill our bodies with glory.
Sonten, great ruler of the Universe, great light, great mover, bestow upon us, who have convened here to pray to you, who toil to touch your heart, a new light and a wonderful light.

We trust Sonten in all things.

Photo 52: Tengu, the hobgoblin

Photo 53: Stairs leading to the main Gate of the Kurama Dera

Traveling to Mount Kurama

At first you travel from Kyoto Station either by bus, subway or taxi to the Demachiyanagi Station. There you take the Kurama Eizan Railway all the way to the last station, Kurama.

As you get off, you are greeted by the hobgoblin, Tengu (photo 52). Judging by his nose, he seems to be a foreigner too; you are in good company.

Next to Tengu, you find a sign that reads: "Watch out for poisonous snakes and bears". Thank God that you don't read Japanese. But, not to worry: In sixteen years and countless visits to Kurama during all seasons, I have never come across either. One of my travel guides warns that Mount Kurama has been a favorite hide out of ghosts and robbers. Yet, those too have not crossed my path, or maybe I just did not pay any attention.

The walk along the scenic village road, meanders between souvenir and traditional sweet shops to the left, until you see the stairs leading to the main gate of the Kurama Temple (photo 53). The distance between the station and the Temple entrance is about 250 meters.

Exploring the Temple Compound

Two stone tigers guard the Temple Gate. One of them has its mouth open, the other, closed. The meaning of this is: from the beginning to the end. In Kurama cosmology, the tiger is one of the helpers of Senju Kannon along with the centipede.

At the Main Gate (Nion Mon, the Gate of Guardians), you pay your entrance fee of 200 Yen (about 2 US Dollars) that permits you to stay all day on Mount Kurama. And, especially if this is the only day you have for the visit, you

Photo 54: One of the tigers in front of the Main Gate

will need it ... I suggest that you take at least two days to explore Mount Kurama. The temple grounds are open to visitors from 9 a.m.-5 p.m., every day. In case you would like to hike all the way up to the top of the mountain and down the other side, you will need about five or six hours—walking leisurely.

Just behind the Main Gate, you are welcomed by Senju Kannon, the Buddha of Love and Compassion (photo 55).

She is one of the three deities of the Kurama Temple, or better, Buddhas: Senju Kannon, Bishamonten, and Gohomaoson.

If you would like to encounter her in the traditional way, please take the ladle that is placed in the small basin in front of her with your right hand. Then, you fill the ladle with water from the basin, or with the water gushing forth from a Lotus flower that the statue is holding. Pour this water in your left hand, cleansing it. Repeat the same with the other hand. Then, take some water in your mouth (without touching the ladle with your lips for sanitary reasons) and either spit it out in the gravel in front of the statue, or drink it down to cleanse your body more deeply. I have drank this water for years and I am still alive ...

Photo 55: Senju Kannon, the Buddha of Love and Compassion

Photo 56: Baby Buddhas

After completing this ritual, you need to cleanse the ladle. This is done by letting the leftover water in the ladle run over its handle. After you have placed the ladle on the edge of the basin with awareness, you fold your hands and bow to Kannon. Only then, you enter the temple …

The First Set of Stairs

This is your beginning of a stair-climbing day. But, not to worry: on one of my last trips, one of the participant's conquered Mount Kurama on crutches. As you climb up the first set of stairs, you find a kindergarten on your right side. You will recognize it by its playground and a sculpture of six Baby Buddhas that is placed in front of it. This sculpture is erected there for the souls of unborn or stillborn children (photo 56).

The first shrine is located in the next building, on your right, called Fumyo Den. It houses the ropeway station for those unable to walk up the mountain. In the back of it, to the left of the ropeway entrance you find a small altar that is dedicated to the three deities of Mount Kurama.

Placed in the middle of the altar, is a statue of Bishamonten. Mounted behind him and above, is a plate with a Sanskrit syllable. On his left, is placed a statue of Gohomaoson only on special occasions, with the plate represent-

Photo 57: The Sanskrit Seed Syllable, Hrih, Japanese: Kiriku

ing him above it. And, on the far right, there is a space for a statue of Senju Kannon, also placed there only on certain days, with the Sanskrit seed syllable "Hrih" (Japanese: Kiriku) representing this Buddha. You will recognize this as the origin of the mental/emotional healing symbol.

Buddhist legend tells us that the Hrih symbol was born out of a tear of the Amida Buddha, who cried it out of love and compassion for the suffering of humankind. Out of this tear, the symbol was born, and, the Senju Kannon (the One-thousand-armed Bodhisattva), the antidote to suffering on Earth. We will encounter the Amida Buddha a little further on our way up the mountain.

In case you are unable to make your way up Mount Kurama on foot, take the ropeway here. It will take you close to the Main Hall of the Kurama Temple. Just after the upper stop of the ropeway, you find a beautiful pa-

Photo 58: The Taho-To Pagoda

goda called Taho-To (photo 58) on your right. If you have two days on Mount Kurama, I suggest that you take the ropeway once, to see it. It is especially beautiful in the spring when the cherries and azaleas flower.

On Foot

Yet, more stairs take you up to two manmade waterfalls (photo 59) that were installed there for meditative practice (This practice, called Mizu Gyo is originally of Shinto origin, but was taken on by the ecclectic Tendai School). Here, you can stand on a stone slab under the waterfall with your hands in the gassho position, letting the water stimulate your crown chakra. But, keep in mind that after your enlightenment there may be neither need nor desire to walk on! In any case, be careful: the stone slab un-

Photo 59: The lower of the two waterfalls

der the waterfall is full of moss and slippery, and it is important for humanity that you survive your enlightenment. Ogawa Sensei suspected that Usui Sensei may have had a Satori here, but this is yet to be proven. Koyama Sensei tells us in her teaching manual that Usui Sensei realized his enlightenment, sitting in a small hut on Mount Kurama. Perhaps it was the Mao Den (see photo 18). I am quite sure that he must have set up camp, somewhere, in the middle of nowhere, in preparation for death.

The Shinto Shrine, Yuki Jinja

After you have climbed an ancient and very steep stairway, you reach the beautiful Yuki Jinja (photo 60), an ancient Shinto Shrine. Next to it, two sacred cedar trees grow all the way into the heavens.

You continue onwards through an invigorating mixed forest until you reach the second gate, called Chuo Mon. Just before the gate, you find a spring on your right where you can refill your water bottle.

127

Photo 60: Sacred cedar trees at Yuki Jinja

The Amida Buddha

Just before you reach the Main Hall, the worlds divide: You come to a large two-story building called Tenporin-do. On the ground floor, you can obtain a cup of Japanese tea, and, if you are a good boy/girl, even an ice cream. My personal favorite is the Häagen Dazs Green Tea Ice Cream. In the floor above, you are in for your second chance of enlightenment, which has its own particular flavor. Before they enter this hall, the worshippers cleanse their hands once more, in the same way it was done in front of the Kannon statue below (photo 61).

The sliding door to this hall is usually closed, but you can open it with a clear conscience. It is closed to discourage the notorious Kyoto monkeys from playing havoc with fruits placed on the offertory altar. Please remember to close it again on your way out.

Photo 61: The spring in front of Tenporin-do

Inside the hall, you find an impressive golden statue of the Amida Buddha, called Amida Nyorai (Sanskrit: Amitabha), the Buddha of Infinite Light. Please do not take photographs in here. This is the perfect place for a silent meditation.

After the mind has become silent, go towards the altar that rests upon the roped off gallery on which the statue rests. To the left, and to the right of this gallery, you can climb on your knees under the gallery. In the center of it, below, you find a rope that is attached to the hands of the Amida. Take this rope in your folded hands, and you are directly connected to the Buddha. Here you ask for his blessings, but never ask for material or spiritual gain.

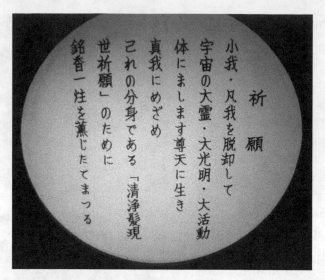

Photo 62: The Kigan prayer in the crypt of the Kurama Honden

The basic philosophical difference between Buddhism and the other Indian religions is that Buddhism accepts the world as real, but does not believe in the existence of the self. Self, or ego, is seen as a mirage—a mental construct that is given "life" by our mental and emotional patterns. In this light, it makes sense not to ask for something, because who is asking, and for what?

From the Tenporin—another steep stairs lead to the Main Hall and its spacious yard. In front of the main Hall, you see a geometrical structure built with flagstones into the ground, facing the main hall (photo 63). There, you stand in the middle of the pattern, facing the temple, with folded hands like my daughter, Christina. It is said that this is a power spot, and the Reiki of the Universe will surge through the crown chakra of the person standing there!

The Main Hall, Honden

The main Hall of the Kurama Temple (photo 64) is constructed of fire resistant concrete because it burned down in its 1300-year history so many times. Even though, it is a beautiful building, and a silent space for meditation and being aware of your true nature.

The Crypt

Situated under the main hall is a magical crypt that houses three beautiful statues, as well as thousands of little urns. Bits of hair of those who would

Photo 63: My daughter Christina and the Reiki of the Universe

like to be connected to love, light and power, and to the deities that represent those qualities, are kept in those urns. Everyday, the delightful abbess of the Kurama temple or her assistant prays for the physical and spiritual wellbeing and happiness of all of those people. This ritual is called Shin Shin Mu Byo (heart/spirit without illness).

Any visitor may take part in this, and it is possible to apply for it in a small office in the main hall on the left (facing the main altar). An urn that will remain there for eternity costs Yen 20,000 (about US$ 200). If you see the urn of Frank Arjava Petter down there, please say hello to him. Please don't take photographs in the crypt.

In front of the first altar upon entering the crypt, you find a small plate depicting the Kigan Prayer for the Shin Shin Mu Byo ritual. In it, you will find the Reiki Master symbol that is used by many Buddhist groups, but has

Photo 64: The main Hall of the Kurama Temple

no relevance in traditional Reiki. Nonetheless, it is a powerful symbol, and at the Kurama Temple it represents the Ultimate principle, Sonten.

Translation of the Kigan Prayer

Small self and worldly self!
We live with Sonten that exists in the Universal Great Spirit.
Great light, great creative body—awaken to my true self.
As support to my prayer in this life, I offer my purified hair
And dedicate this meiko (certified, high class incense).

On the left of the main hall (when facing the main hall), you see a small shrine called Komyoshin Den. The office, called Honbo, that houses the audience rooms of the abbess are located on the far left.

On your way up to the top of the mountain, you pass through a small gate next to the office, and find in front of you, more stairs … you enter the forest again and soon you find a bell house (photo 65) on your right above

132

Photo 65: The bell

the path. If you like, go and ring the bell once while sending good thoughts into the world. Then, you continue onwards to the Kurama Museum.

The Kurama Museum

The museum of the Kurama Temple, called Reiho-Den, is usually open between 9AM and 4PM, and is the home of many beautiful statues that are placed in the top floor. My favorite is the statue of Senju Kannon situated on the far right. Many of my female tour participants fall in love with a statue of Bishamonten ... there is something for everyone!

In case you would like to walk some more and explore the wild side of Mount Kurama, you can continue uphill through another small gate. You can leisurely walk up to the top of the mountain and continue down to the other side until you reach the picturesque village of Kibune. The whole trip should take about two hours. En route to Kibune, you find the Path of the Roots, called Ki no Michi.

Photo 66: Osugi Gongen, the Incarnation of Gohomaoson

Ki No Michi

You remember the story of Usui Sensei hurting his toe on the way down from Mount Kurama. At the Ki no Michi, you see how easily this may have happened (photo 20). After the Ki no Michi, you continue onwards through the woods until you come to a small shrine next to a clearing. Here you may rest or meditate. Once, I sat here with William Rand while two pilgrims were reciting the heart sutra, a blessed moment.

Koyama Sensei tells us that Usui Sensei experienced enlightenment sitting in a small hut on Mount Kurama—this, is the first one of three small shrines on the way down to Kibune. You have now climbed to the top of Mount Kurama.

The Sacred Tree, Osugi Gongen

Photo 67: Geometrical design in the forest looking like the chakras

To the left behind the shrine, you see the roped-off remains of an ancient cedar tree, called Osugi Gongen. This tree is thought to be an incarnation of Gohomaoson. If you would like to take a piece of this tree with you, don't take it from here—you can obtain a small portion at the Main Hall souvenir store.

Chakras

Here and there, on the way to Kibune, you find geometrical structures reminding you of the chakras (photo 67). Whether this is what they depict, I don't know. Next to this, you find the second shrine, dedicated to Fudo Myo, called Sojoga Dani Fudo Do. Fudo Myo is the Buddha responsible for enlightenment, watch out. I have never seen this shrine open-perhaps it is not my time ...

As you walk past the shrine, through the forest, the natural beauty envelops you. Soon you reach the most sacred place on Mount Kurama, the so—called Mao Den (photos 18 and 68).

Photo 68: Okunoin Mao Den

Okunoin Mao Den

This is a very special place, and I suggest that you take your time to soak up the wonderful energy here. It was here that Onisaburo Deguchi had his spiritual experience with Gohomaoson. From here onwards, the path leads down to Kibune—you have almost made it. At the edge of the forest, just before reaching the road that connects Kibune and Kurama, you pass the Western Gate called Nishi Mon, leaving the energy field of the Kurama Temple.

Kibune, Kibune Jinja

Kibune is a picturesque and exotic village that is known for its ancient Shinto Shrines and the many gorgeous, traditional inns (Japanese: Ryokan). The first of the two shrines, Kibune Jinja, is reached after 200 meters, turning right on the road. The entrance to this shrine is especially beautiful around sunset when the traditional lanterns are illuminated (photo 69).

You may continue further up the road to find the second shrine that appears quite sad and desolate, but it is a sad site.

Photo 69: Kibune Jinja (shrine)

Back to Kurama Station

If you like, you can walk back in the opposite direction to get to Kurama Station. About half way, you will find the Kibune station on the Eizan Kurama Railway to return to Kurama or else, back to Kyoto. I suggest a soak in the delightful waters of Kurama hot springs, a five-minute walk beyond the entrance to Kurama Temple. I stay there with my tour participants for three nights, and I tell you, it is paradise …

Special Kurama Festivals

During the Wesak festival coinciding with the full moon in May, the entire Buddhist world celebrates the birth, enlightenment and death of the historical Buddha. The festivities at the Kurama Temple are not to be missed, should you be there in May. The temple's phone number is +81-75-741-2003.

Each October 22, the Yuki Jinja celebrates the Fire Festival (hi no matsuri) in the Kurama Village. This spectacle is mind blowing, and will remain in your memory forever. Huge wooden torches are lit and carried through the village at night, before they are piled up on the temple stairs and burned.

The festival requires some nerves and if you are wary of large crowds and queues, you better stay away.

Both festivals begin in the evening hours.

The Usui Memorial

西芳寺 As far as I am concerned, the second equally important Reiki site is the Usui Memorial in Tokyo. When in Tokyo, don't miss the chance to visit the memorial. Situated at Saihoji temple in the district of Minato-Ku, the Usui memorial is an oasis of silence in the busy-ness of Tokyo.

Photo 70: Usui Sensei's memorial stone

Usui Sensei died on March 9, 1926, while giving a Reiju Kai in Fukuyama, and was buried at the Saihoji temple in Tokyo, a Pure Land Buddhist temple. On the first anniversary of his death, the Usui Reiki Ryoho Gakkai erected the memorial. You can find the translation of the memorial on page 60.

Saihoji Temple is one of several temples with the same name in Tokyo, and it is relatively small. Its name does not appear on Tokyo city maps, it is simply marked by the Kanji for "temple" and not by its name.

Saihoji temple belongs to Jodo Shu (Pure Land Buddhism, see the chapter on historical, cultural and religious backgrounds page 152) and this shows us which religion Usui Sensei and his family belonged to. As it is anywhere on Earth, only a believer of a certain faith is buried at a temple of that particular faith.

The graveyard is public in principle, but foreign visitors are not appreciated by the temple authorities without a Japanese escort—unless they are able to converse in Japanese. This has to do with the fact that a number of foreign visitors have misbehaved at the site. The barrier is mostly cultural and has to do with the fact that most foreigners do not speak Japanese, and may not know how to behave at a Japanese graveyard.

Therefore, you will find a list of the do's and don'ts at the end of this chapter. My suggestion is that you go with someone who speaks the language, to avoid complications and to make sure that more Reiki-lovers can visit Usui Sensei's final resting place in the future. If someone from the temple asks you to do or not to do a certain thing, please follow their advice and be kind and cooperative. Large groups of people with cameras are also not appreciated by the temple authorities, because the graveyard is a place of paying respects to our loved ones.

But first, I would like to tell you the story of my first visit to the temple on September 20th, 1994. I met with a couple of Japanese friends at the airport, who were to help me find the grave. We took the Tokyo Marunouchi subway line and got off at the Shinkoenji Station (photo 71). From there we walked towards Shinjuku. After we had arrived at Saihoji, we asked the monk on duty to show the grave to us. This is what I wrote in my diary that night:

"Usui Sensei has touched millions of people's hearts with Reiki, has purified it, and has

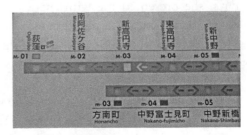

Photo 71: Shinkoenji Station of the Marunouchi Subway Line

given our life a positive meaning. How can I thank him for this in the appropriate way, in everyone's name? I begin by collecting the dry leaves and pieces of refuse that the wind and the crows have deposited there. Afterwards, I cleanse the grave marker, as well as the flagstones leading up to the grave, with water. Wilted flowers are taken away and fresh ones placed in the two vases in front of the grave. Two candles and some incense are lit. The intensive fragrance of the incense transports me into the realm of the dead for a few minutes, and even though it is a cloudy day, I feel like I am sitting in the sun, caressed by its transcendental light. I bow to Usui Sensei silently, and know that he too bows to the Universe, to love and to the Divine. In this bow, we meet and merge for a moment".

After a few minutes, I look around and can hardly believe my eyes. Next to the grave towers a beautiful three-meter tall, stone monument with an inscription in honor of Usui Sensei's life work. This was utterly unexpected, because until this day, no written documents were known to exist about Usui Sensei. I asked my friends to translate the monument for me, there and then. They glanced at each other in the typical, enigmatic Japanese way, and did not say a word. I rephrased my request, but received no reply. The third time my question was filled with emotion and my friend replied, "Sorry, we can not read the inscription." My friend was one of the most well known Japanese translators of spiritual literature of the day, and I thought that he was kidding me. "I thought you learned to read at school, didn't you," I said. He laughed, and replied, "Yes, but this is written in classical Japanese. After a grammatical reform in the 1940's, many of the complex Kanji were simplified. We honestly can not read this text except for a few words here and there."

I was flabbergasted, took out two cameras and a video camera, and started shooting like Billy the Kid. The close-ups of the memorial stone were then presented to my (now ex-) mother-in-law, who was a teacher and had studied classical Japanese. She was very kind and loved me deeply. After a few days, she presented me with the text in contemporary Japanese, and we could begin with the translation into English. For this book, the text of the memorial inscription was translated again, with careful consideration by one of my friends, Akiko Sato, and myself, and some minor changes had to be made.

But, back to the story: Finally, some written document about Usui Sensei was available-and written in stone! You have read the translation of the inscription already, on page 60. As I said earlier, the memorial stone was placed here one year after Usui Sensei's death. In some Reiki books, the

Saihoji temple is called "Bodai" temple. This is not a different name, or a different temple, but it means something like "final resting place".

As stated earlier, the grave of Usui Sensei is also their family grave, and both his wife, Sadako, and their two children, Fuji and Toshiko, are buried here. After his death, Usui Sensei was given the name Reizan-In Shujyo Tenshi Koji. His wife was given the name Tenshin-Ing On Ho Jo Ning Dai-shi. This custom is called Kaimyo in Japanese, and is done to ensure a good journey to the other realm for the deceased. Each Buddhist school does this in its own way; the suffix IN suggests that the person was a great personality.

Now, a few words about the respectful and appropriate behavior at a Japanese graveyard.

Being a Foreigner

A foreigner from a Western country cannot hide in Japan so easily. This can be an advantage at times, and at other times, may make life more complicated. Please be on your best behavior when visiting Japanese cultural sites. Some Japanese still think that foreigners are barbarians. Even though this is not always entirely wrong, it is your responsibility to help with cross-cultural communication!

What You Need to Bring Along to the Graveyard

Please bring along flowers, incense, a lighter and a plastic bag.

Photo 72: Tthe family crest of the Usui Clan

Photo 73: Mikao Usui's tombstone

Flowers

The Saihoji temple does not want visitors to the Usui Memorial to leave flowers (or fruit, as is the custom) at the grave. So, please bring some flowers, (but none with thorns) and place them in the two vases in front of the grave marker. After you are done paying your respects to Usui Sensei, take the flowers home! The reason for taking the flowers home again is, that a mischievous gang of crows who create havoc with the offerings, frequents the graveyard.

Clothes

Please dress accordingly. No shorts and tempting mini skirts.

Silence and Reverence

Please walk and act in silence and reverence. This is a place of worship and devotion like any graveyard at home.

Your Luggage

Please hold on to your bags and don't place them either on the pathways, in front of, or next to any graves. Also, please don't climb on fences and other gravesides even though this might aid you in getting a better photograph.

Pictures

If you are by yourself, or with a small group, it is ok to take a picture of the memorial. But, if you are going with a group, it is better not to do so, in order not to create a circus atmosphere!

Preparation

After you have entered the main gate of the temple, you walk straight towards the large temple hall and the office (situated on your left). On the first path on your right, you see a small hut that houses many small buckets with Kanji written on them. If you can read the Kanji for "Usui", take that bucket. Fill it at one of the taps with water, and take it to the grave. In the hut you also find a number of ladles; take one along with you.

In case that this is your first visit to Saihoji, and you don't know where the grave is located, please go back to the main temple yard. Turn right and walk straight until you reach the overhanging roof of the building in front of you. Take the path that veers off to the right, and walk straight about 50 meters. The Usui Memorial will be on your left.

Upon your arrival, get out your plastic bag and collect debris that may be littering the gravesite. If you find wilted flowers on the grave, take them away. After the flagstones leading to the grave, and the whole area is clean, take some water out of the pale with your ladle and gently pour it over the grave marker. This is essentially a purification ritual, but also cleanses the grave of environmental dirt. Now, gently pour some water on the memorial stone as well. When grave marker and memorial stone are thus purified, light some incense, place them in the receptacle and fold your hands. Now, do what you have come here for.

Perhaps you would like to recite the heart sutra, as the members of the Usui Reiki Ryoho Gakkai do. You can print it out from the text below.

Maka Hannya Haramita Shin Gyo (Japanese Name)
The Great Prajna-Paramita Heart Sutra

KAN JI ZAI BO SA GYO-JIN HAN-NYA HA RA MI TA JI
SHO KEN GO ON KAI KU-DO IS-SAI KU YAKU.
SHA RI SHI SHIKI FU I KU-KU-FU I SHIKI
SHIKI SOKU ZE KU-KU-SOKU ZE SHIKI
JU SO-GYO-SHIKI YAKU BU NYO ZE
SHA RI SHI ZE SHO HO-KU-SO-FU SHO-FU METSU
FU KU FU JO-FU ZO-FU GEN
ZE KO KU-CHU-MU SHIKI MU JU SO-GYO-SHIKI
MU GEN-NI BI ZES-SHIN I
MU SHIKI SHO-KO-MI SOKU HO-
MU GEN KAI NAI SHI MU I SHIKI KAI
MU MU MYO-YAKU MU MU MYO-JIN
NAI SHI MU RO-SHI YAKU MU RO-SHI JIN
MU KU SHU METSU DO-Y
MU CHI YAKU MU TOKU I MU SHO TOK'KO
BO DAI SAT-TA E HAN-NYA HA RA MI TA KO
SHIM-MU KEI GE MU KEI GE KO MU U KU FU
ON RI IS-SAI TEN DO-MU SO-KU GYO-NE HAN
SAN ZE SHO BUTSU E HAN-NYA HA RA MI TA KO
TOKU A NOKU TA RA SAM-MYAKU SAM-BO DAI

KO CHI HAN-NYA HA RA MI TA
ZE DAI JIN SHU ZE DAI MYO-SHU
ZE MU JO-SHU ZE MU TO-TO-SHU
NO-JO IS-SAI KU SHIN JITSU FU KO
KO SETSU HAN-MYA HA RA MI TA SHU
SOKU SETSU SHU WATSU
GYA TEI GYA TEI HA RA GYA TEI HARA SO-GYA TEI
BO JI SOWA KA HAN-NYA SHIN GYO

The Translation of the Heart Sutra

(taken from Edward Conze, *Buddhist Scriptures*, Penguin Classics, ISBN 0-14-044088-7)

1 The invocation.
Homage to the perfection of Wisdom, the lovely, the holy!

2 The prologue.
Avalokita, the holy Lord and Bodhisattva, was moving in the deep course of wisdom, which has gone beyond. He looked down from on high, he beheld but five heaps, and he saw that in their own-being they were empty.

3 The dialectics of emptiness. First stage.
Here, O Sariputra, form is emptiness, and the very emptiness is form; emptiness does not differ from form, form does not differ from emptiness; whatever is form, that is emptiness, whatever is emptiness, that is form. The same is true of feelings, perceptions, impulses, and consciousness.

4 The dialectics of emptiness. Second stage.
Here, O Sariputra, all dharmas are marked with emptiness; they are not produced or stopped, not defiled or immaculate, not deficient or complete.

5 The dialectics of emptiness. Third stage.
Therefore, O Sariputra, in emptiness there is no form, nor feeling, nor perception, nor impulse, nor consciousness; no eye, ear, nose, tongue, body, mind; no forms, sounds, smells, tastes, touchables or objects of mind;
No sight-organ-element, and so forth, until we come to: no mind-consciousness-element; there is no ignorance, no extinction of ignorance, and so forth, until we come to: there is no decay and death, no extinction of decay and

death; there is no suffering, no origination, no stopping, no path; there is no cognition, no attainment, and no non-attainment.

6 The concrete embodiment and practical basis of emptiness.
Therefore, O Sariputra, it is because of his indifference to any kind of personal attainment that a Bodhisattva, through having relied on the perfection of wisdom, dwells without thought-coverings. In the absence of thought-coverings, he has not been made to tremble, he has overcome what can upset, and in the end, he attains to Nirvana.

7 Full emptiness is the basis also of Buddhahood.
All those who appear as Buddhas in the three periods of time fully awake to the utmost, right and perfect enlightenment because they have relied on the perfection of wisdom.

8 The teaching brought within reach of the comparatively unenlightened.
Therefore, one should know the Prajnaparamita as the great spell, the spell of great knowledge, the utmost spell, the unequalled spell, allayer of all suffering, in truth—for what could go wrong? By the Prajnaparamita has this spell been delivered. It runs like this: Gone, Gone, Gone beyond, gone altogether beyond, O what an awakening, All Hail!

This completes the Heart of Perfect Wisdom.

Now, take your leave respectfully. Collect what you have brought along and know that this moment will remain your heart's treasure forever …

The birth village of Usui Sensei, Taniai has already been described in the chapter on Reiki history. At this point, I would like to add some general information, as well as, some photographs. The village of Taniai is nestled in the mountains of Gifu prefecture, about two and a half hours north of Kyoto by car (photo 74). The next bigger city is called Seki. Gifu prefecture has been known since antiquity for the art of sword-making, Miso (fermented soy bean paste), Sake (rice wine), rice, the manufacture of Tatami mats and the traditional Gassho Zukuri Houses (houses with roofs that look like hands held in the gassho position). To get a feeling for Gifu prefecture and Usui Sensei's childhood, watch the film

"The Last Samurai" starring Tom Cruise. Gifu Swords had to yield to incredibly sharp, and beautiful, kitchen knives. Next time you are in Gifu, remember your friends!

As explained in the chapter of Reiki history, a branch of the Usui clan relocated in Taniai (photo 75) with the result that many of the villagers are called Usui. Almost every nameplate says "Usui" (photo 76), this may help you to find the Usui bucket at Saihoji Temple). The first time I visited Tani-

Photo 74: Gifu prefecture near Taniai

146

Photo 75: Place name sign of Taniai

ai was with Tadao Yamaguchi, the manager of the Jikiden Reiki Institute, Hideko Teranaka, Tadao's translator, Ikuko Hirota, two of Tadao's students and my family. Through the village runs a pristine river (photo 77), which must have been the young Usui Sensei's playground.

Several Reiki attractions are left in the village today. The Amataka Jinja (photo 78), the Shinto Shrine that boasts the inscription of Usui Sensei and his brothers as the sponsors. The spring in the forest outside of Taniai, and the Zendo Ji temple in which Usui Sensei received his first six years of schooling (photos 12 and 80, see the chapter on Reiki history).

If you imagine the village (photo 79) without the tangle of the electric lines (a nightmare for every electrician), you will have a good idea of what the village looked like in Usui Sensei's time.

Photo 76: Name plate Kanji of the name "Usui"

Photo 77: The River that flows through Taniai

Photo 78: Amataka Jinja, the local Shinto Shrine

Photo 79: The main village road in Taniai

Photo 80: Tadao Yamaguchi at the spring at Zendo Ji Temple

Part Three: Historical, Cultural and Religious Backgrounds

When the mind is healed, the human becomes god-like or Buddha-like.

—Usui Sensei—

In this chapter, I would like to explain the religious roots on which Usui Sensei based his Reiki Ryoho. By popular request, I would like to begin with the origin of the mental/emotional healing technique, called sei heki chiryo in Japanese. Later on, you'll find an overview of the most well known spiritual and hand healing groups that were active during Usui Sensei's time. These historical and cultural backgrounds shall help you to understand Reiki more deeply.

Due to the multitude of Japanese and Buddhist terms, this chapter may seem overwhelming at first glance. Therefore, I suggest that you imagine being a tiger, and this chapter to be your prey. In this way, you know that you will be able to handle it quite playfully, and perhaps take a relaxed nap afterwards.

A Story

In the year 1997, I was introduced by a friend to a Tendai Buddhist nun, called Myoyu-San. Our mutual friend thought that we might like each other, and she was right. We made an appointment to meet at a bus stop in Sapporo, and it was easy to find each other. A foreigner with a car, and a nun with a baldhead were not so common in Sapporo in those days. She got into the car and we drove to Otaru, the next town, where her grandfather's Tendai Buddhist temple was located. On the way, she casually mentioned that she could not "talk" on an empty stomach. "Talking", I found out later, meant channeling the Buddha. She suggested that we go to a restaurant near her temple. Upon entering, I was thrilled to see that they had Irish beer from the tap, which was unusual in this part of the World. I ordered one, and to my surprise, she did the same while lighting a cigarette. There we sat, a picture out of a stand-up comedy. A foreigner, and a nun, clad in her black robe drinking beer, smoking and enjoying each other's company. The waiter was shocked to his roots. After a delicious meal, we went to her temple and entered the Silence of the Orient. Wherever I looked, I seemed to see a certain Sanskrit symbol that reminded me of the mental/emotional Reiki symbol. I was tempted to ask her about it, but in those days, I was still a good boy. I had learned that the symbols are to be kept secret and should not be shared with the uninitiated. Even though this situation was different, I hesitated until I suddenly came up with a good idea. What if I initiated her into Reiki? This would be fun for her, and good for the members of her congregation that came to her for counseling and healing. She was thrilled by my suggestion, but told me that she, as a nun, did not have money and could not pay for the training. This, I did not mind at all, and we made an appointment for Reiki One in my office. About six months after the first degree initiation, we met at her grandfather's temple for the Reiki Two initiation.

I had asked her to sit in a chair with her eyes closed and hands folded in Gassho. The atmosphere, sitting before the altar, was sacred: two empty human shells being filled with divine nectar, the Buddha, the silence ... Though I had asked her to sit in Gassho, she kept moving her fingers all the time. Once, she was doing the Dhyanamudra (Japanese Jo-in, with the left hand resting upon the right facing the heavens, the tips of the thumbs touching each other). Another time, she held her hands in a different Mudra, in front of her heart. Then, I witnessed a unique stage play: It looked like a mole had gotten under her scalp and was building an underground path from the back of her head to the front! It was difficult not to laugh, but knowing that she was eccentric, I was looking forward to her forthcoming explanation.

In the course of the day, I showed her the mental/emotional healing symbol, and her introduction triggered me to research the subject in depth over the course of 14 years.

The Roots of the Mental/Emotional Healing Symbol

The origin of the mental/emotional healing symbol that is used in the traditional Japanese Reiki teaching as the symbol for the sei heki chiryo (unwanted habit treatment) is found in the ancient Siddham alphabet of the Sanskrit language. The Siddham alphabet is referred to either as the Sacred alphabet, or, the alphabet of the Buddhas.

The symbol that Usui Sensei incorporated into Reiki was a simplification of the Sanskrit seed syllable, hrih. Usui Sensei knew this symbol from childhood from the religious tradition of Jodo Shu, Pure Land Buddhism, the religion of the Usuis. He may have seen it on the grave of one of his forefathers (see photo 15, the grave in the center, second row), and would have come across it, time and again, during his later years. In Jodo Shu Buddhism, the principle Buddha is the Amida Nyorai (Sanskrit: Amitabha) who is represented by this symbol which the Japanese call "kiriku". The change of name has to do with the fact that the Japanese cannot pronounce its Sanskrit name. If you ask a Japanese to repeat "Hrih", he will answer, "Did you say, kiriku?" The Japanese phonetic alphabet does not allow any word to end in a consonant, except for the consonant "n". It is also not possible to have two consonants next to each other—a vowel must be placed in between them. In this manner, the name Frank for example, becomes "Furanku".

Photo 81: Kukai or Kobo Daishi

Buddhist History in Japan

You may wonder how a Sanskrit seed syllable ends up in Japanese religion and culture? The answer to this question requires a bit of background information. Please bear with me for a little while.

Buddhism arrived in Japan from China and Korea in the fifth century. The first person who brought Tendai Buddhism (out of which many other schools evolved) to Japan, was the Chinese master Ganjin, the founder of Toshodaiji Temple in Nara. As mentioned earlier, his student, Gantei, founded the Kurama Dera in the year 770. But, Ganjin was not to be the one who spread the Tien Tai (Japanese: Tendai) Buddhism, which he brought from China. This was privileged to one of his spiritual successors called Saicho, who lived from 767-822, and dedicated his entire life to this cause. He was also known as Dengyo Daishi (great teacher Dengyo). Saicho was a contemporary of the, perhaps, most well known Japanese Buddhist reformer in its entire history, called Kukai or Kobo Daishi, 774-835 (great teacher Kobo, photo 81).

In favor of an in-depth understanding, let's take one step backwards. After the outstanding efforts of the Indian Emperor, Ashoka (273-237 BC), Buddhism developed in two geographical directions and took on the culture and customs of the people it encountered. The first was the Southeastern route, and, this school became known as Theravada Buddhism (the way of the elders, the old school). The Northeastern route, which developed a little later, became known as Mahayana Buddhism (the great vehicle). Later, the older Theravada school was referred to as Hinayana (the small vehicle), which is actually a derogatory term. More about that a little later.

Mahayana Buddhism arrived in Japan via China. In the course of the Buddhist prevalence in China, the original texts were translated from Sanskrit and Pali into Chinese.

This fact helped the spread of Buddhism in Japan, initially. The Japanese did not have an appropriate written language of their own, and imported the Chinese Kanji in the fifth and sixth centuries, giving them a Japanese pronunciation. Yet, the characters were identical, and the Japanese could read the Buddhist texts arriving from the mainland. In the Japanese language, there are three different ways of writing. The first one is the Kanji that were imported from China, then Hiragana and Katakana. The latter two are simple phonetic alphabets, each made up of 46 characters. Hiragana is used to explain complicated Kanji phonetically, helping even an uneducated person to read. It is also used to fuse certain Kanji together. Hiragana is the first alphabet that a Japanese child learns at school before having to tackle the complex Kanji. Nowadays, Katakana is used exclusively to write foreign words and names. You remember that some Reiki practitioners in Japan write the word Reiki in Katakana, to avoid misunderstandings.

Kukai and Saicho both traveled to China in the year 803 to find original Buddhist texts that were not translated into Kanji. They suspected that some of the essence of Buddhism had gotten lost in the translation, and wanted to gain a deeper understanding of Buddhism by learning Sanskrit, allowing them to read the original texts. Four ships left Japan from the Southern Island of Kyushu; two of them were never seen again. The other two anchored in different places in Chekiang, or Zhejiang Province, in Southeast China. Kukai was on one boat, and Saicho on the other. Both found what they were looking for with different teachers. Kukai became a disciple of the well-known Master, Hui Kuo, who taught esoteric Buddhism and made Kukai his spiritual heir.

Saicho found himself on the Tien Tai Mountain where the legacy of the Indian Master, Nagarjuna, was taught, emphasizing the Lotus Sutra. Saicho learned from a master called Tao-Sui, about whom nothing further is known. It is said that he also studied with some other teachers.

Both men had found the object of their heart's longing. Saicho did not learn Chinese, but could read the original texts. Kukai became proficient in Chinese during his stay.

After their return to Japan, Saicho became a student of the charismatic Kukai, until their paths clashed due to irreconcilable differences of a religious nature.

Saicho later founded the Tendai Buddhist school (Tendai is the Japanese word for Tien Tai—where he previously studied). Kukai founded Shingon Buddhism, which became known as esoteric Buddhism then. Tendai Buddhism developed its own esoteric rituals and practices over the centuries. Nowadays, both schools are referred to as Mikkyo (Mi is a simplification of the word himitsu/secret, and kyo means teaching).

The Jodo Shu School, the Usui clan's religion, later on developed from Tendai Buddhism.

Now, let's go one step ahead again, and talk about the two main Buddhist schools of thought: Theravada and Mahayana Buddhism.

Even though Buddhism was born in India, (actually in present day Nepal), it did not stand a chance to develop further in its religious climate. India was a Hindu heartland, and the gentleness of Buddhism propelled itself toward other shores.

Theravada Buddhism

Theravada Buddhism moved over the Southeastern route to Sri Lanka, Birma, Cambodia, and Thailand, onwards to Indochina. As mentioned earlier, Theravada is the original school and is based upon strict moral concepts. Its basic teaching suggests that women are essentially impure, and that enlightenment is only possible for a male monk. This fit in with the culture of the Southeast Asian countries, and Theravada Buddhism flourishes there until this day. The goal of the teaching is that of the Arhat, an enlightened monk sitting under a tree, smiling to himself. Because of this limitation, Theravada Buddhism is often called Hinayana (the small vehicle) by its opponents, as it is intended for men only.

Mahayana Buddhism

Mahayana Buddhism travelled on the Northeastern route across the Himalayas. It developed in China, Tibet, Bhutan, Nepal, Korea and Japan. When Buddhism reached the Himalayas, it encountered a sociologically different society. The women in the mountains were strong and proud, and there was no way for them to accept a religion that promised enlightenment to men only. Accordingly, Mahayana Buddhism developed into a new direction. Its basic teaching proposes that enlightenment is possible for all human beings, regardless of their gender, social status or age. It is the birthright of all, lay person, nun, or monk. The goal of the teaching is that of the Bodhisattva, (a Buddha in Seed), who postpones his own perfect enlightenment for the sake of humanity. When Buddhism arrived in Japan it mixed with the long established Shintoism, and this proved beneficial. It provided a social and worldly strength to the teaching that was necessary for the Japanese way of life.

If you ask a Japanese citizen what his religion is, he will probably answer that he is Buddhist. If you ask the same person a few minutes later if he is also a Shintoist, he may answer that Shintoism is not a religion, but a way of life. He IS Shinto. The Mahayana Buddhist schools in Japan are: Jodo, Kegon, Tendai, Shingon and Zen.

In order to explain the underlying principle of the sei heki chiryo, let me go into more detail. In Mahayana Buddhism there exist two types of Buddhas; you can look at them as two Buddha Families.

The Nyorai

The first family is that of the so-called Nyorai (Sanskrit-Tathagata), the supreme Buddhas. The Buddha taught that eons ago, long before his birth, five blessed beings had reached perfect enlightenment. When they reached this absolute state, their existence on Earth was complete. They each created their own Pure Land, or Paradise, in the center of the Universe, and in all of the cardinal directions. Later on, other Nyorais came into being as well.

So a Nyorai is one who has reached the Jodo, the Pure Land. However, the Pure Land is a one-way street. Once it has been entered, there is no way back, unless one explicitly wished to come back for the sake of humanity. In this case, a re-entry permit is granted, once only. This return does not add further karma, and, therefore, does not start the wheel of karma again. The Nyorai has completed the circle, and, therefore, there is no need for further learning. Because of his supreme nature, a Nyorai emits such light that would burn up the beholder instantly. Therefore, we cannot look at him directly, and, for this reason, the other Buddha Family came into being—the Bosatsu (Sanskrit Bodhisattva).

Below is a list of the five principle Nyorais, followed by the secondary Nyorai.

Sanskrit:	Japanese:
Gautama Buddha (the historical Buddha)	Shaka
Vairocana, the ruler of the Middle Kingdom	Dainichi Nyorai
Bhaisajya	Yakushi Nyorai
Lokeshvara Raja	Sejisaio Nyorai
Maitreya (he is also a Bodhisattva)	Miroku Nyorai
Aksobhya, the ruler of the East	Ashuku Nyorai
Ratnasambava, ruler of the South	Hosho Nyorai
Amogasiddhi, ruler of the North	Fukujyoju Nyorai
Amithaba, ruler of the West	Amida Nyorai

The most important are the principle Nyorai, called Godai Nyorai (the five Nyorai), the five Buddhas of Wisdom

Dainichi Nyorai in the center
Ashuku Nyorai in the East
Hosho Nyorai in the South
Amida Nyorai in the West
Fukujyoju Nyorai in the North

As far as I know, the only one of the Nyorai that plays a part in Reiki teaching is the Amida Nyorai, the Buddha of Infinite Light and the Ruler of the

West. In his teachings, the historical Buddha described a monk of antiquity by the name of Dharmakara (Japanese: Hozo Bikku). He had taken a vow long before the Buddha to attain enlightenment and to create a Buddha Land. Through eons, he worked upon himself and he become known as the Amida Buddha after he attained enlightenment. The Buddha Land that he created is known as the Pure Land of Bliss, Jodo (Sanskrit: Sukhavati). In Jodo Buddhism, the Amida Buddha is the principle Buddha and is referred to as "The Nyorai". The Amida Nyorai rules from the western Pure Land and is responsible for the West on earth, as well. In large Japanese cities, like Kyoto for example, a temple for the Amida Nyorai is always erected in the West, in order to protect the city spiritually. The temples for the other four principles Nyorai are built in the middle, the North, South and East.

The Amida Buddha has a special place in the human body as well: he lives on top of the crown chakra. You probably remember the initial story in this chapter, about my friend Myoyu-San. Her scalp was moving because she felt the presence of the Amida Buddha there ...

The legend says that the Amida Buddha was looking down on Earth one day, from his seat in the Western Pure Land. When he saw that everyone below was suffering, he shed a tear of Love and Compassion, knowing that he could not help as he wanted from up there. This tear dropped down onto the Earth and out of it was born the Bodhisattva Avalokiteshvara (Japanese: Kanzeon or Kannon Bosatsu) and, the Sanskrit seed syllable Hrih/Kiriku. Therefore the symbol is often depicted as resting within a teardrop in esoteric Buddhism. Since the Bodhisattva Avalokiteshvara is born out of the tear of the Amida Buddha, he is seen as his child—with the same DNA! He represents the Amida's qualities of love and compassion and is one with him. However, he has one important characteristic: He is able to help us humans directly and meets us face to face in our daily life. So, watch out ... he could be the gas station attendant, or the lady at the bakery.

Let's continue with the second Buddha Family, the Bodhisattvas.

The Bodhisattvas (Japanese: Bosatsu)

The Bodhisattvas came into being because of the god-like divinity of the supreme Buddhas and their inability to interact with humans directly, without hurting them with their luminosity. The Bodhisattva is able to meet you face to face and help you to find your essential being, thus ending your suffering.

A Bodhisattva is a human being who has actualized his potential and has reached enlightenment, but, by choice, does not enter the Pure Land. He opens the door to the Pure Land, and keeps it open for all of us who are suffering. She can be a housewife or a bank teller, a homeless person or an athlete—so, keep your eyes open and treat everyone you meet as if he/she were the Bodhisattva who has come into your life to save you. He/she has gone through the entire evolutionary cycle from suffering to bliss, and, therefore, knows how to help us do the same.

The Bodhisattva promises that he will only enter the Pure Land after everyone else has entered before him. This can never happen, so the Bodhisattva stands at the gate for all eternity. To illustrate this principle, I have written an inspirational text that I would like to share with you here:

The Promise

I have been to your house a million times, yet I fail to recognize you every time we meet. Your fragrance should remind me, but for reasons beyond my comprehension, my senses are blocked in your presence. You marvel at my inability, but let me tell you this:

Your heart and mine are one from the moment we first met. But I have vowed not to lock the door of your palace behind me, because of a promise made a long time ago.

My ways may seem unusual, yet I am your faithful agent. I work for you by taking care of others. I carry what is their's, and what is mine is their's to take. They need my hand in order to find your's. I take you there, for they don't know how to find you.

Please do not mind if I will never stay for dinner. I must not quench my thirst, nor satisfy my hunger. The longings of my heart require a bitter medicine; while in your arms the sweetness may deter the soaring spirit from coming back again, another time.

Kwan Yin

A beautiful Buddhist legend that clarifies the principles of Mahayana Buddhism is that of Kwan Yin, a Buddhist nun. Kwan Yin was a disciple of a Buddhist master from the old school. Like Usui Sensei, she was close to finding her essential being, and she asked the master when it would happen. He answered that she was indeed close to home and prophesized, "The next time that you are born into a male body you will experience enlightenment." Many Eastern Schools believe that one is born as man/woman alternatively to ensure proper balanced learning in the evolutionary cycle. Kwan Yin was not happy with the answer of her teacher at all. If the physiological difference between men and women was a prerequisite for enlightenment, then it was not for her. She took a vow to always be reborn as a woman. This way, she would not reach the final goal and would be able to help her fellowman, forever …

One of the main ethics of Mahayana Buddhism is that enlightenment is not for yourself, but for the wellbeing of humankind. Upon ordination, a Mahayana nun or monk must take the so-called Bodhisattva Vow that proclaims:

The Bodhisattva Vow

May I help all beings to find enlightenment, and may I be the last to find liberation, after all beings have found enlightenment, as the Bodhisattva Avalokiteshvara does.

In Mahayana Buddhism, there are many Bodhisattvas, but with respect to Reiki they are less important with the exception of the Kanzeon Bosatsu. Still, I would like to mention their names below in Sanskrit and Japanese.

Sanskrit:	Japanese:
Bodhisattva Dharanipala	Soji Bosatsu
Bodhisattva Ratnapala	Ho o Bosatsu
Bodhisattva Bhaisajyaraja	Yakuo Bosatsu
Bodhisattva Parabhaisajya	Yakujo Bosatsu
Bodhisattva Avalokiteshvara	Kanzeon Bosatsu
Bodhisattva Mahasthamaprapta	Daiseishi Bosatsu
Bodhisattva Avatamsaka	Kegon Bosatsu
Bodhisattva Sutralamkara	Dai Shogon Bosatsu
Bodhisattva Dharmakaya	Hozo Bosatsu
Bodhisattva Silakaya	Tokuzo Bosatsu
Bodhisattva Vajrakaya	Kongozo Bosatsu
Bodhisattva Akashagarbha	Kokuzo Bosatsu
Bodhisattva Maitreya	Miroku Bosatsu
Bodhisattva Samantabhadra	Fugen Bosatsu
Bodhisattva Manjushri	Monjushiri Bosatsu

The common characteristics of all the Bodhisattvas are Compassion (Sanskrit: Karuna) and Wisdom (Sanskrit: Prajna). Compassion is seen as the seed of enlightenment. Please take a moment to consider the fifth Reiki Principle: Hito ni shinsetsu ni.

Photos 82 and 83: The seed syllable Hrih on wooden plates and etched in stone

The Kanzeon Bosatsu

千手観音

Now I would like to spend some time with you and the Kanzeon Bosatsu; please let him/her into your heart. The Kanzeon Bosatsu, Kannon Bosatsu or simply Kannon, is the most loved figure in Japanese Buddhism—and not only in Japanese Buddhism. You will find him in other Buddhist countries under the following names:

Avalokiteshvara (India)
Chenrezig (Tibet)
Kwan Yin (China)
Kannon (Japan)
Kwan Um (Korea)
Quan Am (Vietnam)

Some scholars even suspect that the existence of our beloved Mother Mary may have been borrowed by ancient Christians from the Buddhist Kannon. Be that as it may, the quality of love and compassion is in every human's heart, and must be unveiled sooner or later in each and every one of us.

As we saw above, Kannon can manifest in many forms. In Reiki, the relevant form is that of Senju Kannon (千手観音), the patron saint of the Kurama Dera. Senju Kannon, like her father the Amida Nyorai, is also associated with a cardinal direction. He is responsible for the North. The Kurama Temple for example, was built in the North of Kyoto to protect the city spiritually. You can make use of this knowledge at home. If you have a statue of Kannon or the symbol Hrih that represents her, place that in the Northern corner of the room or property, looking towards the South (photos 82 and 83).

The Word Senju (千手) is made up of two characters. The first character, Sen, means one thousand, and stands for "countless". Ju means arm. Kannon means Bodhisattva. Together it means the "One thousand armed Kannon". The reason for Kannon having a thousand arms is obvious: so many humans suffer that he needs all the hands he can get! The statues/drawings of Senju Kannon often are shown with 40 arms with which he works upon the 25 worlds, giving it a total of 1000. In each arm he holds a tool for transformation; this can be a scroll to signify the Buddhist teaching that will bring illumination. It can also be a sword that means cutting through untruth and illusion—and repelling evil spirits. Depending on the era and artist, each hand may feature an eye in the center of the palm. This is to encourage us to be honest with Senju Kannon: she has seen it all, so we might as well place our misery at her command without trying to hide the ugly truth.

Most Senju Kannon statues seem to be female, though some are male, while others are hermaphrodite. This tells us that the Bodhisattva, as well as spirituality, doesn't have a gender. Our essence is ... a moment of silence while writing these lines (photos 84 and 85).

The most impressive temple that I have visited in this respect is the Sanjusan Gendo-Temple in Kyoto. It houses 1001 life-size Kannon statues—an unforgettable sight and feeling.

Photo 84: Lovely Kannon, Kyoto

Photo 85: Ryozen Kannon, Kyoto

Photo 86: Kurama tiger

The Kurama Temple philosophy says that the Tiger (photo 86) and the centipede are the helpers of Senju Kannon. So, if you meet a tiger on the road, be kind to him ... Both the Amida Nyorai and the Senju Kannon are represented by the Hrih/Kiriku symbol. Whether you are aware of it or not, you call on him every time you draw this symbol in the sei heki chiryo. From now on, do it with full awareness and devotion.

The Sei Heki Chiryo

Usui Sensei taught that the origin of all illness is found in the mind, as you recall from the interview on page 67. He says that all healing must begin with the mind, and he gave his students two techniques to do that. The first technique is living the Reiki principles. The second one is the so-called Sei Heki Chiryo. After the mind is healed, Usui Sensei tells us, a person becomes God-like or Buddha-like, and happiness radiates from him, making himself and the people in his environment happy. Once the mind is healed, the human is healthy, even when he is physically unwell. Please think about illness in this way and you will find that it has very little to do with the body.

The Japanese word "Sei Heki" is made up of three characters (性癖) that mean "(unwanted) habit". In case you would like to verify what I say, make sure that you divide the word sei heki in two kanji before you look them up in a Japanese dictionary. To make sure that you look up the correct Kanji, we have included them here. Some people have mistakenly divided the word sei heki in three words, but by doing this you enter hell's kitchen, and this is a hot place ...

During Usui Sensei's time, the word Sei Heki meant the whole bandwidth of habits whether physical, emotional, mental or karmic. Ultimately, it does not matter because all of this is One!

To combat these unwanted habits, the simplification of the Hrih/Kiriku symbol is used in combination with a Kotodama. Chiyoko Sensei taught this Kotodama during Okuden and her students continue that tradition. With the symbol, you call on the Senju Kannon and he performs the healing together with the soul of the recipient. In this way, you pass on the healing to a higher instance, and watch the healing process as a mere spectator, just like when you perform a physical treatment. When concerning the healing of the soul of another human being, the Japanese find it presumptuous to attempt this in person. It is not beneficial for us to pretend that we know what the soul of the other needs. In our German tradition of faith healing, we use the same principle and give the power of attorney to a higher instance.

The duration of a Sei Heki Chiryo is not set, according to Chiyoko Sensei; however, she suggested that it should be at least 30 minutes, and if possible, longer.

I am glad that you managed to read this far; before we end this chapter and go on to Reiki related spiritual groups in Usui Sensei's time, I would like to give you a concise overview of Jodo Shu (Pure land Buddhism). As we have discovered earlier, Usui Sensei and his clan were members of Jodo Shu school of Buddhism. He received his basic education at the Terakoya (elementary temple-school) of the Zendo-Ji in Taniai.

Jodo Shu

The roots of Pure Land Buddhism are to be found in the fifth century AD in China. Only many centuries later it took root in Japan through the efforts of the (then) controversial Buddhist reformer Honen Shonin (1133-1212). Nowadays, he is celebrated as one of the greatest Saints in Japanese history. As a young man, Honen lived as a monk in a temple on Mount Hie, the citadel of Tendai Buddhism. He referred his teaching to the Chinese Buddhist Master Shan Tao (Japanese: Zendo Daishi). This was the same saint, Zendo Daishi (538-597), who appeared in the dream of Kanemaki Usui and Chitsu Bosatsu (see the chapter on the life of Usui Sensei, page 30).

The origin of Jodo Buddhism is found in the Sukhavati Viyuha Sutra (Infinite Light Sutra) that states that the repetition of the name of the Amida Nyorai ten times during one's life-time, will ensure rebirth in the Pure Land. Reborn in the Pure Land, life is lived without illusion and automatically leads to enlightenment. Once the believer has entered the Pure Land, the wheel of karma stops forever.

Jodo Buddhism developed at a time when it was not possible for most common Japanese to follow Buddhism for obvious reasons. Membership in the congregation, and therefore, the promise of enlightenment and salvation, were dependent on either making a generous donation to the church, or else to become a monk/nun for a while. The people were thirsty for something that they could be a part of, and that was Shintoism-back then as it is today. Honen's timing was perfect: he taught that it was enough to repeat the name of the Amida Nyorai, even in worldly activity. This became known as Nembutsu, and the followers of this path were called Shinjin (devotee of Amida Nyorai). The Nembutsu is the practice of chanting: Namu Amida Butsu (save me o Amida Buddha).

Nowadays Jodo Buddhism with all its sub-divisions is the largest Buddhist school in Japan, with roughly 20 Million followers.

Zendo Daishi taught that everyone who repeats the name of the Amida Nyorai is escorted by him to the Pure Land, upon his death. This automatic process was called Ojo (the heavenly rebirth in the Pure Land. According to Honen this rebirth takes as much time as it takes to cut a single hair.). With this in mind, you understand why Usui Sensei entered Mount Kurama to end his life.

A Jodo Buddhist follower is asked to devote himself fully to the Amida Buddha. In a Jodo Buddhist text by Tada Kanai from 1907 it is said that so doing, Heaven and Earth fill with infinite light and the devotee is instantly relieved from all his suffering.

Reiki-Related Groups in Usui Sensei's Time

As I mentioned in the chapter on Reiki History, a multitude of spiritual groups existed during Usui Sensei's life. Some of those groups practiced hands-on healing. This seemed to be the mood of the moment.

Most of these groups either had a Shinto, Buddhist or Confucian background. Some groups broke from their original fold later on; some remained with it.

A minimal number of these spiritual groups of the day, like Reiki, don't fit into a religious category. The philosophies of all these groups revolve around the trinity of Kokoro (heart/spirit/mind), Tamashi (soul, spirit) and Ki (energy). Many of the groups worked on and addressed issues such as social reorganization, a spiritual renaissance, and the dream of creating a better world.

Shintoism is the original Japanese religion that is seen as a way of life rather than organized religion by the Japanese. It is based upon animistic and shamanistic principles. It is believed that the Universe is ruled by gods/spirits that live in places of special beauty on Earth; they are worshipped in trees, rocks, waterfalls and other natural wonders.

Buddhism was introduced in Japan around the year 552 AD, before finally taking root firmly in the eighth century. The final effort to establish Buddhism in Japan was due to a smart feat by the monk Gyoki, who pronounced that Amaterasu, the highest goddess in Shintoism (the goddess of the sun, represented in the Japanese flag) was identical with the historical Buddha.

As a result, Buddhism and Shintoism fused to a typically Japanese cocktail, mixed with Buddhist, Shinto and Confucian elements. A strict Buddhist may not even consider Japanese Buddhism as Buddhism. But, being an island, Japan is the perfect breeding ground for a synthesis that suits its geography and people.

Many of the groups described below worked predominantly with psychic healing which was until then a specialty of Nichiren Buddhism and Shugendo practitioners (mountain ascetics). They named their techniques after one of the following:

1-Seki (life energy)
2-Kiai Jutsu (healing with the thrust of the spirit)
3-Reiki (soul energy, therefore Usui Sensei added his own name to Usui Reiki Ryoho)
4-Reiho (spiritual technique) or
5-Reishi (spiritual atom).

The focus of the other spiritual groups that were not involved with healing was based upon spiritual and esoteric practices. They are called Shin Shukyo or Shinko Shukyo (new religions). An estimated 25 percent of the Japanese population belongs to one of these groups today.

All together, there are literally hundreds of these groups. They developed in three waves: 1-between 1800 and 1860, 2-around 1900-1920 and 3-after World War II (due to the change in Japanese laws). The most important groups during Usui Sensei's time were the following:

Shinto Groups
Omoto Kyo

Founder Nao Deguchi (1837-1919), headquarters in Ayabe Town, North of Kyoto

Photo 87:
Nao Deguchi

Photo 88:
Onisaburo
Deguchi

The Omoto Kyo is a Shinto group under the leadership of Nao Deguchi (1837-1919) and her son-in-law, Onisaburo Deguchi (1871-1948), who took on her family name[6].

The Omoto Kyo is comparable to the Theosophical movement. One of their main tenets was the arrival of the Miroku Bosatsu, the Buddha of the Future, of whom the historical Buddha had spoken. He said that he would return as the Maitreya, "the friend," in 2500 years. This last Messiah would herald the start of a new golden age. The Omoto Kyo had strong nationalistic elements, and was convinced that Japan and its people would play a leading role in this golden age.

Nao Deguchi had a spiritual experience on January 30, 1892 (incidentally it is the 30th of January as I translate this!). She experienced that the Shinto God, Ushitora no Konjin (the Master of the Universe), entered her being and began acting and talking through her from that day onwards. In the nineteenth and twentieth century, this type of experience was known as Kamigakari (possessed by God).

Nao Deguchi began her career as a healer. Both her and her son-in-law, Onisaburo, were noted psychics, the most well-known in recent Japanese history. In the autumn of 1900, Onisaburo had a vision that was presented to him through a poem:

Yo no naka no
Hito no kokoro no

[6]Japanese society is based upon the preservation of the male family line. In this way, the family name remains, and the family grave that is passed on to the eldest son of a family will be taken care of in the future. The ancestors play an important part in the life of the Japanese. Every year during the Obon Season in August, every Japanese visits his ancestors' grave. At the grave, a ritual is performed in which one prays for a good life for the ancestors in the other world; and the ancestors are requested to pray for the living.

Kurama Yama
Kami no hikari ni
Hiraku kono michi

The translation is:

In the middle of the night (perhaps an allegory of society in the dark age)
On this path
Opening the heart of humankind
With the light of god
Of Mount Kurama

Nao, her daughter Sumi, her husband, Onisaburo, and one of Nao's disciples made their way to Mount Kurama on foot. They spent the whole night with spiritual rituals in front of the Mao Den, the most sacred place on Mount Kurama (see photo 68) when they encountered Gohomaoson, the demon king. He is said to have descended upon Mount Kurama 6.5 million years ago from Venus and rules the world from there.

It is not known whether this may have been the reason for Usui Sensei to choose Mount Kurama to prepare himself for death. It is disputable whether Usui Sensei was a member of the Omoto Kyo, but he was most certainly acquainted with their practices. There is no proof of his membership. We know from Koyama Sensei that Usui Sensei was a Shinto missionary for a while, but which group he belonged to is unknown.

However, in Fran Brown's book on Takata Sensei (title: Living Reiki) as well as in Helen Haberly's book (title: Reiki, Hawayo Takata's Story) it is told that Usui Sensei travelled through Japan carrying a burning torch during the day. When asked why he did so, he reportedly answered, "I am looking for a healthy and happy human." This story points towards a common practice of the Omoto Kyo around the year 1900. They walked the streets of the cities with burning torches during the day and preached that the world was in darkness and needed renewal and light. Both Fran Brown and Helen Haberly state in their books that Usui Sensei was a Christian missionary. The word "missionary" is always associated with Christianity in our parts of the World, but in this case it was wrong. Usui Sensei, as Koyama Sensei told us on the telephone in 1994, was a Shinto missionary.

Another clue that Usui Sensei was associated with the Omoto Kyo, is the first name of Sumi and Onisaburo's daughter, Naohi, which reminds the Reiki initiate of a symbol used in the traditional teaching. A further indication may be the name of a group that Onisaburo founded in 1908, called Choku Rei Gun.

Around 1917, the Omoto Kyo recruited high Navy officials in their ranks that supported the group financially and otherwise. Whole naval fleets donated large amounts of money. A similar situation repeated itself years later in the Usui Association. In 1919, the Omoto Kyo had an estimated 100,000 members. In the same year the Taisho government fired some of those officials because of their involvement in the Omoto Kyo. It had become too powerful.

The Omoto Kyo was the spiritual group of the day. In the year 1920, the membership increased to about 300,000. Fifteen years later in 1935, it was about 800,000. Nowadays, the membership is estimated at about 150,000.

Notable members that are known outside Japan as well were:

1-Morihei Ueshiba (1883-1969), the founder of Aikido
2-Mokichi Okada (1882-1955), the founder of the Johrei Movement
3-Masaharu Taniguchi (1893-1985), the founder of Seicho no Ie.

It is said that Onisaburo felt the illness of his clients in his own body. This reminds me of our work with the byosen (page 180), knowing that many of us have the same skill. He also proposed that culture was an oral tradition, which was also taught by Takata Sensei in respect to Reiki. Words, Onisaburo taught, were Kotodama, a word or phrase with spirit-power (see page 24). This, too, is similar to our Reiki practice where Kotodama play an important role in the recitation of the gokai, the sei heki chiryo and the distant healing symbol. The Omoto Kyo was wrongly charged with lese majesty, which was the worst offense in Japanese society back then. Onisaburo Deguchi spent two terms in Jail, the last one from 1935-1942 before being publicly acquitted from all accusations. Besides being a psychic/healer and prolific writer, he was a gifted artist as well.

The Omoto Kyo was active in the peace movement as well as in the spread of Esperanto in Japan.

Kurozumi Kyo

Founder Munetada Kurozumi (1780-1850), with its headquarters in Okayama City

This group is one of the first of the New Japanese religions. During the Meiji period this group had many members, nowadays it is estimated at about

200,000. The founder of the group, Munetada Kurozumi had contracted tuberculosis, which was not curable back then. He swore to himself to be reborn in the heavenly realm as a "Reijin" (a healing spirit), from where he would help suffering humanity. Before the onset of his illness at age 19, he had decided to grow into a Kami (a nature-god, nature-spirit, not in the sense of the Almighty) during his lifetime to be able to heal his fellowman.

He was convinced that the root of all illness was to be found in the kokoro (spirit, heart-mind). When this was healed, the spirit was to become god or Buddha-like. The exact words are to be found in the Usui Reiki Ryoho Hikkei (see page 66)—without the reference to Kurozumi. Kurozumi inspired and warned his disciples with the following words: "When the kokoro becomes god-like, you become god. When the kokoro becomes Buddha-like, you become Buddha. But when the heart is poisoned …"

Kurozumi was healed twice when he prayed to the sun as a last resort asking to be healed from his deadly illness. Upon the second prayer he went into complete remission, and the third ritual shift changed into a spiritual experience that turned his life upside down. On his 35th birthday, he sat down at dawn facing the East and breathed the sun's rays into all the cells of his body. This he performed with such devotion that he had the impression that the sun came into his being from the heaven and that this unity cleansed him to the core. This ritual may inspire you to a meditation … In Shintoism the sun represents Amaterasu Omikami, the highest goddess.

Kurozumi gave his students several precepts, just like Usui Sensei. The most important was: kansha shite, be grateful. His main teaching centered around the purification of the kokoro, kokoro naoshi, the healing of the spirit/heart/mind.

The healing methods of the Kurozumi Kyo remind one of Reiki. The practitioner first purifies himself with a sun ritual in which he breathes in the Yang energy of the sun and retains it within. This energy is called "Yoki". The afflicted body part of the recipient is then blown on, while the practitioner rubs that body part with his hands lightly. In this way the "Yoki" is brought into the body of the recipient with the breath and light touch. Chiyoko sensei taught us a couple of techniques called Gyoshi-Ho and Koki-ho that are quite similar. In the Kurozumi treatment this is called Majinai (faith healing). This is done to treat physical as well as psycho-emotional illnesses, but is performed exclusively by a priest of the group.

The Kurozumi Kyo displayed no anti-government tendencies (unlike some of the other spiritual groups), and was therefore given the right to be recognized as an independent religion.

Konko Kyo

Founder Bunjiro Kawate (1814-1883), later known as Konko Daijin, with its headquarters in Konko, Okayama prefecture

Bunjiro Kawate grew up only a few miles from Munetada Kurozumi's hometown, and was adopted into a wealthy family when he was twelve. The name of his birthplace, Otani, was later changed to Konko in his honor. The Konko-Kyo was founded only after Kawate's death.

After a spiritual experience in which he was transformed by a Shinto deity, he called himself Ikigami Konko Daijin (the great teacher Konko, the living god!) The deity in question is the same one that was mentioned in the chapter on the Omoto Kyo, Ushitora no Konjin. Ushitora no Konjin, the metal god of the Northeast and the guardian of the demon gate was a greatly feared god, whom many spiritual seekers tried to soothe through a variety of rituals.

Bunjiro Kawate's life story reads like that of a person in whose life spirituality and faith took first place, overshadowing everything else. He proposes again and again that salvation lies entirely in the steadfast trust and faith in God and the Buddhas. In his teaching, we find two of Usui Sensei's principles: Be grateful and don't be angry. He also teaches to live in the present moment, kyo dake wa ... "If this morning is the first of the year and this evening the last, you always live in the present." Kawate taught that there is no need for ascetism, if you meet all the challenges of life. This sounds just like the fourth Reiki principle. In respect to healing he preached that only God could grant healing; yet, when someone had recognized their divine being, this alone could set spontaneous healing in motion.

Tenri Kyo

Founder Miki Nakayama, born around (1798-1887) with its headquarter in Tenri City, Nara prefecture.

Miki Nakayama, a wealthy landowner, was possessed by a Shinto deity called Tenri o no Mikoto in the year 1838. Nakayama gave all her wealth to the poor, and later on, Tenri City was built by her disciples near Nara. An amazing place!

Other groups

Sekai Kyuusei Kyo

Founder Mokichi Okada (1882-1955), with headquarters in Atami, between Tokyo and Nagoya.

Mokichi Okada became a member of the Omoto Kyo after the devastating Kanto Earthquake in 1923. In the year 1926, he had an experience in which Kannon the goddess of Love and mercy/compassion took a hold of him. At first he remained in the Omoto Kyo, but founded his own group by the name of Dai Nihon Kannon Kyo (The great Japan (ese) Kannon Congregation). According to various sources, the date for the founding of this group is thought to be either in 1928 or 1934/1935. After several name changes of his group during his lifetime, the name Sekai Kyuusei Kyo (the religion/ congregation for saving the world) remained. Like many other gifted healers, Okada, too, was arrested and jailed for breaking the Japanese medical law.

Okada taught a healing technique that is practiced by millions all over the globe, called Johrei (purifying the Spirit). When administering Johrei, the hands are not placed upon the body directly but held about thirty centimeters in front of the client's physical body. Okada taught that the soul is the center of the being and that it rules over body and mind. He also proposed that the three great sufferings of mankind, sickness, poverty and conflicts are of a spiritual nature. He labeled those as clouds, and these clouds would be erased with Johrei. When giving Johrei, divine light is emitted from the practitioner without his doing, and the clouds, whether physical or psycho-emotional are banished.

On the physical plane Okada taught that the body deposits toxins at strategic places (see the chapter on byosen on page 180). When a saturation point of toxicity is reached in a certain body part, the result is illness. Therefore, Okada placed importance on the cleansing of mind and body. He said that many chemicals like medication, pesticides and artificial fertilizer couldn't be processed and eliminated by the human body. He was the first advocate of organic farming in Japan and his students operate a health food store chain all over Japan, called Moa.

Koyama Sensei tells us that Okada's wife was a student of Usui Sensei (this must have been his second wife, because his first wife and child died in 1919 already). Chiyoko Yamaguchi was a student of Okada, but left his association after his death. Okada used the so-called Reiki Master Symbol and gave this handwritten on a scroll to some of his students. In 2002, I was shown a wonderful original of this at Chiyoko Yamaguchi's home. Ray Toba, the head of the American Johrei Fellowship writes in a letter that Iris Ishikuro, a cousin of Takata Sensei, was a member of the Johrei Foundation in the 1970's. Perhaps this is how the "Master Symbol" found its way into the Western Reiki Tradition. Both Chiyoko Sensei and Ogawa Sensei told me that the symbol was not part of the original teaching.

Mokichi Okada advocated the brotherhood of mankind, regardless of their religion or nationality. His association has countless followers worldwide, from all confessions.

Seicho no Ie

Founder Masaharu Taniguchi (1893-1985) with its headquarters in Tokyo.

Masaharu Taniguchi was a member of the Omoto Kyo as well. While performing an Omoto ritual called Chinkonkishin in 1923, he had a spiritual experience. He describes: "One day a bright light descended upon my heart. I felt a rain of flower petals fall upon my head, my hands and my feet. I was covered by this light, and breathed it in to the point that I almost choked. Then I realized that this light was life …"

In 1930, he founded his own group with the name Seicho no Ie (the house of (inner) growth). He thought that man was a son of God, and therefore, free. The real essence of reality, he proposed, was God. According to Taniguchi, three types of darkness obscure the hearts of men: Sin, illness and death. The light of life that he experienced lights up this darkness, thus dissolving it. The Seicho no Ie group works with spiritual healing that is meant to awaken the spirit so it will recognize its divine essence.

Taniguchi mentions Usui Sensei casually in one of his books published (in English) in 1963 with the title Recovery From All Diseases (Tokyo, Seicho no Ie Publications, Divine Publication Department). This fact shows us that Usui Sensei was a known personality in insider circles, and that his work continued in Japan after his death, even though it was practiced in secret. Like Usui Sensei, and other contemporary spiritual teachers, Taniguchi speaks of the human Buddha-nature—the Enlightened Spirit: "When you are One with the Buddha-spirit, the grace of God flows without delusion."

An additional similarity to Reiki is found in his book with the title "The Truth of Life" published in 1964 in which he employs an analogy for the mind that Hayashi Sensei used in regards to the Byosen. Hayashi Sensei called this analogy, "the muddy river" (see page, chapter Byosen 180). The description of Taniguchi is rendered here in a condensed form:

"When an ill person reads the Holy Scriptures, it is possible that he may suddenly experience an acute deterioration of his physical situation. The wrong thoughts responsible for his suffering are being uprooted by the truth and roughed up, like a vessel with muddy water that is ruffled by adding clear water. This may lead to the impression that only muddy water is present in this vessel, but after a while the clear water prevails."

Taniguchi was well known abroad and was friends with personalities such as Joseph Murphy, and the likes.

Tairei Do
Founder, Morihei Tanaka (1884-1928)

It is difficult to research this group nowadays, even though it must have been widespread in Usui Sensei's time. Ogawa Sensei told us that Tanaka was one of Usui Sensei's teachers; his method was called Reishi Jutsu.

Noguchi Seitai
Founder Haruchika Noguchi (1911-1976)

Haruchika Noguchi attracted attention already at the tender age of five when he was observed to heal the business partners of his father. After the Kanto Earthquake in 1923, he became well-known for his healing abilities. He was twelve years old at the time. It is told that he used to insert a finger into the ear of a heavily injured person, and if the body reacted to his healing touch, the injured was taken to the hospital. Some people say that Noguchi was a disciple of Usui Sensei, but Noguchi was only fifteen when Usui Sensei passed away.

Photo 90: Haruchika Noguchi

The Noguchi Seitai has branches all over the world. During Koyama Sensei's presidency, the Usui Reiki Ryoho Gakkai included one of Noguchi's healing techniques into their practice. The original technique was called Katsugen Undo, while the Usui Association renamed it as Reiki Undo (see chapter, Japanese Reiki Techniques on page 213). This is one of the most profound healing techniques I have come across.

The healing method founded by Noguchi is called "Yuki".

Three of his books that are available in English with the titles "Colds and Their Benefits", "Order, Spontaneity and the Body", and "Scolding and Praising" all published by Zensei Publishing, Tokyo, are well worth reading.

Buddhist Groups

Reiyukai (The association of the friends of the soul/spirit)

This group was founded by three people, Kakutaro Kubo (1892-1944), Ya-sukichi Kotani (1895-1927), and his wife Kimi Kotani (1901-1971).

I heard that Usui Sensei was supposed to have been a member of this group, but this has not been verified. The group was formed between 1919 and 1930, a long process in politically difficult times. Reiyukai is a Buddhist lay organization whose philosophy is based upon the Lotus Sutra. Psychic healing is an important cornerstone of their practice. This group has several million followers and is a sub division of Nichiren Buddhism.

Soka Gakkai

Founder Tsunesaburo Makiguchi (1871-1944).

Originally a lay form of Nichiren Buddhism, the Soka Gakkai was founded after Usui Sensei's death around 1930. Nowadays, it has about 20 Million members! In the 1960's and 1970's, the group was active in Japanese politics. Their party, called Komeito, made up about 30 percent of the seats of the Japanese Parliament. Their mouthpiece was the Asahi Shinbun, Asahi Newspaper, one of the most widely read, and still, partly, in the hands of the Soka Gakkai. I hope that this chapter on Japanese spirituality during Usui Sensei's time has given you an inkling of the spirit of the times that he lived in, and we can now devote our attention to practical matters.

Part Four:
The Practice

Usui Sensei went to Mount Kurama to die.
Practice Reiki with the same devotion.

— KOYAMA SENSEI —

Body and heart/mind are one, and when we try to divide this unity, we cut ourselves into pieces. To reassemble those pieces later on becomes difficult, if not impossible. Imagine a photograph that you have cut into a thousand pieces with a pair of scissors: don't do the same to yourself!

The Japanese point of view in this respect lies in the theory that every human being has been breathed into or given a soul by the divine. Usui Sensei refers to this in his interview on page 67 when he is asked whether or not only spiritually evolved and special people could practice Reiki. He answers that anyone who has a soul can do Reiki—and that is all of us.

This soul aspect is lodged in the center of the head according to the Japanese, where the third eye and the crown chakra meet, if you were to draw a straight line through both of them. Anatomically speaking, this area corresponds to the pineal gland, but I guess we are not able to find the soul if we look for it with scientific techniques. Indian meditation masters, too, work with this point in a ritual called Shaktipath (which I received several times in my youth from Osho).

This soul aspect is eternal. It reincarnates, again and again, until the evolutionary process is complete and the lessons to be learned on Earth are understood. Then, one enters the Pure Land (Jodo) … The sum total of all the experiences undergone in all the lives lived is stored in this soul aspect, like on a giant hard disc. Good and bad experiences are thus recorded and, out of these, certain habits are formed. Some of those are bound to be good, others, perhaps unwanted. You recall that we already discussed the so-called Sei Heki Chiryo, which is meant for the healing of those unwanted habits.

In the Interview with Usui Sensei he also states that Reiki can be seen as a psychic healing technique, as well as physical therapy. Seen in this light it becomes clear to us what happens when you treat someone's head.

When the hands are placed upon the head, the Reiki does not only flood the physical body, but it also touches, rejuvenates and purifies the soul aspect. You are touching the eternal, and this might give you a feeling of awe and humility. This also means that you are working on the present, the past and the future at the same time. Habits that were acquired in this life, or in past lives, are released and this changes the future. So, the most important work in Reiki that is so often forgotten is to give hands-on treatments. With Reiki, the recipient is purified and once again reconnected to heaven and Earth, becoming like a Miko (see page 11), a medium of the divine.

Body and soul are connected to one another like a swinging door at an old fashioned restaurant: you enter the soul through the body, and the body through the soul.

The Western Way of Treatment

In case you have solely learned the Western Treatment method devised by Takata Sensei, you might especially enjoy the following chapter on the Byosen.

A treatment using standardized hand positions may be helpful for a beginner. It has its use for someone who does not have much chance to practice and does not see his teacher often. The whole body is energized and the common diseases of civilization are often successfully healed. Stress related complaints, insomnia and general physical discomfort disappear quite readily, even during or after a single treatment. As we will see below this is not magic: once the body is energized it detoxifies immediately. So, please don't misunderstand that I am suggesting to you not to work in this way, it is good sometimes.

However, the image that I have about the difference between using a standard way of working and listening to the byosen is this: Imagine that a house is on fire. You can either flood the whole place with water, or just put out the fire in the burning pot that was left on the stove too long.

In case you work in the standard Western way, it is useful to add several hand positions to the lot. It is important to treat the lymph in the groin area, as well as, under the knees. Also, the ankles and the soles of the feet (for the treatment of the kidney meridian) should be treated regularly.

Self-Treatment

Self-treatment is an important issue. In the Western style, you follow the standard hand positions prescribed in countless books. This way of energizing certain positions daily is a wonderful tool to tune into your body, and to get to know its needs. It will also help you to become more sensitive to Reiki, and your perception will be heightened.

In the original teaching, there is no prescribed hand sequence. You place your hands where they are needed. Every one of us has a weak spot or a little pain, here and there. Place your hands there and leave them there for at least an hour a day, the longer the better. This is especially important if you have a health issue. I have met so many friends that have cured themselves of the most serious illnesses. If you are one of them, please tell it to your friends!

Personally, I do this every day, whenever one or two hands are free. When I awaken in the morning, and when I go to sleep at night, I give myself

Reiki. During the day, whenever I remember, I place my hands on my belly. While I watch a soccer game, or a movie, the hands are busy doing nothing! While teaching Reiki or jetting across the globe on an airplane, the hands are always where they belong: On the Body!

The Byosen

The original teaching applies no standard treatment. Both Usui Sensei and Hayashi Sensei gave manuals to their students with a treatment guide for common illnesses, but these were meant for the inexperienced beginner.

More experienced practitioners learned an advanced technique that is, unfortunately, unknown to most of us outside of Japan.

According to Chiyoko Sensei, Koyama Sensei, and Ogawa Sensei, both Usui Sensei and Hayashi Sensei worked according to what Usui Sensei termed Byosen. Even though the word Byosen (病腺) is a Japanese word, you will not find it in the dictionary—it is Reiki-specific. As far as I know, it is not used in any other healing modality either. Usui Sensei created this word from two kanji. The first is Byo (病), meaning sick, sickness, ill, illness. The second character, Sen (腺), stands for accumulation, or blockage of vessels, in terms of lymph or blood vessels. Together, it describes the accumulation and blockage due to toxins in the vessels of the bodily fluids. The practical Byosen work will be described in detail below.

How Reiki Works

According to Chiyoko Sensei, Hayashi Sensei often explained how Reiki works. He said that Reiki detoxifies the body. To illustrate this point, he used an analogy that he called "the muddy stream." Reportedly he said, "When you look at a stream it looks clear and beautiful.

But when you rough up the waters (give a Reiki treatment), the mud from the bottom of the stream comes up and the whole stream looks muddy. In terms of the body, this means that the toxins that have accumulated have entered the bodily fluids. Those toxins now flow downstream to be eliminated through the blood, the lymph, the sweat and the gastric juices. In the course of the treatments, the body is cleansed more and more, until the river is clean and free of toxins. The mud particles that are dissolved in the detoxifying process are siphoned off. But some of them escape and fall back to the bottom of the stream. In the next treatment, these particles are again brought to the surface and eliminated. The body of the client returns to his natural equilibrium, and when more toxins have accumulated in the future, they are eliminated by further treatments. Once the stream is in its original state, the client is healthy." Now you know why both daily self-treatments and treatments for someone else are so important.

The Toxicity of the Body

The accumulation of toxins is a natural process called Shizen Joka Sayo in Japanese (自然浄化作用). The word shizen means natural, joka means cleansing, and sayo means process. This process is essentially good, and the body does us a great favor with this. If the toxins were not accumulated in certain strategic spots, the whole system would be toxic. It is the natural wisdom of the body that aims at keeping the damage as minimal as possible. To illustrate this principle, I would like to share an image with you. Think of the garbage disposal in any modern habitation. You collect the garbage in your garbage bin. If you are a good boy, you recycle and separate it. When the bin is filled, you bring what is to be discarded to the road or into a larger bin outside of your house. Once or twice a week, the city's sanitary department comes by with a truck to collect everything that has accumulated. They have calculated how many men it needs to take care of their area (manpower=energy). If one of the workers is ill, the rest of the crew cannot handle all the garbage and must leave some of it behind. In terms of the body, this means that if there is not enough energy, the elimination of toxins cannot be executed. When the garbage has not been disposed of for awhile, you know what happens …

Heikin Joka, Balanced Cleansing

The accumulation of toxins in the body does not happen at random, but it is carefully planned and executed. The body is such a miracle. The system of accumulation depends, like everything in life, upon balance. In Japanese, this is called Heikin Joka or "balanced cleansing" (平均浄化). This means that the body accumulates toxins at about even measure on both sides of the body. So, if one shoulder hurts due to over-exertion or repetitive wrong movements, you can be certain that the other shoulder, too, will be almost equally affected, even though you don't feel it. You may have experienced this yourself, or heard it from a friend or client. For instance, someone has a hip replaced, and, after the surgery wounds have healed, he feels like new. But, after a while, he begins to have discomfort with the other hip. Sooner or later, that will have to be replaced as well. In every day language, we say that the pain has moved—but, pain does not move! After a successful surgery, the pain eases and only after it is gone do you feel the discomfort on the other side, which was there all along. This is a neurological trick of the brain, and you can experiment with this to see how it works in your own body—without being sick. Let's say you have hurt yourself while cooking and cut your finger (no need to do it on purpose now ...). Your finger hurts, and if you bite into another finger hard enough, the pain in the wounded finger disappears.

All of this tells us that we always have to treat both sides of the body to avoid later complications, and to eliminate toxins left and right. But, even if there is no corresponding organ or body part on the other side of the body, the body still deposits toxins evenly. So when you treat the liver, you must treat the spleen as well.

Energy Loss

The body needs a certain energy level to be able to detoxify periodically. But, sometimes there just isn't enough of the elixir available. Reasons for this lack of energy can be many: insufficient diet or sleep, lack of—or wrong movement, the ingestion of strong medication or drugs, environmental hazards, toxic thoughts and emotions, the whole gang! All of this creates toxicity in the body and these toxins are deposited in strategic places, which are:

1–The large joints
2–The inner organs
3–The lymph
4–The head
5–The problem area, if there is one

These are the parts of the body that are moved the most, or move on their own. The inner organs oscillate continuously to be able to function correctly. Their tissue is similar to that of muscle tissue. If they don't move adequately, they begin to atrophy. This lack of movement is due to the accumulation of toxins in the blood vessels surrounding the organs. The blockages inhibit the natural movement of the organs, and when the organs begin to atrophy, their function is impaired.

When body, mind and spirit and its surroundings work well together the body will eliminate the accumulated toxins on schedule. The inner pathways of elimination are the gastric tract, the lymph, the liver, the kidneys, the bladder and the bodily fluids. Some toxins are eliminated through the sweat glands, and when something along the line does not work well, the body detoxifies through the skin.

When the accumulated toxins cannot be eliminated for some reason, the toxicity increases until the balance tips from health to illness. The first step to illness may be tension. We have noticed that one of the first places the toxins accumulate in the body is in the shoulders and in between the shoulder blades. This, at first, is felt as tension, and if it is not dealt with, the toxins travel downwards, creating potential trouble for an inner organ below.

Someone who has been properly trained in the art of finding and working according to the Byosen, will be able to witness the process described above. According to Koyama Sensei, this art may take years to perfect. When I was given her teaching manual in the 1990's and read her evaluation, I was suspicious and I thought that she paints the picture too black. I figured that I could teach what I thought to be a technique to my students on a weekend. But, over the years I had to realize that I must be more humble, because the art of Byosen is quite complex and multi-layered.

Chiyoko Sensei often said that someone who does not know the Byosen couldn't work with Reiki effectively.

In the Usui Association, Ogawa Sensei told us, the prerequisite for learning Okuden was that one would understand the Byosen. Usui Sensei states this in the interview on page 67 saying that once you have brought good results after learning Shoden, one could learn Okuden. What he referred to was the art of Byosen.

Anamnesis

Before you can take care of a client well, you must first understand him and his life-situation fully. For this reason, it is vital that you take an in-depth anamnesis. An illness is often a sign of imbalance, or of psycho-emotional stress. It usually points towards an unhealthy way of life, in all respects. One of my friends always says to his students that three aspects of your life must be taken care of: your work, your family (including the place you live) and yourself (which means that you, too, need some time for yourself).

Medical Diagnosis

The first question you ask your client is whether or not he has any discomfort. Why did he come to you? If he does not feel well and has not been diagnosed by a medical doctor, ask him to go and have himself checked out. I don't suggest this solely for legal reasons, but also because you will be able to work in a relaxed way, once you know what is going on. Even if you are a Byosen specialist already a medical diagnosis is always helpful.

The client knows what is going on with his body and can get accustomed to it, and you will know where your focus during the treatment ought to be. And, most importantly, his health care practitioner can periodically check the client again and you will see the improvement on paper, as well as with your hands.

The Prognosis

Please ask your client what prognosis his doctor has given him. In case this has been devastating to the client, it is your first job to rebuild his confidence and will to live. We have often treated medically infertile women with Reiki and positive imagery, with beautiful results. Their husbands at home did the rest! When a young woman is told that she will never have children this often works as a self-fulfilling prophesy. Out of respect for the doctor and medical science, they will comply and remain without children. They may even stop using contraceptives, knowing that nothing can happen. We have two beautiful children, and my wife was diagnosed infertile when she was a teenager ... So, please be careful and caring about what you say to your clients, it may heal them or make them sick! More about this issue in the next chapter.

A Holistic View

Once you have heard the diagnosis that your client has been given, think about what his body is trying to do with the "illness". The body is not stupid—it is a genius. It tries to keep the person alive with all tricks of the trade. If the body would not react with illness to a certain mismanagement, the client might be dead already. The accumulated toxins would not be stored in, or around one organ but would have poisoned the whole body.

Please consider this issue carefully. A pathology handbook or a quick internet-research may help you understand the dynamics of an illness better. Now a few questions worth asking:

1–What is the body trying to achieve, and how can you help it to do that better?

2–Which bodily functions do not operate well?

3–What does your client do for work?

4–When did the symptom appear for the first time?

5–Do other family members suffer from the same or a similar illness?

6–Did any traumatic event precede the onset of the illness?

7–Did the client move to a new house or location, a new job?

8–How is his physical and mental/emotional constitution?

9–What is his family situation? Is he married or single, does he have children?

10–How is his complexion, his posture and facial expression?

11–What impression do you have of him as a person?

12–What do you feel when you shake his hand, when you are in his physical presence?

13–Is he sad or happy, or is there any special emotional quality that he displays?

Look at your client in depth, without judgment. I suggest you look at him the same way you look at a beautiful landscape, with an open mind but without trying to change or improve on anything that you see. Look at him how he is, and love him the way he is, without compromise.

After you have completed the anamnesis, in written form, if possible, begin with the treatment.

Let's say the client has asthma. This is one of my favorite illnesses, and in the last nineteen years countless clients have come to me with it and left without it. In the case of asthma, there usually is no problem with the lungs, though this must be verified first. Instead, it may be a digestive disorder. The gastro-intestinal tract of the asthmatic cannot digest certain foods that create mucous. This mucous moves up and is eliminated through the lungs. But the lungs are not made for the elimination of mucous, causing the client to breathe with difficulty, and this may make his life a living hell. The first thing you should do is to help the client heal his digestive tract. Find out what he does for work. Perhaps he works in heavy industry or he paints cars? Maybe he lives in a polluted environment, or is a chain smoker? If the client is a child, perhaps his parents smoke? Perhaps the problem lies in the family history. I once treated a young Israeli who had heavy asthma attacks with a family constellation (systemic family therapy). It turned out that her whole family was killed in the gas chambers of Nazi Germany, and the asthma attacks were her way of feeling a part of her clan, her nation, and her heritage. After the constellation, the asthma disappeared for good.

When you have gathered all the necessary information, the treatment can begin. In the case of the above, the diet of the client must be adjusted, at least temporarily. The client should avoid milk products altogether, or at least until all the symptoms have gone. Also, other food that create mucous must be avoided for a while. Soymilk and other soy products, for example, have the same effect as milk products. Everything that creates mucous is placed temporarily on the black list.

Then you ask your clients to take one tablespoon of the following mixture, three times a day, before or after meals:

–500 grams of honey, if possible organic—and, collected within a 30-mile radius of the client's home. The honey will have all the pollen from the flowers and trees of the environment. This alone can sometimes have an immediate positive effect also for allergies.

–50 grams of freshly grated horseradish. The best is if the client can grow it in his own garden, organically.

–The juice of three large lemons.

This is mixed well and kept in the refrigerator. It will not go bad, if the client takes the prescribed three tablespoons a day. During the treatment, concentrate on stomach and intestines and use the Gedoku-Ho detoxification technique described on page 246 until he is complaint free and can breathe well without his inhaler. If you don't get the desired outcome, send your client to me.

Psychological and Neuropsychological Aspects

Bringing the Mind of the Client Over to Your Side

Even though Usui Sensei says in the interview on page 67 that the client does not necessarily have to believe in Reiki for it to have a good effect, it does help. The desire to get well and the trust in Reiki magnify the healing curve in your favor.

I suggest that you help the client to think and feel positively. This way, his mind is on your side and together you can watch his recovery. The basis of thinking positively is to have positive inner images. When someone asks me if Reiki will make him or her well, I answer with conviction that it will always have a good effect. Whether this good effect will be physical, psychological or emotional cannot be said in advance: you will see. It is not up to us, and I suggest that you trust and let go. Chiyoko Sensei and Koyama Sensei both said again and again that Reiki would always have a positive effect; categorically, there is no contra-indication.

Yet, you don't work exclusively with Reiki: your life experience, your heart and mind are able to help the client on his path to recovery. At times, a therapeutic intervention may be called for. The subconscious works with images and listens to clear instructions. Use this knowledge with love and creativity. The body and mind of the client are healed by (positive) Reiki energy.

To aid this process, a positive image may work miracles.

Be Positive

Reiki is a one-way street. You are connected to the cosmic circuit, and the energy that comes through you is not your own. You are merely the channel for the cosmic energy that flows through you and fills you entirely. When your being is filled with the cosmic nectar, there is no space for anything else. Negativity and an anticipated backflow of negative energy need space, and there is none. Everything is full of light.

You don't have to fear that negative energy will flow back from your client and make you sick. Here, apply general "rules". First: the higher energy always transforms the lower. Second: soul energy does not give space to negativity in whatever form.

The international Reiki world is filled with fear of negativity. Please know that negativity is only truly destructive when it is in your own heart. It is my suggestion that you begin at home and purify heart and mind with constant effort. Once that is done, you will never be afraid of the negativity of others again.

To banish negativity from your own being, allow your being to be filled and permeated with Reiki. Koyama Sensei suggests in regards to receiving Reiju (attunement), that you should focus your attention upon the movement of Reiki in your energy body. So doing, you become more and more egoless, peaceful and silent.

One of the main Buddhist scriptures, the Dhammapada, begins like this: "We are what we think. All that we are is decided by our thoughts. With our thoughts we make the world." Later on in the text it is said, "Speak and act with a clear mind and happiness will follow you as a shadow, consistently and unwaveringly."

When this is understood, your life begins anew. This new beginning and the choice to walk into the right direction are possible through the gate of

Reiki. To let go of your negativity requires hard work, but this is a rewarding endeavor: it will cleanse your heart and mind along with your life, and awaken creativity and the joy of living.

Above all, negativity is a bad habit that originated in negative inner and outer experiences. It grows and flourishes by the constant repetition of negative feelings and thoughts. Be aware of the fact that these negative feelings and thoughts are yours and they are nourished by you. Take responsibility for it, even though the origins may be found in your upbringing, your society and social, religious or cultural conditioning. You are the only person on earth who can help you get rid of this vice. You cannot remain a child forever …

Every time a negative thought or feeling visits you, you have the option to either nourish it with your awareness and thought process, or to let it go. Make the right choice and take responsibility. The word responsibility is beautiful: it means the ability to respond. It is easy to give the responsibility for what happens to others. This way you remain a victim, and a victim can never come out of the miserable situation he finds himself in. Being responsible is the first step in the journey to happiness and a zest for life. Remember the fourth Reiki Principle: gyo o hage me. When the container for the cosmic blessings (see the kanji for the word Rei on page 16) has been converted into a garbage bin, it is your job to give it back its original purpose and purity.

Letting Go of Mental-Emotional Patterns

It is your choice. Once you have become aware of a negative pattern within you, let it go. Your thoughts and emotions are like the electric lines in your house. They determine whether it is hot or cold, dark or light. From now on, chose light and warmth, for this moment only, kyo dake wa …

When I notice a negative pattern repeating itself, I imagine that I rewind the mental tape to its origin. Having reached there, I look at it, acknowledge it as it is, and say to it in my mind: "Not today." If this is repeated over and over again, you starve the pattern to death. It will probably revisit again only to receive the same treatment. Think of riding your bicycle on a flat surface. It will continue rolling as long as you pedal, and will continue only for a little while after you stop pedaling.

The Neuroplasticity of the Brain

Your thoughts and emotions, your consciousness alters body and mind/spirit. Recently, modern science has accepted this as a fact. The human brain actually changes depending on what is thought and felt. By disciplining heart and mind, the brain mass is stimulated and modified. This process is known as the neuroplasticity of the brain. It entails the development and redevelopment of nerve cells as well as synapse formation, and the development of neural networks. I am quite sure that this can be applied to all the body, and Reiki may play an important part in this[7]. In a Reiki treatment, the whole body is flooded with light and changed positively. This can be witnessed in each and every treatment, especially when treating children. Besides that, the client takes his health into his own hands once more, positive images override negative patterns, and life is fun again.

The human brain and the whole organism constantly have to get used to new circumstances and adapt to the current ones in order to survive. These life situations are known to change with Reiki, resulting in a restructuring process of body and mind. In the human brain, this happens through the strengthening and re-connection of already existing synapses, and the formation of new ones. The nerve cells are connected by tiny hairs called dendrites that enable communication between the cells. Whether or not the capped dendrites re-grow in a damaged nerve cell, and how many of them re-grow, seems to depend upon the stimulation of that particular part of the brain. One more reason to treat the heads of your clients intensively! There are speculations that even the connection of a single dendrite may be enough to connect different parts of the brain.

This reconnection of the neurons can be watched if you treat a neurological client over a long time period. Sometime ago, I treated a child in a waking coma in Latin America. At the first treatment, her whole body was rigid. After several days of daily treatments with several other practitioners, her limbs relaxed. She was able to move the right part of her face after a week. After two weeks, the feeding tube was removed, and she was increasingly present and she smiled ... The injury had happened 18 months previously, yet daily progress could be watched.

The cross-linking of the neurons had been stimulated by the daily treatments of head and spine. Reiki is not only energy and light—it is love. By receiving a loving touch, positive physical and emotional responses are triggered and brain and body change. Mental and emotional processes find new avenues of expression, and life becomes joyful and worth living.

---

[7] *More detailed information about this subject can be found in* Train Your Mind, Change Your Brain, *by Sharon Begley.*

But, not only the brain of a child is able to recover. Countless treatments of stroke patients have shown that the brain of an adult is able to interconnect and reorganize itself. My latest experience in this respect was the month-long daily treatment of a stroke victim. When she came to me, we were only able to help her up a couple of stairs with great effort. After one month, she was able to climb 60 stairs to my office with a little help, and on the last day she tied her shoelaces for the first time in five years.

The myth that the brain cells of an adult, once destroyed, will not be able to multiply again has been disproved by science recently. Apparently, this has to do with positive mental, emotional and physical stimulation and the environment that the person lives in. The recuperation, however, does not always occur in the same magnitude. It seems that the most important aspect of neuroplasticity is spiritual awareness.

The new mental and emotional pathways must be walked consciously; one more reason to live positively and healthy in all respects. In this sense, you are the architect of your destiny.

For this reason, all spiritual schools (and Reiki is no exception) pay special attention to tutoring the mind. In Tibetan Buddhism, for example, this is called "to put the bridle on the mind." In this way, the animal is disciplined, and mental/emotional patterns cease to be the master in the house and become the servants. The Master is the spirit/soul, pure consciousness, the inner emptiness or spaciousness that is focused upon itself. In this spaciousness, there is room for everything under the sun.

Byosen—the Core of Reiki

 The byosen is the frequency that is emitted from a tense, injured or ill body part when the blood and lymph vessels are blocked due to the accumulation of toxins. But that is not all there is to it. It is also the reaction of the body to the incoming Reiki energy—the healing process!

By evaluating the above, an experienced practitioner can estimate the time needed for a treatment or a series of treatments and the time needed for the recovery of his client.

All the above sounds a little negative, but the good news is that the byosen is not a bad boy: It is a sign of Life. Our body is in constant movement searching for its natural balance. This balance does not remain forever; it changes moment by moment—and so do we!

In regards to the byosen, we are dealing with five aspects, which I would like to explain below.

The Different Processes in the Body

The first step is to become aware of all the different processes in the body. These inner processes are not the byosen, and with a little practice you will be able to distinguish them from it.

–Whenever you place your hands upon the client's body or your own, you feel the energy flowing through your hand and into the body that you are touching. Later on, I will show you how you can increase the perception of the Reiki-flow.

–Perhaps you feel the pulse of your client. It is easily felt at the carotid artery, around the chest, and the wrists. If you are not certain whether what you feel is byosen or the pulse of your client, take his pulse with your watch with one hand and compare it to what you feel in the other hand.

–You may be aware of an energetic pulse in the body that you are touching. Please experiment with this: Place your middle finger in your navel without pressure, and pay attention to what you feel. You may feel a very fast and subtle pulse, comparable to the heart rate of a child in the mother's belly. This is an energetic pulse, and not byosen.

–You may feel the peristaltic movement of the inner organs. Every time you place your hands upon the stomach and intestines of a client, the body reacts with rumbles and movement to the incoming energy, the warmth of your hands, the loving touch. But all the inner organs move and you may feel this movement when you watch out for it silently. Next time you treat someone's kidneys, pay attention.

–You feel the temperature, the texture and the density of the body, as well as the temperature of your own hands.

Because of the multitude of the impressions, it is easier to feel the byosen in someone else's body. Because of that, it is easier to begin practicing by treating others. The easiest way to practice is with a client who is seriously ill, because the byosen will be strong and tangible. But I am not saying that you should not treat yourself; with practice you will be able to feel the byosen in your own body as well. It is probably easier to feel the byosen in your own limbs before you feel it in your torso. Generally speaking, it seems to be easier for women to feel their own byosen because they are more in touch with their own bodies than men.

Areas Where the Byosen Shows Itself

The accumulation of toxins happens in certain designated areas of the body. As mentioned earlier, it is those places in the body that move a lot or are moved a lot.

- The large joints
- The inner organs
- Where the lymph flows
- The head
- The problem area, if there is one

Looking at the hand positions taught by Takata Sensei, you find exactly these body parts. Takata Sensei called the systematic treatment that she taught "foundation treatment." This "foundation treatment" was her addition to the original teaching.

Byosen often accumulates on the upper part of the body first. If someone has a strong byosen in between the shoulder blades for example, it is vital that you treat him intensively before the byosen moves downwards and accumulates around an inner organ.

The Five Levels of Byosen

The byosen has five levels, all of which you probably have experienced in your practice previously. But you may not have been aware of the fact that there is a system to it. In general, the following is universally true. But you may discover your own individual way of experiencing the byosen on top of what is described below. Let it teach you the secrets and magic of the body.

The five levels are:

1 – Heat, called Onnetsu in Japanese. Onnetsu means temperature, heat or fever. This temperature is perceived as higher than the normal body temperature of the client. This perception means that toxins have accumulated which need to be eliminated. The incoming energy supports the elimination process.

2–Strong heat, called Atsui Onnetsu. The word Atsui means hot, and this heat makes your palms sweat; you may also feel as if your hands are burning hot, on fire! The hands may turn quite red, the circulation working on full power. You may worry that you may burn a hole in the client's clothes! At this level, more toxins have accumulated but it is still in the green zone.

3–Tingling, called Piri Piri Kan. The word Piri Piri describes the sound and movement of the energy in your hands, as if ants are crawling all over them. The word "Kan" means perception.

This tingling may hardly be tangible, but can also be experienced as pins and needles, as a magnetic feeling, or as your hands becoming numb. Numbness is a strong byosen level three. When treating the kidneys of a client who is lying on his back and your hands are under his body, it is possible that the numbness is due to the circulation in your hands being disturbed. Ask the client to turn over and check if you still perceive the same numbness in your hands. If only one of your hands tingles and you are not certain whether it is a byosen or tension in your own hand, exchange hands and see if you get the same sensation in your other hand. The third level of byosen is the dividing line between health and sickness. If you feel a piri piri kan in a certain area you know that this body part needs Reiki-attention to avoid further complications.

4–Pulsation, throbbing, cold, called Hibiki. The word hibiki means pulsation or throbbing. The pulsation can be perceived as strong or weak, slow or fast. It may be perceived as being just under the surface of the skin, or way down in the deeper tissue. A hibiki byosen is clearly felt in your own body, when you have a dental infection, or an infected nail. You feel the blood vessels contract and relax in a rhythm of their own—this is the pulsation that you perceive.

When the body-part you touch feels cold, it is not necessarily the fault of your hands, but a sign of strong byosen level four. If you are not sure, interrupt the treatment for a moment, warm up your hands with hot water and then place them on the body again. If you feel the same sensation again, you can be sure that it is a byosen that you feel. When the body displays a Byosen level four you know that it has accumulated too much toxin. It does not always mean that there is something pathologically wrong, but it is likely. An acute infection or extreme tiredness can also provoke this type of byosen.

5–Pain in the hand of the practitioner, called Itami. The word itami means pain. This pain may be felt in the hand, in the fingers, fingertips or on the back of the hand. It may move up your hand into the wrist, towards the elbow, and may continue all the way up to your shoulder. If that happens, don't worry. Koyama Sensei said that pain is the result of positive Reiki Energy flowing into a strongly negatively charged body area. All that is needed is to stay in this position until the pain goes away. Change your hands if it becomes too uncomfortable, or take them off for a while. Then place them again on the same spot. Don't be afraid of being contaminated by "bad" energy, remember, Reiki is a one-way street ... I have noticed over the years that a level five byosen always shows itself to me in the triple warmer meridian. It moves on the outside of the arm towards the shoulder. But perhaps this is different for everyone. Chiyoko Sensei suggested that we should not panic when we feel a strong byosen. Byosen is the healing process of the body, and any reaction is good. The body reacts to the incoming energy, and its inherent healing abilities are awakened. Instead of worrying, Chiyoko told us she thinks of the Japanese battle cry "Yosh" which means, "I am going to give it all I got!" However, if you feel a strong byosen in a vital area for a couple of days and the client has not been to see a doctor, send him there with emphasis, without alarming him.

The above levels are experienced by everyone initiated into Reiki. The levels are not clearly defined. You may feel a mixture of a byosen two and three for example. In this case, you would feel heat and tingling at the same time. When levels four and five mix, you may feel pulsation and pain. It is also possible that you perceive something that is not mentioned above. In this case, please note it down and once you have gathered enough data, find out for yourself in which level of byosen your perception fits. Suppose you feel a magnetic feeling, a push or pull, or you feel that your hands have become one with the body of the client. Which level would you designate this perception to?

It is also possible that you may see, smell, hear, taste or just know the byosen. That may sound a little outlandish, but it is possible. If you ever perceive something that is not mentioned above, don't disregard it. Place your hands on the indicated body-part and wait. Let the byosen reveal itself to you. This needs time, and more time—no need to hurry.

Please don't misjudge Byosen for something bad. The body tells you with the help of the byosen how long, how often and how intense a certain area needs to be treated. Be grateful for that. Koyama Sensei taught that the byosen attracts the hands and the attention of the Reiki practitioner. This is a good way of looking at the byosen. Please integrate the above five levels of byosen into your practice. It will help you understand what is going on in your client's body, and will give you tremendous self-confidence. Two examples from my personal practice: Once a lady asked me to check a node that she had discovered in one of her breasts. The byosen that I felt there was a light level two. I told her not to worry and to go to her gynecologist shortly, who gave her an "all-clear." With another client the opposite happened. She asked my advice and I urged her to see a doctor. She died within a few months, and I was not surprised. A byosen level five in the breast is not a good sign. Since we are talking about the issue, I would like to share something of Chiyoko Sensei's wealth. She treated many women with breast cancer, and told us that if the node hurts upon being touched, you can relax …

The Movement of Byosen

The byosen does not remain constant in almost all cases, but it moves in cycles. Usually, these cycles come and go in intervals of 10-15 minutes. That means that you must stay in one position for a long time to be able to detect and watch the byosen. The first three levels of byosen are a sign of tension or light toxicity. This is nothing to worry about, but it is time to give plenty of Reiki, and, if possible, daily treatments until level two or one have been reached. A Takata Sensei style foundation treatment is good for general wellness or stress related issues that display a low level byosen. In this way the whole body is energized beautifully.

However, if your client is seriously ill, I suggest working with the byosen. When you place your hands on a body part that is ill, you will feel the byosen in that area.

It may come up right away, or may take some time to develop. An experienced practitioner will feel it instantly. Let's say you feel a byosen level five right away. It increases and the pain you feel in your hand soon moves up your arm. When it is most intense, you know that it will soon diminish. So, after each peak comes a valley. Sometimes the byosen flat lines completely and you feel nothing, except for the constant flow of Reiki. Stay where you are and don't move to another position. Perhaps you will not feel anything at all for another 10 minutes. Suddenly, you are surprised by the next wave, which increases, peaks and then diminishes or disappears again.

Chiyoko Sensei found out for herself that she felt most comfortable when she could perceive the rise and fall of the byosen four, or better, five times per treatment. This made her treatments at least 90 minutes long. "But I never look at the clock during a treatment," she said. "You get so curious watching the healing process that you don't want to stop. And, you look forward to tomorrow's treatment! If the byosen is just in the process of coming up again when you are about to stop, continue until after the peak. It would be a pity to miss this chance for a deeper healing …"

During the treatment, especially during the initial treatment move your hands as little as possible so you can watch the byosen in the problem area. Once the intensity of the byosen diminishes, the healing process is on its way and you can include other positions as well. It is not over until the byosen peak is at the intensity of level one or two, Onnetsu or Atsui Onnetsu. If the byosen peaks in the problem area do not diminish, keep working on this area intensively, the longer the better, and, if possible, daily.

Koyama Sensei says in regard to the byosen, which she often refers to as Hibiki, "During the initial treatment, move your hands as little as possible (if a certain illness has been diagnosed, and you know where to put your hands). It is not good to change positions. By keeping your hands on the problem area for a long time the illness is healed from deep inside". But don't overdo it so you don't get tired from sitting or standing too long. If possible, stop the treatment only after the byosen has disappeared.

As long as you are not yet able to feel the byosen clearly, always begin with the head. After a while, the part of the body that is ill moves internally all by itself. Tell your client to let you know when this happens, and then treat the indicated body part until the byosen is gone. The byosen is not necessarily a result of a discomfort or health complaint: it may appear before the client feels anything. In this case,

Reiki works like a vaccination, you prevent the illness from erupting. Always ask your client before the treatment if he has any discomfort. Let's say he complains of pain in his shoulders. You place your hands on the shoulders, but if your hands move to the stomach on their own, this is where the origin of the illness comes from. Keep treating the stomach until the byosen is gone.

Even when the doctor can not help anymore, it is often possible to be and remain pain-free and free of complaints with Reiki."

Sometimes the movement of the byosen is atypical. The peaks and valleys may come in a two-minute tract, like the subway! This is a sign of an acute illness, like an infection or food poisoning or the like. The peaks can be quite violent and give you a great deal of pain. Don't worry unless this type

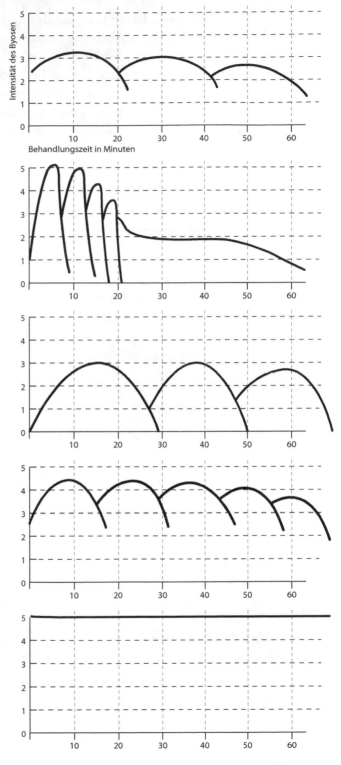

Graphs 91: Five examples of the perception of the movement of byosen during a sixty-minute treatment. From the top to the bottom.

1. *A lazy byosen, typical of a chronic illness. The peaks and valleys are all of the same intensity. The time-distance between them is more or less the same. This type of byosen tells you that the treatments will take time, but it is not life threatening.*

2. *A typical acute illness. Intense peaks that come, go and disappear quickly. Most probably this illness will be healed rather quickly.*

3. *A slowly forming byosen, the beginning of tension, or the beginning of an illness. High time to work preventatively, as Koyama Sensei suggested—before the onset of the illness.*

4. *Intense Byosen, that diminishes very slowly or not at all for a while. Probably due to a serious illness.*

5. *Permanent byosen level five, often encountered with terminal cancer patients..*

197

of byosen is felt when placing your hands on an inner organ. For an acute illness the rule usually is: what comes quickly goes quickly.

Usui Sensei and Hayashi Sensei as well as Chiyoko Sensei taught a special symbol to their Shoden students to be used almost exclusively for the byosen. Chiyoko Sensei too taught us this symbol, to be used perhaps four or five times during a treatment. When the byosen is at its peak, you draw the symbol on the body part with your hand and so doing dissolve the accumulated toxins so they can be eliminated. In Jikiden Reiki every Shoden student learns this symbol and the accompanying technique. The philosophy behind this is similar to a homeopathic principle. First, you build up the energy. When there is little or no energy, there is no possibility of healing to occur. After the energy has reached its highest point—when the byosen is at its peak, you use that energy to dissolve the toxins.

Since Chiyoko Sensei and Takata Sensei had the same teacher, we know that Takata Sensei too learned this symbol. Upon researching with some of her students we found out that some of them learned it while others didn't—or forgot. If you would like to learn this way of working, please find a suitable teacher near you. A book is not a suitable medium when talking about the Reiki symbols: they belong in the Reiki-classroom with its special atmosphere.

The Body as a Unity

When we suggest that a problem area is treated specifically that does not mean that one organ is necessarily treated by itself. I would like to explain this approach with the example of a client who had neurodermitis on the palms of her hands and the soles of her feet. Her condition had been chronic since adolescence and hurt just by looking at it. She was treated during two consecutive trainings by my students and myself for a duration of 15 days. I usually invite someone who is ill to receive treatments for free: this way the students will be able to feel the byosen and the clients usually get well quickly—because there are several people working on them daily.

When she asked me whether Reiki could help her, my standard answer sprang forth. Then I tricked her with a positive image: I told her that I would bring my camera to take pictures before and after Reiki. If I had said to her that Reiki would cure her, she would not have believed it, but in this way we bypassed the conscious mind with the power of suggestion. She was working in the cafeteria of a meditation center and I gave her the following conditions. First, she had to come for the treatments every day, for about an hour and a half each. Then she was instructed not to use any cleaning products, no soap, and was not to get her hands wet. Every time she went to the restroom I told her to wash her hands with her own urine. That did not sound appealing to her, but it is an old trick; all the old cultures used their urine for the treatment of skin conditions, infections and the like. We began with treatments after I had made an in depth anamnesis. When the body detoxifies through the skin, it is clear that the liver is not working as it should. So in the first week I concentrated on both her liver for 30-45 minutes and her head for 15-30 minutes. One of my students took care of her kidneys for the whole duration of the treatment, a second one touched the hands and another the feet. On the days that we had more participants we covered additional areas: the stomach and intestines, the shoulders, heart and solar plexus, as well as the lymph glands around the groin area.

After a few days her hands began to tingle, which made her worry and me smile. I knew that she was on the way to recovery and told her that, keeping in mind Hayashi Sensei's analogy of the muddy stream.

Her hands and feet had turned bright red now, and the skin that was cracked deeply had healed. The byosen of the liver had diminished from level five to three, and now I included the stomach and intestines more intensively. On day nine, she suddenly had a bleed outside of her regular cycle, and for the next few days I mainly treated her ovaries. The others kept up covering the vital organs. After the ovaries, the liver and kidneys, stomach and intestines showed a byosen of level two—the treatment was ended. She has not had any problems since three years.

Byosen, the Energetic Diagnosis

It must be said at this point that our "diagnosis" when working with the byosen is of an energetic nature. This has several interesting implications. First of all, those of us who are not medical practitioners are not permitted to diagnose medically. Second, we diagnose something that may not yet be or not anymore noticeable by medical science. This point is vital in the aftercare of cancer patients. When the client is discharged from the hospital "cancer free" but you still feel a strong byosen (level 4 or 5) in the afflicted area, you know that it is too early to celebrate. It is important to continue daily treatments until the byosen is at level two or one.

It is possible that Byosen may suddenly increase after a couple of weeks of treatments. This does not necessarily mean that his health is deteriorating. It is possible that the body shows its real state only now. After the body has been energized, the byosen comes up and shows its real face.

If a client takes or took strong medication/drugs, such as chemotherapy, the immune system shuts down. When the immune system is down, the body does not react to the incoming energy and the byosen hides deep within the body. Once energized, the body wakes up and begins to work. As explained above, it is essential to keep up the daily Reiki treatments until a low level Byosen is reached.

The same is true for someone who has depleted himself physically and mentally/emotionally so that no byosen can be found. In most cases, this is relatively easy to remedy. Hayashi Sensei suggested treating the head of such a client for at least 30 minutes. By doing so, the byosen—the healing process—would be jump-started.

A case history of a diabetic I treated in Caracas years ago will elucidate this principle. The man was very seriously ill, had gone blind and lost parts of his foot due to the diabetes. We treated him with six or seven people and none of us felt any byosen whatsoever. This happened to be the first experience of this kind for me, and I was insecure. Did I lose my skill or was it too late to help this man? I placed one hand on top of the body above the pancreas and the other below, but felt absolutely nothing, as if touching a piece of plastic. After the first treatment, I was tempted to tell his wife that we could not help, but luckily I didn't and asked him to come the next day again. When he came for the third treatment, his wife told me that he did not need his pain medication for the first time in months. The byosen did come up from then on, but I did not have the chance to continue the treatments for long because I had to leave again …

Byosen Work with the Seriously Ill

Even in seemingly hopeless situations, working with the byosen is rewarding. Chiyoko Sensei suggested that a seriously ill person should be treated with Reiki daily for at least one month. After the initial months, the result of the Reiki could be evaluated and a treatment plan for the following months could be made. Perhaps one would continue giving three or four treatments per week in the second month, and a little less in the third. After three months, Chiyoko Sensei said, most illnesses were healed or at least kept at a manageable state. In any case, she always suggested to the family members of the client to learn Reiki so they could work on their relative daily.

After a lecture in Rio de Janeiro, someone asked me for advice. Her husband, she said, had total kidney failure and had to go to dialysis three times a week, for five hours. He was a diabetic and had to inject insulin five times a day. Soon a bypass operation was to be performed. I thought that he would be the perfect client for my trainees and I invited him to come for daily treatments over a couple of weeks while I was in Brazil. After a week of treatments with ten students, he told me one morning with a mischievous smile that he hadn't slept well. When I asked him about it, he told me that he had to go to the restroom all night: the kidneys had begun to work again. He was flabbergasted because he was a medical doctor and this shook his medical views greatly. Soon afterwards, him and his wife were initiated into Reiki. Later, the nurses at his hospital took Reiki classes. The kidneys started doing what they do best and the blood sugar counts improved about fifty percent.

Before we talk about increasing your perception to feel the byosen more intensely, a tip about treating cancer. Koyama Sensei suggests that you begin by treating the area around the tumor. In this way, the cells around the afflicted area become strong and healthy. Once the byosen diminishes, you close in on the tumor until after a while you place your hands on top of it. She says that one can live quite well with a tumor and you want to make sure that it does not spread.

In regards to the byosen, there is no health and no illness. It is only a difference in degrees. The accumulation of toxins in the body can be little or severe. If the body deposits toxins in one area, it does you a favor and keeps you alive by doing this. Please look at illness with love, and thank your body and that of your clients for keeping you/them here as long as possible. If the client wasn't sick, he might be dead! In this sense, illness is not bad, but an unenlightened way of the body to stick around. Now enlighten it by giving Reiki.

Increasing the Perception

The art of byosen is neither intuitive nor psychic. Finding and following the byosen is possible by becoming acutely perceptive and anyone can learn this, no need for special skills. The art of being perceptive is best learned in the presence of a good teacher.

We noticed that the skill and expertise of the teacher is naturally absorbed by his students. This is the natural law: the higher energy transforms the lower.

To be able to increase perception two things are necessary. First, you need to pay attention, and second, you need to become empty inside. Begin by attentively gathering all the information about the client that your senses provide. Look at his body, his posture, and his character. Even though the client may not know what he needs, his body may display it. His body will provide you with the five levels of byosen. This is the body's way to ask for what he needs. Byosen attracts your attention—now, it is your turn to give it. The byosen also tells you about the result of your treatment, and allows you to watch the healing process of the body—one of the most beautiful natural phenomena. Enjoy it!

The Inner Emptiness

Human consciousness becomes most powerful when it is empty of thoughts. Imagine that you are calculating complex mathematical formulas while talking on the phone, skating and having a vegetarian hamburger all at the same time. You will not be able to do any of it right. The same rings true for Reiki—the more you are present, the better it works. But, being present and concentration are two different things.

Know that you don't need an effort to give Reiki; it flows through you without your doing. Stop thinking while giving Reiki and become your hands. In this way, several things happen: First, more energy flows through you. Second, you don't get tired. Third, you are not tempted to have egoistic thoughts. Fourth, you discipline your mind while giving Reiki, and the treatment becomes a meditative experience of emptiness.

Troubleshooting

1—You Don't Feel Anything

Don't worry if you don't feel any Byosen in the body of someone afflicted with a serious illness. It may be due to the abovementioned ingestion of strong medication or drugs. Learning to feel the byosen takes time and practice. Don't be in a hurry and trust that it will reveal itself to you. It is the most rewarding gift for any Reiki practitioner, and—his clients!

Practice the wonderful Joshin Kokyu-Ho technique described on page 221 that will surely get your perception going. Additionally, think about which representational system you use predominantly. Are you a kinesthetic, an auditory or a visual person? I once talked to a friend who is a musician. She told me that she had learned Reiki Two, but did not feel the energy. I thought it would be impossible to be a musician and not feel anything. So I asked her to listen to the body of the next client, as if it were a song. She called back to say that she listened, she heard and now she feels ...

If you are auditory, listen, if kinesthetic feel, if visual, see (inner and outer as well as etheric images).

2–One Hand is More Sensitive than the Other

Train the less sensitive hand. Choose an area with a strong byosen and place the hand that is more sensitive on it. Wait a while to let the byosen develop. Once you receive a strong signal, change hands and, again, let the byosen develop. If the signal lessens, change back to your more sensitive hand. With a bit of practice, both hands are able to feel the energy equally well.

3–You Feel a Different Byosen in Both Hands

Since there are many areas in the body where toxicity accumulates, you may feel a different byosen in both hands. This is not due to the sensitivity of your hands, but rather, that's exactly what is happening in the body. The area that one hand rests upon may be more toxic than the other. The movement of byosen, too, is different from one part of the body to another, even if they are close in proximity. You may perceive a byosen peak in one hand, and a valley in the other.

4–You Feel the Client's Byosen in Your Own Body

Don't worry about this, but be grateful instead. The byosen attracts your attention. This is a wonderful way to find out what is happening in the body of the client. I am sure that this has happed to you before, but perhaps you misjudged it, or rejected the feeling thinking that it is your own problem that you are suddenly aware of. Perhaps you have felt a pinch in one of your kidneys, or a sudden shooting pain in your tooth while administering a treatment. Don't disregard it right away.

You are simply using your body as an instrument. Touch the respective body part of your client, and if the itch in your body goes away, and you feel a byosen, you know what to do. No need to worry about receiving negative energy from your client: Reiki is a One-Way Street.

5–You Feel the Byosen Only in One Finger, or, in the Back of the Hand.

This is possible when the afflicted area is very small. Let's say your client has a cavity in one of his teeth and you place your hands on both cheeks. You may feel the byosen only above the injured tooth. An example: when our daughter was teething, she often awoke at night from the pain. In order not to wake her fully, I then sent her distant Reiki and always knew which tooth was about to be "born". I validated it the next day.

6—You Don't Feel the Byosen in Your Hands, but Somewhere Else in Your Body

A friend of mine who is an electrician perceives the byosen in his feet, instead of in his hands. Perhaps he received too many electric shocks in his life! Be open to anything you may perceive, trust your inner wisdom, and, if in doubt, ask your teacher for guidance.

Words of Encouragement

The ways of the byosen are still relatively uncharted. Keep working with the mind of a pioneer. Every client, every illness, and every fate is unique. Know that the only thing required of you is to have a heart filled with love and to do absolutely nothing … the more you disappear, the more Reiki takes over to do the job.

I trust that the combination of the abovementioned techniques and receiving Reiju will have a wonderful effect on your students and clients. Your students and clients are blessed and Usui Sensei's last wish becomes true: that Reiki may heal the earth and its inhabitants.

Three Traditional Byosen Techniques

1—Working on the Problem Area

To be able to work with the byosen effectively, we are aided by three techniques: The first technique is really not a technique at all. A client comes to you and tells you what his physical problem is. A healthcare practitioner has diagnosed him, and maybe he experiences pain or discomfort. You place your hands on that body part and feel the byosen. If you feel a strong byosen, level four or five, you know that something serious is happening there which needs serious and possibly time-consuming attention. As you keep your hands on this area, you watch the peaks and valleys of the byosen. It comes and goes in waves.

You keep working with the client until the peaks have diminished to level two or one. One example: A seminar participant was supposed to have her gall bladder removed a few days after the workshop. She had developed very painful gall bladder stones and the doctors saw no other way for her than surgery. Everyday for five days, I worked on her with the other students. On the first day, I felt a strong byosen, level five. During the treatment, one of us held her head, one held her feet; two or three held other positions and I placed my hands on the gallbladder for the whole duration. I kept one hand on top of the body and the other underneath. The byosen changed after two peaks and dropped to a strong level four. I felt the area cold, and imagined the stones turning to dust. The next day, we began again with a light level five byosen, and from then on the byosen dropped dramatically. On the third day, all I felt was a strong tingle—level three. By the end of the training, after five days, there was only heat to be felt. I asked her, quite strongly, to have a checkup before surgery, because I knew that the body was taking good care of itself. The body's healing powers were activated and I was confident that it would now heal itself. All the others felt it too. The surgery was cancelled by a surprised physician.

2–The Reiji-Ho Technique

The second technique is called Reiji-Ho in Japanese. It comes directly from Usui Sensei, who taught it to his students. In the Usui Reiki Ryoho Gakkai (Usui Reiki Healing Method Association) this technique is thought to be one of the Pillars of Reiki. They suggest to practice and perfect it over the course of many years. This may seem strange to you, because the technique is rather innocent looking. But I promise you, it is a tiger in a sheepskin. The words Reiji-Ho mean "indication of the spirit" or, in our case, indication of the Reiki Energy. Because this technique is so important, I will talk about it more in the chapter on the Japanese Reiki Techniques on page 213.

Instructions for the Reiji-Ho Technique

Step One: Fold your hands in Gassho and bow lightly. Now become aware of the Reiki flowing through you. (Someone who has been attuned to Reiki will feel this instantly. Most of us feel a pulsation, or waves of energy in between your palms.)

Step Two: Pray for the healing and wellbeing of the client on all levels (without judgment).

Step Three: Lift your hands up in front of your forehead, thus activating the third eye, and ask the Reiki energy to take your hands to where they are most needed in this moment.

Now you will receive an inspiration that tells you where you shall place your hands. This may come in a variety of forms. It may come to you as a thought or as an emotion. You may see an inner image, or an etheric one. You may just know where to go. You may hear an inner voice telling you where to go. You may sense what is happening to your client. Or you may feel a subtle sensation in your own body, pointing you in the right direction. Once you follow this perception by placing your hand on the client's respective body part, the sensation in your own body disappears.

After you have received the information in whatever form, you place your hand on the body, and pay attention to the byosen. Depending on the strength of the signal, remain there until it decreases to level one or two. The first part of this technique is linked to your intuition, but the second part is perception. And this is what I personally like about working with the byosen. You can always verify what you intuit by placing your hands on the body. I am not comfortable with the emperor's invisible clothes ...

Several years ago, I showed this technique to an old friend who is an internationally well-known physician, Dr. Klinghardt. I stood behind him for a couple of seconds, and then told him which areas of his body needed attention. He could not believe his ears, and immediately invited me to a congress. This technique turns Reiki into a very serious healing art, and should be learned by everyone who practices Reiki.

After you have worked with this technique for a while, you may not need to go through the motions anymore, or you may find your own way of doing it. Maybe you just need to look at someone to be able to tell what is happening to his body. Personally, I am not very skilled at these things—and, if I can learn it—I promise you that you will be really good at it!

Another part of the Reiji Ho technique is for psychic development, but this is something to be learned from a teacher, and does not belong here. I teach it exclusively to my Shihan students. Koyama Sensei said that the learning of the Reiji-Ho technique requires a lot of practice and patience. So please begin here, and be sure that this technique will change your life and your clients' lives for the better. This is my promise: your intuition will open its doors, not only in terms of Reiki but in all aspects of life.

3–Scanning the Body Within and Without

The third technique is scanning the body. This is usually done by running your hands over the body through the aura of the client, slowly and consciously. Begin at the head, holding your hands a few centimeters above the body. While doing so, you pay attention to the subtle changes in the perception of your hands. Scan the whole body and remember or write down the areas that were indicated. After you have covered the whole body, go to the place where the impulse was strongest, place your hands on it and wait for the byosen to develop. In both the second and the third technique, the byosen pulls your hands to the place that needs attention.

You can also scan the body from the inside. Place your hands on the body and listen carefully. Listen with love and devotion and you will hear the melody of the body you are touching. Body and mind will reveal their secrets to you.

Your hands may already be sensitive, or they may require some perception training. One hand may be more sensitive than the other at the moment, but eventually both are able to feel the energy equally well. It is possible that you may feel the byosen with one hand or with both, depending on the size of the area that is afflicted. You may also feel it only in one finger, or, in the back of the hand. You will be surprised how accurate it can be.

The byosen is a powerful tool that can help you get better results and work more effectively. I would like to encourage you to experiment with the techniques mentioned above and thus experiencing how exciting it is to work in this fashion. You will see that your efforts will be rewarded beyond your expectations.

Perception Training

In the end of this chapter and in the beginning of the next chapter on the Japanese Reiki Techniques, I will talk about how you can make your hands more sensitive to be able to feel the byosen clearly and be able to help your clients effectively.

Sensitivity and Perception

Your hands are already sensitive after you have been initiated into Reiki, yet they may require some additional perception training to feel the byosen clearly. The traditional way to increase the perception in Reiki is divided into two pathways. One depends upon your teacher; the other depends on your personal practice. Usui Sensei sometimes demanded that students practice on their own before he was ready to give them an attunement.

Training with Your Teacher

Reiju

The most precious gift your teacher can give you is the attunement. The Japanese word for attunement is Reiju. In this case, the word Rei means soul or spirit. The word Ju means to grant or to give. When the soul forces that are dormant in your being are activated by your teacher, the energy awakens and your hands become super-sensitive. After receiving a Reiju is a good time to practice perceiving the byosen for that reason. In the original Japanese Reiki teaching it is said that it is good to repeat the Reiju at least once a month—until you yourself become a teacher. My personal favorite Reiju ritual is what I learned from Chiyoko Sensei in 2002. But any ritual that is well proven to activate Reiki and is close enough to the original will do. In Japan, not only human beings are given Reiju. Chiyoko Sensei reported that both Usui Sensei and Hayashi Sensei initiated Reiki certificates and Quartz crystals. Koyama Sensei adds in her teaching manual that she also gives Reiju to table-salt that is later given to her students for healthy cooking!

As we have seen above, Reiki awakens the soul power in the initiate. But this soul power must be awakened so that you can use it for yourself and others. Imagine that your grandmother had buried a treasure under your house in her youth. As long as no one knows about this treasure and its location is unknown, it is of no use at all. It needs someone who knows the whereabouts of the precious treasure. This someone is your Reiki teacher, providing that he has learned the sacred art of awakening the treasure.

This ability has been passed on to him by his own teacher, and he has been given permission to perform the Reiju ritual with his own students.

The Initial Spark

Spiritual growth usually is sparked by a spiritual teacher. Once the flame is burning in your heart, you can work by yourself even though you might still need the guidance of your teacher, as well as the support of other students of the way. In this way you see where the path leads and this gives you confidence and trust. When I give public lectures, this is what I do. I show the audience through my words, my gestures, the openness and love that has grown in my heart through the years, how someone develops on the path. Because I know that we are all made of the same stuff, I give the listener a view of his own future for a little while. This gives the beginner courage and serenity.

The Reiki teacher has two functions. First, he is to light the initial spark. Second, he is supposed to be a role model showing the student how to integrate the Gokai, the Reiki principles. He is to follow the Bodhisattva Vow in his own way (see page 161) and should nourish love and compassion in his heart and actions. Part of the initiation is to pass these virtues on to his students.

The teacher has heightened his energy level and purified his own heart. This higher frequency is conferred to his students. Therefore, it is suggested to choose your teacher carefully. If the teacher himself has not found happiness, he cannot help you out of your suffering.

A Successful Reiju

Technical know how is also required for a successful Reiju. The teacher must have learned to know when the soul power is activated in his student. Once this is certain, he teaches his students by practicing Reiki together. He explains the Reiki philosophy and history to bring Reiki in its original light. Only then can he let his student loose on the public with a smile.

Later on, the student himself will get a feeling of the flow of energy in his hands and body. Takata Sensei says in her diary about this issue: "Fold your hands in Gassho, focus on your Tanden, and wait for the sign." She does not specify what she means by "the sign", but I suppose that she refers to something that we all know. Your folded hands become warm, and soon begin to pulsate in a peculiar rhythm that is unlike the heart rate. I call this sensation the Reiki-Pulse. In order to strengthen your perception of this pulse, please refer to the Hatsurei-Ho techniques in the next chapter. At first this pulse is felt in your hands only. After a while, it is possible that you feel it all over your body, and even beyond the confines of your physical body.

The Responsibilities of the Teacher

The Reiki teacher is responsible for his students and for the quality of his work. Once, when Tadao Sensei was asked about this issue in my presence, he said that he is also responsible for the students of his students. So, in this respect there ought to be no compromise whatsoever. Either I give myself to the role as the teacher fully, with heart and soul, or I better wait until this readiness has grown in my being.

A Reiki initiation is never without positive results. For many students, it acts as a door towards the discovery of their inner world. The initiate is reminded of his essential nature and this has a great impact upon his physical, mental and emotional being. He sees himself in his true light for the first time and will experience transformation in many ways. Perhaps he finds the strength to get out of a disruptive relationship, or he leaves a job in favor of something he wanted to do all his life. Perhaps he does not change his life at all but finds long lost happiness and changes only his attitude. Quite possibly he begins to nourish body and mind in a healthy way; in all those changes he receives the love and support of his teacher. The teacher shows him how to let go of dependency (also the dependency on the teacher!) and shows him by his own example how life can be lived joyfully.

The Responsibility of the Student

Ultimately, everyone is responsible for himself, but one grows into being and acting responsibly slowly. I call this the process of becoming human … We arrive on Earth with potential that we are able to actualize in the course of our life. This process is filled with happiness and sadness, success and failure. It leads through peaks and valleys, health and illness, joy and sorrow. In short, this is our journey through life and death.

Giving Treatments Together with Your Teacher

When I trained with Chiyoko Sensei, the participants practiced giving Reiki to each other daily. Under her guidance it was easy to learn: she was an expert in giving treatments with 65 years of actual experience and a heart full of love. I felt like a Reiki baby in her presence …

We, her students, noticed that we felt the byosen more easily when working with her. In the physical presence of the teacher, your vibration is raised to that of your teacher temporarily. If your teacher is capable, his capability (temporarily) becomes yours and you learn rapidly. By repeating this experience as often as possible, you will be able to work on your own later on in the same way.

The best way to practice on your own is to work on someone who is seriously ill, because the byosen is felt strongly. If someone "just doesn't feel well" the byosen is often minimal and hard to catch for a beginner.

Your Individual Practice

After you have received a good education from your teacher, you are able to discover the wonderful world of byosen by yourself. You can practice the techniques we talked about earlier and, above all, please give treatments to others. I suggest that you keep a written journal of all of the treatments you have given, especially in the beginning of your practice.

Note down in great detail what you have felt during the treatment. Keep a notepad next to your treatment table and a clock. As soon as you feel the byosen arising, look at the clock and write down the time. When the byosen is peaking write this down too. As soon as the byosen diminishes make a note of it. After the treatment you will see the characteristics of the byosen, and you'll be able to understand it better in the following treatment. The Byosen has its own signature, its own character. When that changes, the healing process is on its way. Understanding the signature of the byosen is especially important when you treat someone distantly. Chiyoko Sensei told us that her husband was missing in battle towards the end of World War Two and for a long time afterwards. She sent him Reiki distantly every day and knew that he was still alive because she knew his byosen well …

After Each Treatment

Hayashi Sensei used a technique called Ketsueki Kokan-Ho Technique after each treatment. Ketsueki means blood/ blood flow and Kokan means exchange. I have translated this word in a previous book with Blood-circulation technique. This is not entirely wrong because the technique increases the blood circulation. But what is truly meant is blood-exchange. The reason for performing this technique at the end of each treatment, described in detail (on page 246), is that during a Reiki Treatment the toxins are dissolved and have entered the bodily fluids. This means that the system is superficially more toxic and the client may experience a healing crisis. He may get a headache or feel nauseous. Pain and other symptoms have also been known. With the Ketsueki Kokan Ho, all the bodily fluids are exchanged, and the client is all "new"!

Chiyoko Sensei suggested that this technique could also be used if there was no time for a Reiki Treatment; it takes four to five minutes. It is also indicated for illnesses of the metabolism, or for stroke victims, as well as for kids who don't want to get up in the morning due to low blood pressure.

Case Histories

On the next page, you will find an example of what your Byosen notes may look like. You can copy it out of this book and use in your practice, or make your own. It will help you understand the byosen better—bon voyage!

Reiki Treatment Sheet to Register the Byosen

Client's name:		
Age:	Date of birth:	Gender:
Address and phone number:		
Place and date of the session:		
Illness history, if known:		
Symptoms:		
Notes:		
Byosen:		
Note about the client:		

The Reiki treatment sheet can be downloaded at: www.reikidharma.com

The Japanese Reiki Techniques

In this chapter, I would like to share the traditional Reiki Techniques with you that Usui Sensei taught to his students. They are still taught in the Usui Reiki Ryoho Gakkai today. In their meetings, they are practiced together and integrated in the Reiki work. Chiyoko Sensei taught some of these techniques as well, while she disregarded others as not so essential. For completion's sake, I would like to include them all at this point.

I have been practicing these techniques for many years and have had the privilege to experience beauty, love and inspiration through them. I trust that you, too, will find pleasure in them. My friend, Shizuko Akimoto, who had learned them from Ogawa Sensei, initially taught them to me. Later on, I found them described in detail in Koyama Sensei's teaching handbook.

But, before we begin, I would like to make it clear that Reiki is not a technique, and does not depend upon techniques. Energy simply is! But, perhaps it is useful to learn a ritual or a technique that allows you to bypass the conscious mind. In this way, Reiki can unfold freely and heal your world and that of your clients and students. The less you are, the more Reiki is …

The Best Technique

The best technique is the one that you don't need anymore. This is not because the technique is not good or not good anymore, but because it has taught you to arrive at the desired goal without it. In India they say: The Master Musician destroys his instrument. The prerequisite for this is year-long, single-pointed devotion and practice. Reiki is the most simple thing in the world, yet it requires all your love and attention.

As is true for meditation, the effect of a good technique does not necessarily reveal itself immediately. Learning and practicing a technique is a challenge to your wholeheartedness and a great chance to discipline your mind. One, or the other technique may yield immediate and stunning results, which seem to disappear again after a while. This may make you think that the technique has lost its power and impact, but this is a misconception. By practicing, you may have gotten used to the increase in energy. At first, when it was new to you, you over-reacted like a pendulum swinging to the other side of the spectrum. After a while, the energetic pendulum finds its equilibrium and you may not feel it anymore or not as strongly, but the people in your surroundings will. If you should experience it, don't give up, and keep practicing at least for another three months—then you can let it go.

Some of the techniques below are designed to increase your perception so you can feel the byosen more clearly. Usui Sensei called these techniques Hatsurei-Ho, and they are to be practiced daily, until your perception is acute. For this reason, I will embark upon this chapter with the Hatsurei-Ho techniques.

Please focus your initial attention on those techniques, the Reiji-Ho technique and everything that has to do with byosen. Together, they compose the heart of Reiki. You will be richly rewarded for your efforts.

If you have not learned these techniques previously, I suggest you find a local teacher who can guide you with this. A book can only inspire you and is no substitute for a teacher whom you can touch and who can touch and teach you in his own original way.

The reason for this is clear. Reiki means transformation and realization of your true nature. If your teacher has done his own inner work, he will be able to transfer it to you with love, awareness and ease.

In case it is difficult to find a suitable teacher, begin by yourself and keep your eyes open: when you are ready, life will present you with a suitable teacher. Trust that …

The following techniques have been described by me previously in the book "The Spirit of Reiki" (Lotus Press). Now, eleven years later, I would like to share them with you again with a deeper understanding and bathed in the light of transformation. I teach these techniques worldwide and many others teach them in workshops and on the Internet. Sometimes they are mis-represented as a tool lacking the practical aspect. To remedy this, please read on.

What follows is a description of each technique, with an explanation of its esoteric background, as well as a wealth of practical experience that has shown itself over the years. Some of the techniques have the suffix "Ho" meaning technique; the others have the suffix "chiryo" meaning treatment.

1. The first Hatsurei-Ho technique: Gassho Meiso (Gassho Meditation)

Preparation

The first technique to increase your perception is the Gassho meditation. You sit with your eyes gently closed in a quiet, and preferably, darkened room. It may be helpful to place your tongue against your front teeth, and to breathe through your nose as you breathe in and through your mouth when you breathe out. When breathing out, the tongue automatically drops down. If you like, imagine that you are looking at something beautiful through your closed eyelids, about ten inches in front of you. This focuses the energy on the third eye and makes it easier to be single-minded.

Make sure that you are not disturbed, and that there is nothing that needs to be done. Turn off the telephone, and, for half an hour say goodbye to all worldly activities.

If you can sit quietly without any movement of body and mind, the results are best. But if you have a backache and your knees are pinching you, don't hesitate to practice anyway. The occasional thought will not disturb you much. Everything is subject to change, even pain, and you can be certain that it is not going to kill you.

Make sure that the area just above and just below your navel is relaxed and not tight. Wear comfortable pants or open the top-button, if necessary, so you can breathe easily into your Tanden (two or three fingers width below your belly button). If necessary, you can support your back; it is ok to lean against the wall or a cushion.

Fold your hands in front of your heart. The word Gassho means two hands coming together. The correct way to practice Gassho is to hold the hands up, with the palms touching. Each finger is supposed to rest upon the respective finger of the other hand. The hands are held so that the fingertips are held just below the nose. The elbows don't touch the body, but there is enough space in between the inside of the upper arm and the armpit to fit an egg. The back is held erect and the head floating up by itself, as if held up by a helium-filled balloon.

Ogawa Sensei suggested that the hands are held in such a way that the out breath (through the nose) touches your fingertips. This tells you how high the hands are to be held. This meditation is meant to transport you into an ego-less state, a state of Silence and contentment. If your body hurts too much, relax and be kind to yourself: this is not supposed to be a torture.

The Esoteric Background of the Gassho Meditation

In traditional Reiki, it is believed that the middle finger has the most energy output. For this reason, this finger is used when working on a small body area, as described below concerning the hesso chiryo or the treatment of the auditory canal. In this case, you place the middle finger in the auditory canal, and place the other fingers around the ear. This technique is also used for treating the eyeballs and individual teeth.

In esoteric Buddhism, the left hand represents the moon, the right hand the sun.

> Each finger represents one of the five elements:
> The thumbs represent the Void
> The index fingers represent Air
> The middle fingers represent Fire
> The ring fingers represent Water
> And the little fingers represent Earth
> According to esoteric Buddhism, the fingertips:
> Of the thumbs represent discernment
> Of the index fingers represent operation
> Of the middle fingers represent perception
> Of the ring fingers represent reception
> And of the little fingers represent form.

From a standpoint of meditative science, sun and moon and all the elements come together when we fold our hands, the circle is complete. Focusing our attention on the middle finger stresses the fire aspect of meditation, awareness burning unconsciousness.

Your fingertips also are the home of many nerve endings and meridians. The meridian that ends in the middle finger is the pericardium meridian of the hand Jueyin. It runs from the chest along the medial side of the arm, past the wrist, through the palm of the hand and it terminates in the tip of the middle finger. If your hands should get tired while meditating, allow them to gently come down and rest in your lap, still focusing your attention on the point where the two middle fingers meet.

Meditation Clues

It has been the experience of meditators all over the world, that meditation comes easiest when the spine is held erect, in a ninety-degree angle towards the pelvis. If this does not come naturally to you, tip your pelvis backwards a little.

This does not mean that you can't meditate sitting in a chair or lying down. Once you have the knack of it, you can meditate anywhere, anytime with closed or open eyes. Then, meditativeness has entered every action, filling your life with serenity, grace and invigorating silence. Everything is perfect as it is. Nothing must be changed, improved upon or banned out of your experience. After a while, this becomes second nature. One of the things that people always say to me is, "You are so silent inside, and relaxed."

I, myself, don't really notice this anymore because there is no separation between the experience of silence and the one who is experiencing it.

If possible, keep your eyes closed the whole time in order to keep the energy within; this also helps you perceive the energy, and you may actually be able to see it in front of your inner eye. If this is difficult or makes you prone to increased mental activity, keep them half-opened in a 45-degree angle without looking at anything in particular.

We are so used to looking around and getting drawn into our thoughts that arise through visual or other sensory impulses. Impulses then lead to a train of thought that is automatically followed, leading us into a jungle of unconsciousness.

Meditation with Open Eyes

So, if you feel uncomfortable with closed eyes, keep your eyes open but unfocused and avoid blinking altogether. After a few minutes, your eyes will start to tear—keep going. When you have practiced this a few times, you will be able to not blink your eyes during the whole meditation. The idea behind not blinking is that the blinking of the eyes and the arising of thought often go hand in hand. No blinking—no thinking! You could also use a blindfold to keep your eyes gently closed.

Letting the Breath Come and Go by Itself

Let the breath enter your body by itself, no need to regulate it in any way. The only thing you should do is to breathe deeply into your belly. If you don't know how to do it, either ask someone to show you how, or put one hand on your belly and breathe into the area that you are touching. After a short while, you will get the hang of it. Make it a point to practice daily, and within a little while your breath will reach deeper and deeper into your belly. An exercise that will help you experience belly-breathing almost instantly is the Joshin Kokyuu-Ho technique described below.

Tune In

The Gassho meditation is practiced to increase the energy level of the practitioner and to put you into a meditative space. It is to be practiced daily either in the morning or the evening (or both), alone or in a group for at least twenty to thirty minutes.

We all know how difficult it is to forget everything when we sit down to meditate. I remember a friend of mine asking my spiritual master, Osho, why it was that her inner dialogue had started to go absolutely crazy every time she meditated. Osho told her that the actual fact was that she had only become aware of the fact that her mind was crazy when she started to meditate.

Our "normal" state of mind is in reality absolute chaotic madness. The knack to get out of this madness is to first become aware of it. Then, without intending to make the craziness go away, you turn the poison into nectar. There is a beautiful story of Mullah Nasruddin, a humorous character in mystic Islam, whose stories are used to illustrate the human nature:

The Mullah had a beautiful apple tree in his garden that bore many delicious fruits. It was well known in the neighborhood, and, in the season, many children sneaked into the Mullahs garden to steal his apples. Every time the Mullah saw a child coming up to the apple tree, he would charge out of the house screaming and yelling at the offender. One day, one of his neighbors, who had been watching the daily drama took the Mullah by the arm and said: "Mullah, you are such a peaceful man, and the tree in your garden yields so much more than you could possibly eat—why do you chase the poor kids away?"

"Children", said the Mullah, "are like thoughts. When you chase them away, you can be certain that they will return."

Keep this story in mind when you are meditating. Don't chase away the thoughts that cloud your mind's eye. Look at them, acknowledge them, and bring your attention back to the point where the two middle fingers meet.

It has been our experience with hundreds and hundreds of seminar participants that this meditation fits the Eastern, as well as, the Western mind very well. It is well received by old and young regardless of their background.

One remark that is usually shared with us after practice is that it seems to be easy for many of us to watch our internal dialogue and be less fidgety than usual.

The Technique

Fold your hands in the gassho position as described above.

Focus your attention on the place where the two middle fingers meet. In the Japanese Reiki Tradition, it is said that the middle fingers have the strongest current of Reiki Energy. (Remember this when giving treatments in an area too small for the whole hand). Now pay attention to what is happening in the palms of your hands, as well as in all the fingers. You are probably going to experience a pulsation or tingling sensation in some or in all parts of your hands and fingers. This is the Reiki! Keep your attention on this process and on your middle fingers for at least twenty or thirty minutes. When the time you have given yourself for this meditation is up, take your hands down, rest for a few minutes and then continue with your daily activities. If you have more time, continue as follows:

Additional Practice

This can be done with open or closed eyes, preferably in a darkened room, because you may actually be able to see the energy that is generated. Koyama Sensei says that you can

Photo 92: Gassho Buddha

see the energy playing around your fingers in purple rays. You may be able to see this with open or closed eyes—experiment. If darkening the room is too time-consuming, do it in daylight or outside in a beautiful quiet place in nature. Personally, I perceive Reiki as a deeply violet ball of energy that increases and decreases before the inner eye, like the moon on a clear night.

The Technique

Your hands are in the Gassho Position. Move the palms of your hands slightly apart, so that there is a space of about one or two inches in-between them. Feel the energy between your hands and when you do, compress the air/energy between your palms by moving your hands slowly away from each other, and then again closer to each other. You may also move your hands towards or away from your body slowly, as if forming a ball of energy.

Slowly let your hands come further, and further, apart. Each time, make sure you take enough time to feel the energy between your palms.

If you don't feel the energy anymore at some point, let your hands come closer together again. Then, when you feel it once more, let them move further apart again. Continue to do so until your hands are about shoulder-width apart, or more.

Then, in your own time, return very slowly and consciously to the Gassho Position. Remain with your hands folded for a minute or two, and then let them come down. Take a few minutes to return to life …

This exercise can be done on the train, or in nature, at home or at the office when you have a few minutes of time. When visiting a power spot (like Mount Kurama, for example), you may feel the energy instantly, just by moving your palms apart. There is no time limit for this exercise: you alone decide the length of it in any given situation.

Partner Exercise for Strengthening the Perception

Exercise One: Do the same as described above with a partner, placing the palm of one of your hands on the palm of your partner's hand. Then continue with your partner as in your individual practice.

Exercise Two: Place one hand on your partner's body and one hand on your own upper thigh. It does not matter which hand you place on your partner's body. If your partner has a physical problem in his body, place your hand on that area. If he does not have a problem, or is not aware of one, place your hand on his shoulder. You probably remember that we said earlier that toxicity accumulates around the large joints of the body, the inner organs, the head, the lymphatic system and the afflicted area(s). On the shoulders or between the shoulder blades, the byosen readily shows itself in every one of us.

Now pay attention to what you perceive in both hands. Knowing the pulse of Reiki will help you distinguish what is going on.

Whenever you touch the body—whether it is your own, or someone else's, the energy immediately begins to flow. As I told you earlier, Chiyoko Sensei always said when she touched the body, "On" and when she took her hands off, she said "Off". Once initiated into Reiki, this is what happens whatever you do, awake or asleep, conscious or unaware … in good spirits or when you're having a bad day.

You will now feel different sensations in both hands. The hand resting on your thigh will probably pulsate with the Reiki pulse slightly. It will feel warm, relaxed, comfortable and neutral (unless you have just run the New York Marathon). The other hand will perceive something entirely different: you will become aware of the byosen of your partner's shoulder. You may feel a tingling sensation, a strong pulsation or even pain in your hand.

Exercise Three: Partner exercise. One partner sits quietly as the other prepares himself.

Begin as in Technique One and let the energy build up between your palms for a few minutes. Let the palms move away from one another slowly. When your hands are about fifteen inches apart, move them to the left and right side of your partner's head, making a Reiki Burger out of his head. Move your hands slowly, to and from the head, feeling the subtle changes in the flow of energy. In this case, you are not scanning for anything, but administering a treatment—and being aware of the energy flow at the same time. If there is enough time, you can move your hands in front and back of the head of your partner, or any other body part.

The same exercise can be done distantly. Follow the standard procedure for distant healing.

Switch over after ten or fifteen minutes. Now, you rest and your partner prepares himself, before commencing the treatment.

These exercises can be done without the previously described Gassho Meditation. But make sure you do begin with folded hands in the Gassho position. Wait until you perceive the Reiki-Pulse, and only then, begin ...

Besides increasing your perception, this exercise is a lovely treatment for general wellbeing and relaxation. If continued for thirty minutes or more, your partner will enter a deliciously relaxed state and will be flooded with light from head to toe. Another reason for practicing this exercise is that you realize that energy is not some esoteric dream, but it is tangible—a fact of life. Every time you place your hands on someone, all the atoms in his body are en-lightened!

Remembering Compassion

While practicing the above techniques, please remember that you are doing it for your clients. Practicing with this attitude, you don't get too involved with the phenomena that you may experience. The utmost goal of Reiki is not the fireworks, but compassion. Remember the fifth Reiki Principle: be kind to others (hito ni shinsetsu ni).

 **The Second Hatsurei-Ho Technique: Joshin Kokyu-Ho, the breathing exercise to purify the spirit**

Preparation

This is the second of the exercises to strengthen your sensitivity, as well as, the Reiki output. Remember the principle law of energy: whatever you pay attention to, grows ... Pay attention to sensitivity and energy and you have more of both.

The Japanese term Joshin Kokyu-Ho means "breathing technique to purify the spirit." This exercise will strengthen your energy. It teaches you to draw in cosmic energy consciously and to collect this energy in the Tanden.

From the Tanden, the energy is brought up on both sides of the chest towards the hands, from which it is then passed on to the body that is being treated.

This technique increases your energy and helps you to be like a hollow bamboo—a clear channel for Reiki. Practicing this technique, you realize that this energy does not belong to you, it is supra-personal. It is the all-pervading energy that gives life to everything in existence and pulsates in all living things, sentient and insentient. With a little practice, you might become aware of the fact that what you previously considered as yours, melts and merges with the whole. Experiencing this, it becomes impossible to draw the line between the cosmic and your small self. Heaven and Earth have become one.

It is a great pleasure to teach this technique especially to a Reiki beginner. He may think of himself as insensitive; he may believe that everyone else will feel it, but does not trust in his own inborn ability. In my experience, I have never met anyone who did not manage to feel the energy flow using this type of breathing.

Sit in a comfortable position with closed or open eyes in a quiet, and preferably, darkened room. To find out what is easier for you, test both ways. Some of us are visited by more thoughts when the eyes are open; others are busier with the eyes closed. To make matters more complicated, this may change according to the inner seasons! In any case, testing it just takes a minute or two.

It may be helpful to place your tongue against your front teeth, and to breathe through your nose as you breathe in, and to breathe through your mouth when you breathe out. When breathing out, the tongue automatically drops down. If practicing with closed eyes, imagine you are looking at something beautiful through your closed eyelids, about ten inches in front of you.

Make sure you are not disturbed, and there is nothing that needs to be done. Turn off the telephone and, for fifteen minutes say goodbye to all your responsibilities.

If you can sit quietly without any movement of body and mind, keeping your back erect, the results are best. But if you have a backache and your knees are pinching you, don't hesitate to practice anyway. When not concerned with pain, it disappears after a few minutes all by itself.

Make sure the area just above and just below your navel is relaxed and not tight. Wear comfortable clothing and open the top-button of your pants if necessary, so you can breathe easily into your Tanden (two or three fingers width below your belly button).

The Tanden

The Tanden is a point two or three fingers width below the navel. It is not identical with the second chakra, but is a point of its own.

If you have never felt this energy center in your own body, I invite you to experiment with the following techniques. If you are well acquainted with the Tanden, you can skip the next paragraph, as well as the exercises.

Exercise One: getting centered in the Tanden

You may already know this exercise from Tai Chi or another martial art.

–Stand in a comfortable position, feet shoulder-width apart.

–Tilt the pelvis backwards about an inch.

–Take a few deep breaths.

–Let go of all the tension in your body and think of something pleasant.

–Let your mouth open slightly.

–Let your tongue rest on the roof of your mouth upon the in–breath. Breathe in through your nose. When breathing out through your mouth, let your tongue naturally come down and rest on the bottom of your mouth.

–Let your knees bend in slow motion focusing your attention on your lower abdomen. Do this very, very slowly.

–Suddenly you become aware of a point in your lower abdomen, two or three fingers width below your navel. This is where your life-force dwells—the center of your being.

–Now begin with the breathing technique.

–It may help to put one or both of your hands on your lower abdomen and breathe into the spot you are touching.

We do not only breathe through our lungs, and, we do not only breathe in a mixture of gases commonly called "air" either. Modern medical science understands that each cell is able to breathe and that we would die if that ability were suspended for a certain period of time. For example, in the case of severe burns. All the esoteric sciences have known that we do "breathe in" energy, ki, chi, prana—whatever you may call it—through our lungs and through the skin, our largest organ.

As I mentioned in an earlier book of mine, certain fakirs of old, and nowadays, the breatharians, have been known to sustain their bodies without eating. Some fakirs survive without breathing for a long time.

It is a well-known fact that those of us who are in good physical shape could easily fast for as long as six weeks without further complications (please don't try this out by yourself—fasting should be done only under the supervision of a capable health-care practitioner). To keep the body alive we do need only a minimal amount of food—it is the actions we perform that require us to supply the body with the necessary fuel.

I personally don't see a great value in not eating or not breathing. You are perfectly fine the way you are, even with a lung full of air and a stomach full of food! And both of the above can give such pleasure and zest for life.

But the point is, that we are able to use the subtle energies that surround us, more efficiently. And the more we grow on the spiritual path, the more subtle fuel we need to keep a clear mind and a pure heart.

To achieve the above, it is vital to learn how to breathe deeply into your belly, all the way down to the Tanden. Breathing in energy consciously will put both you and your client into a higher state of consciousness.

Exercise Two: swinging in the Tanden
  –Stand in a comfortable position, feet shoulder-width apart.
  –Tilt the pelvis backwards about an inch.
  –Take a few deep breaths.
  –Let go of all the tension in your body and think of something pleasant.
  –Let your mouth open slightly.
  –Let your tongue rest on the roof of your mouth upon the in–breath. Breathe in through your nose. When breathing out through your mouth, let your tongue naturally come down and rest on the bottom of your mouth.
  –Let your knees bend in slow motion, focusing your attention on your Tanden. Do this very, very slowly.
  –When the Tanden is felt, let your body swing from one side to the other. The direction of your swings does not matter. Extend both arms while you swing, to give you momentum.
  –Pay attention to the Tanden as you swing and you will notice how the body swings around an axis—the Tanden.

Exercise Three: breathing vigorously into the Tanden
  This exercise, too, is taught in the martial arts.
  –Stand in a comfortable position, feet shoulder-width apart.
  –Tilt the pelvis backwards about an inch.
  –Take a few deep breaths.
  –Let go of all the tension in your body and think of something pleasant.
  –Let your mouth open slightly.
  –Let your tongue rest on the roof of your mouth upon the in–breath. Breathe in through your nose. When breathing out through your mouth, let your tongue naturally come down and rest on the bottom of your mouth.

224

–Let your knees bend in slow motion, focusing your attention on your Tanden. Do this very, very slowly.

–Place your hands in front of the Tanden with the thumbs and fingertips of both hands creating a triangle pointing downwards.

–Breathe in through your nose and imagine breathing out through your Tanden.

–When breathing in, pull the folded hands up to your solar plexus.

–When breathing out let the hands come down in front of the Tanden once more. While doing this make a strong noise imagining that you bring down all the air and energy into the Tanden with this movement of your hands. At the same time imagine that you are breathing out through your feet, sending roots deeply into the Earth.

Breathing in this way, nothing can disturb your peace of mind. But not only the mind has become steadfast. The body, too, is strong and unmovable. This exercise shows the power of the Tanden beautifully. Even a small girl cannot be lifted by a couple of strong men, if she breathes as is explained above.

Exercise Four: walking from the Tanden

When clear about the location of the Tanden, practice the following walking meditation. There is no need to turn this into a special occasion. You can do it anytime. I prefer to take my shoes off, and walk either on grass, wood or a nice stone surface. Wearing shoes walking on gravel can be quite an experience as well. Take a few minutes and walk in slow motion.

Pay attention to the Tanden and imagine that you are walking from the Tanden. Imagine that the Tanden walks you. For a good posture, imagine that the Tanden and the tip of your nose are aligned.

The Esoteric Background of the Joshin Kokyu-Ho

The breath is the gate to consciousness. If you breathe deeply into your lower abdomen/Tanden, the spiritual heart opens up and you become strong in all respects, mentally/emotionally and physically. The deep meaning of the Tanden is pure Japanese culture and spirituality. If you would like to do further reading, I suggest you read the book called "Hara" by the German Zen Master, Karlfried von Dürkheim.

The Perineum (Chinese: Hui Yin) situated between the sexual organs and the anus is seen as one of the most important energy gates of the body, along with the Tanden. Because the life energy can quite easily leak out of this point, the Hui Yin is contracted in Taoist and yoga traditions, coupled with breathing exercises.

The aim of the contraction is to keep and accumulate life energy in the Tanden first, and then, allowing it to rise to the higher energy centers, filling them with divine nectar. This is done by breathing properly into the Tanden while the perineum is contracted. At the end of the in-breath, the breath is held for a few seconds before it is released. At the same time, the perineum, too, is released and that gives the air/energy mixture a catapulting movement, bringing it up the back of the spine on the out-breath.

This breathing technique is useful for the prevention of prostate related complaints, because it tones the muscles in that area. For the same reason it is pure magic for men with premature ejaculation problems. I suggest about thirty or forty in and out-breaths, contracting and releasing the Hui Yin, per day for both complaints. Some Reiki teachers practice this while giving an attunement, but this is useful only in connection with Tanden breathing- and unnecessary during an attuement.

The Technique, Joshin Kokyu-Ho

This technique should initially not be practiced for more than three to five minutes. If you find yourself dizzy or light-headed, you know that you have overdone it already. Stop the exercise immediately, breathe normally and take a few minutes before you resume whatever you were doing before.

Breathe in through your nose and imagine that you are breathing in a mixture of air and Reiki-Energy through the top of your head—your crown chakra. Pull this breath into your lower abdomen, into your Tanden.

Hold your breath and the energy there for a moment or two. While you are holding it, allow this energy to fill your body and energy body, reaching all the corners of it and nourishing it. Let the nectar flow … and then slowly and consciously, breathe out. Make sure that you hold your breath only for a few seconds. No need to aim for a new world record! Find your own rhythm.

Breathe out through your mouth and imagine that you are simultaneously breathing out the accumulated energy through your hands, your fingers and fingertips, as well as your feet and toes.

You can do this exercise alone, to increase "your" energy, or practice while giving a treatment. When practicing during a treatment, imagine that you breathe out the energy mostly through your hands as they are resting upon the client's body. You will be surprised by the "Turbo Reiki" effect. If you are feeling cold or tired and you would like to energize yourself, please experiment with this: Place your hands upon your kidneys and pay attention to what happens when you breathe out. You will probably feel waves of energy stimulate your kidneys. After a few minutes, your hands and feet will warm up and you'll be filled with energy and good spirits.

Gradually increase the time you spend breathing like this, until it becomes second nature.

Side effects: be careful, breathing properly will change your life!

Precaution

During pregnancy, or if afflicted with high blood pressure, take it easy with this exercise, because it may bring the blood pressure up even more. I suggest you take two or three normal breaths, and then one as described above. If in doubt, measure your blood pressure while practicing. Increase the time for this exercise slowly—begin with 2 minutes.

A hint for the lowering of high blood pressure: Yogic breathing has been seen to decrease the blood pressure dramatically. You can combine this with the Joshin Kokyu-Ho technique by counting the duration of your breath. Begin with breathing in to a count of three. Hold your breath to a count of three, and then breathe out to a count of three. Hold the breath again to a count of three. Increase the numbers over a few weeks until you reach up to eight. By this time your blood pressure may be back to normal. Another healthy but perhaps questionable way of combating high blood pressure is consuming large quantities of garlic. In case you can't find enough garlic or the right company where you live, come to Greece and we'll eat it together!

 ## The Third Technique: Reiji-Ho, The Indication of Reiki

The Japanese word Reiji means indication of the spirit, or in our case, indication of Reiki. In Takata Sensei's diary, this technique is described as the "utmost in the energy science".

This technique teaches you to learn to follow your intuition. Intuition is not something that you have to develop, it is already given to you at birth as a divine gift. All you have to do is to learn to listen to it—and—then, to follow it. You will agree with me that so many times in your life when you did not follow your intuition, which often is the first impression that you have about someone or something, you do regret it greatly afterwards! So, listen to your inner wisdom! The more I learned to trust myself and life as such, the more acute my intuition has become, in all aspects of life.

It is very ego-gratifying to think that we create our own reality, and that we manifest things and situations in our lives, but this theory does not match my experience at all. Of course, one needs to be open to be able to receive abundance, but ultimately life goes on its course, in spite of us. What we can learn here and now is not to obstruct the flow, to step out of the way and let life live itself. In the case of Reiki and the Reiji technique, that means that we become a hollow bamboo for the energy to flow through us, no matter where, when and how. The instructions for this technique are, once more, simple and to the point:

Sit or stand in a comfortable position and close your eyes.

1–Fold your hands in front of your heart in the Gassho position and ask the energy to flow through you unobstructedly.

2–Ask for the healing and wellbeing of your client on all levels, whatever that may be.

3–Bring your folded hands up to the third eye and ask Reiki to guide your hands to wherever they are needed.

Now wait and see what happens. You may be guided to a certain body part right away. This can happen in many different ways. If you are a visual person, you may see a particular body part in front of your inner eye, or, the body part to be treated may "jump" into your eyes.

If you are auditory, you may hear which part of the body to treat.

If you are kinesthetic—the feeling type, you may simply feel where you should touch your client.

Some people feel it in their own bodies. Use all the cues available to you. Use all your senses and your knowledge of the body to tune into your client. You can also ask your client to ask his body as to where it needs to be treated. Often it is quite obvious to see what is going on with someone's body by simply looking at the way the body is laying on the massage table in front of you. See how the head is resting, is it straight or laying to one side? Is the body twitching, are the limbs straight, or does one leg appear longer than the other? Is the spine twisted? If you can see a twist in the body, but cannot figure out where the tension stems from, gently try to recreate that tension in your own body and feel where it is. For example, an imbalance in the left shoulder area may have its origin in the right lower back. When you have found the tense body part, treat it.

If you do not get a clear message with the Reiji technique right away, hold one or both of your hands over the client's crown chakra, either touching or just above the head, and tune into her/him. Ask your client to pay attention to any movement in his body and tell him to let you know when and where he feels it. When he tells you where he felt movement, place your hand(s) upon that body part. Koyama Sensei tells us that the byosen attracts the attention of the practitioner in this way.

After years of training—or, if you are very skilled in listening to your intuition already—you may be able to "see" ailments in your clients just by glancing or looking at them.

When you have your client lying on the massage table in front of you and your hands are guided to the abdominal cavity, it may not be clear to you which vital organ is attracting your hands. Koyama Sensei suggests that the easiest way to check it is by simply asking yourself: is it the gall bladder, or is it the descending colon, the pancreas etc. Then let your hands answer your mind's questions. The way the answer is given is for you to find out. It may be a tingling in your hands, warmth, a magnetic feeling, or simple knowing … It is also possible that the hands stop above the organ in question and don't want to move further.

The idea that we are separate from the rest of the world is an illusion. Realize that wisdom is infinite and available to all. All you have to do is to learn to tap into the collective knowledge of humankind. And in the case of the Reiji-Ho, all you need to do is ask …

Once you have mastered the art of Reiji for healing, you can expand it into other areas of your life. Expand it into your creativity, your art, or answering questions that you feel stuck with. I wrote my first books using this technique … and have had a history of finding things that were lost with it as well.

4. The Fourth Technique: Kenyoku, Dry Bathing

The Japanese word kenyoku means dry bathing. Over the years I have been taught three different versions of this magical technique, and it is hard to say which one is "right". Please experiment with it and find out which one suits you best. Different situations may require a different version. Follow the inner wisdom of your body/mind. My inner image in this respect is this: when taking a shower, there is no premeditated system as to which body part you wash first. It depends upon the individual situation.

Kenyoku is done to purify body and soul. It strengthens your energy and helps you to disconnect from your clients, situations, thoughts and emotions. It brings you into this moment, disconnected from the past. Many times during the day, we get lost in our own minds, our thoughts, problems, joys and emotions. Or else, we get drawn into the same of our fellowman. Neither one helps us on the path to self-discovery. When you are drawn into your own daydream or that of another, you loose yourself and enter an automatic train of thought. This cannot be called thinking because it is absolutely involuntary. Like a monkey swinging from one branch to the next, ad infinitum. During this time we miss the present moment, the only time that really does exist.

What a waste of quality time! It is difficult to break the identification with ones thoughts, for identification is what keeps us engaged in mental or emotional activity.

But Kenyoku is not a technique to cut ties: you disconnect from the past to be present for this very moment.

The Esoteric Background of Kenyoku

When researching the background of Kenyoku, I came across Zen Buddhist and Shinto techniques that are quite similar.

> A–In Zen Buddhism, a Kenyoku-like technique is used. You stroke with your right hand from the collarbone under the left shoulder diagonally to the right hip, twice. Then you repeat this with your left hand. Now you draw the kanji for "Dai Shin" (photo 93) above your own head and work it into your aura. In this way, you reconnect to the whole, and disconnect from the little ego, the unessential.

> B–In Shintoism, the priest performs a ritual that looks almost exactly like Kenyoku before certain ritual acts, like the blessings of objects.

> C–In Shintoism, there exists a cleansing ritual for body, mind and soul by the name of Misogi. The practitioner either stands under a waterfall in a white kimono (woman) or a white loincloth (man). He or she lets the water fall upon his crown chakra allowing the nectar of the mountains to cleanse his being from head to toe.

In Reiki this technique is used instead of the old fashioned way of splashing ice-cold water over oneself for purification. So if you don't have your pocket-waterfall with you today, kenyoku will do just fine. Use it before and after treatments and every time you want to disconnect from thoughts and emotions.

Version 1: I was told that Usui Sensei taught it this way: Place your right hand on the left side of your chest, over the collarbone. Now stroke down gently across your chest to the right hip. Do the same with your left hand, starting on the right side of your chest, above the collarbone. Stroke down gently towards your left hip. Repeat the movement with your right hand.

Now gently stroke with your right hand from your left wrist over the open palm of your left hand, past your fingertips. Then gently stroke with your left hand from your right wrist over the open palm of your right hand, past your fingertips. Repeat the movement with your right hand.

Version 2: Nowadays, it is widely practiced like this: Place your right hand on the left side of your chest, over the collarbone. Now stroke down gently across your chest to the right hip. Do the same with your left hand, starting on the right side of your chest, above the collarbone. Stroke down gently towards your left hip. Repeat the movement with your right hand.

Now put your right hand on your left shoulder and stroke down gently over the outside of your arm and the outside of your hand, down past your finger tips. Do the same stroke with your left hand over the outside of your

Photo 93: Dai Shin calligraphy inside Tenryu Ji Temple, Kyoto

right arm and repeat the pattern once more with your right hand stroking along your left arm.

Version 3: This is my personal favorite version: Place your right hand on the left side of your chest, over the collarbone. Now stroke down gently across your chest to the right hip. Do the same with your left hand, starting on the right side of your chest, above the collarbone. Stroke down gently towards your left hip. Repeat the movement with your right hand.

Now put your right hand on your left shoulder and stroke down gently over the inside of your left arm and the palm of your hand, down past your finger tips. Do the same stroke with your left hand over the inside of your right arm. I was taught this technique by someone who used to be a Buddhist monk. In his school of Reiki, they add a gassho at the end of the ken-yoku technique. (Try it out and see if that feels good to you, too.)

As I said, I personally practice technique number three. However, I suggest that you find out which technique clicks with you by practicing it yourself. At the end of the day, you are your own best teacher. If you are shy or unable to go through the motions of this technique in public, experiment with doing it mentally. You'll be surprised!

念達法
5. The Fifth Technique: Nentatsu–Ho, Detoxification Technique

I was taught this exercise when I took the first class with Chiyoko Sensei in the year 2000. It is meant for detoxifying one's body and mind.

The instructions go like this: Place your left hand upon your Tanden and the right hand on your forehead. Now gather your energy in your forehead, allowing it to rise from the Tanden. Visualize that your forehead is filling up with Reiki. When the forehead is filled with Reiki, bring it back down to the Tanden. Cross your hands in front of the Tanden with the back of the hands facing up, the hand chakras on top of one another. Do this as long and often as you like.

靈氣回し
6. The Sixth Technique: Reiki Mawashi, Reiki Current Group Exercise

The Japanese word mawashi means current. In this exercise, a current of Reiki energy is passed through a group of practitioners in a similar way that you may already practice it in your Reiki share groups.

Sit in a circle and hold hands, or hold your hands a few inches above/below the hands of your neighbors. Your left hand is facing up, the right one facing down. The teacher starts the energy flow, sending energy to his/her right hand. The receiver receives the energy from his/her left hand, lets it flow through his/her body and passes it on to the next person through his/her right hand. Practice for 10 minutes. Try it the other way around as well.

In the Usui Reiki Ryoho Gakkai, it is taught that this exercise increases the practitioner's perception of energy. It is also practiced to maintain the health of all the members of the group, if performed at least once a week for ten minutes or more. The youngest member of the association is in his late sixties, so it seems to be working! After the Reiki Mawashi, you will feel the energy flow more clearly, and you'll be able to feel the byosen of your clients readily. The more you practice this, the more permeable for Reiki you become.

Left or right?

I don't know whether or not it matters which way around the energy is directed. There are many theories regarding the Earth magnetism, and that it should be done to the right above the equator and to the left below the equator. Theories are great but they should not limit us in any way. So I suggest that you try out which way feels the most natural for you and your Reiki friends. I can't help but feel that our preference may be rooted in what we are used to, and that both ways will work anywhere on the planet—and maybe beyond! We have embarked on the path to learning how to direct energy, and it should not make any difference to us whether we direct it to the left, the right, above or below.

The energy of a group often exceeds the sum of the energy of the participants, and spontaneous healing on all levels may occur. I usually practice this exercise for about ten to fifteen minutes in my seminars. There is no need to use Reiki symbols while practicing this.

 **7. The Seventh Technique: Shu Chu Reiki, Concentrated Reiki Group Exercise**

The Japanese word shu chu literally means "concentrated".

This technique is practiced during a Reiki workshop or at a Reiki share group. One client or workshop participant lies on a massage table or sits in a chair while the other participants give him Reiki. Experience suggests that it is important to treat the head, the soles of the feet, the Tanden, the heart, the liver, the kidneys and the lymph. How this is performed depends upon the size of the group. If three people treat one client, the treatment should take at least 30 minutes. If the group is large, 10 or fifteen minutes may be sufficient. I have done this a few times with a hundred people treating one client, who later on floats off the table. If the client is seriously ill, you can help him tremendously in a matter of minutes.

This can be an intense experience for the client, and I would not recommend treating clients who are emotionally unstable with many practitioners. In large groups, it may not be possible for everyone to touch the person to be treated. What we do, in this case, is to form several rows of healers around the massage table. The first row touches the client directly, and the second and third rows touch the shoulders of the people in the first row. This way, the energy flows and surges through everyone administering the healing, and finally into the client as well. This is a wonderful experience for everyone involved.

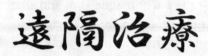 ## 8. The Eighth Technique: Enkaku Chiryo (Also Called Shashin Chiryo), Distant Healing Treatment

Usui Sensei was apparently fond of distant healing, because it helped him greatly in the aftermath of the Great Kanto Earthquake. He used it even though the recipient or the recipients were in the next room. He taught this technique at Okuden Koki (last part of Okuden—our second degree). The Japanese word enkaku means "sending" and the word chiryo means treatment. This method has also been known in Japan as "shashin chiryo", or photographic treatment. Ogawa Sensei told us that this technique was a privilege of the wealthy, because poor people did not own photographs of themselves in the old days. How grateful Usui Sensei would be if he knew that nowadays literally anyone can receive distant treatments!

There must be as many distant healing methods as there are Reiki practitioners, all of which are designed to help us focus our minds. Below, I would like to share with you three traditional methods from three different sources.

1-Chiyoko Sensei

Chiyoko Sensei taught us to use our own upper thigh to perform the distant treatment. With the help of a Jumon (magic formula), the thought form of the client was brought to the here and now. We were asked to imagine the client lying on our thigh, and this is where he was treated. If the client was known, we were just to think of him and imagine him lying on our leg. If the recipient was not known, there were some prerequisites to be taken care of: his or her name, the date of birth, the gender and the body part to be treated were written on a separate piece of paper. This helped us to focus our energy on the unknown person.

Using ones own thigh has the advantage that you can feel the byosen of the recipient (represented by your thigh) quite readily.

2–Koyama Sensei

Koyama Sensei suggested, additionally, to use a photograph of the recipient and to perform the distant treatment by touching the photograph directly. When using a photograph, it is easy to treat body parts that you cannot touch due to cultural reasons, or because it would be too painful. She said that the byosen can be felt on the photograph as well. I suggest that you begin with Chiyoko's technique before experimenting with photographs.

3–Ogawa Sensei

Ogawa Sensei said: "If you don't have a picture of the recipient, draw an image representing them on one of your fingers or on your knee and use that. It does not matter which finger or which knee you use." Some Western Reiki teachers say that you should not touch your own body when sending distant Reiki, because you might send your own ailments to the recipient. I find this idea amusing: please don't worry about it. When you use your own body to send energy to another, you use it simply to focus your mind.

In all the above techniques, the philosophy is the same. You bring the other person here by using the Jumon (the distant healing symbol); so, Reiki does not travel from A to B, and you don't need the recipient's address.

I suggest not sending energy to a person who has not asked you specifically for it. Reiki energy cannot do any harm to anyone, but I feel that we must respect the personal space of another and not interfere with the other's freedom uninvited. But then there are always exceptions!

性癖治療

9. The Ninth Technique: Seiheki Chiryo, Habit Healing Technique

The Japanese word Seiheki means habit, the word chiryo means treatment (see the chapter on the roots of the sei heki chiryo on page 164).

This technique is used to treat habits, preferably, what we would label as "bad" habits. Many of you have learned a technique known as the deprogramming technique in the Western Reiki hemisphere, which is a method adjusted to the Western Mind as described in my first book, "Reiki Fire". It involves the use of the other two Reiki symbols of the second degree, whereas, this technique doesn't. If you are working on yourself, make a suitable affirmation. If you are working with a client, help her or him make an affirmation. Remember that affirmations must be short, precise, and positive, in the present tense, and in the words and language of the person who will use it. Also, remember that an affirmation should never be limiting in any way.

To find out what a person really wants in his/her life, you will need to take your time. Our desires usually have deeper meanings that are hidden at first.

Someone who desires a million dollars, for example, may really desire to be loved and cared for. Or, someone who wants to become enlightened, in my reality, may be trying to escape from him/herself!

Now to the instructions: Place your non-dominant hand on the forehead of the client (or on your own forehead) and place your dominant hand on the back of the head. Draw the second symbol over the back of the head with your dominant hand.

Keep your hands there for two or three minutes while you intensely repeat the affirmation in your mind. Then, take your non-dominant hand away from the forehead and simply give Reiki to the receiver with your dominant hand still resting on the back of the head. While doing this, forget the affirmation.

Usui Sensei is said to have used the five Reiki Principles, or a poem of the Meiji emperor, with this technique as well. Instead of making an affirmation, he would repeat the principles/poem when touching the recipient's forehead and back of the head.

Chiyoko Sensei taught a powerful kotodama to perform this technique that is not used in the Western Reiki lineages.

凝視法　呼気法

10. The Tenth Technique: Gyoshi-Ho and Koki-Ho, Healing with the Eyes and the Breath

The Japanese word Gyoshi means staring, the word Koki means blowing. These two techniques are like your left and right hand. If you want to succeed in something that you do, they have to work together. You always begin with the Gyoshi-Ho. Usui Sensei is reported to have used this combination of techniques for small and big injuries. He suggested to his students that they work best when used immediately after the injury has occurred. This he said guarantees success: the wound heals quickly and no scars remain. In the interview on page 67 he says that you stare at the body part, you blow at it and stroke it gently, in this sequence. He explains that Reiki is radiated from all body parts of the initiate, especially the hands, the eyes, through the breath and the feet. We are used to throwing our energy out through our eyes, but with this technique we learn to use it creatively. In order to heal, we must first defocus our eyes and learn to look into the void. Staring is aggressive, and an aggressive look does not heal—it intrudes.

It may be helpful to practice this technique with an object first, for example, a flower. Take the flower in your hand, or place it one or two feet away from you on a table at eye-level. Defocus your eyes. Now relax your eyes and look at the flower as if looking through it, or behind it. After a moment, you will notice that your field of vision has become peripheral. You can see almost 360 degrees now!

Now look at the flower and let the image come to you, instead of sending the arrows of your visual attention towards it. After a while, you may become aware of a very subtle form of breathing that happens through your eyes, connected with the in and out-breath. Practice this for ten minutes every day until you feel comfortable treating a person in this way. If you are in love, this comes easily: look at your beloved in the same way.

Now to the instructions for the Gyoshi Ho: With a soft focus, look at the body part you want to treat for a few minutes. While you are looking at the recipient, let the image of the person enter your eyes instead of "actively looking". Notice how a circle of energy between you and the other person is created when you let the energy of the other enter your eyes.

If you enjoy this technique and would like to experiment further, I suggest the following Hindu meditation technique.

Tratak Meditation

Place a burning candle about three feet in front of you, at eye-level. Sit in a comfortable position for forty-five to sixty minutes and stare at a candle. Don't blink your eyes. After a few minutes, your eyes will begin to tear while you keep staring at the flame. With a little bit of practice, you will be able to do this for one hour. Your consciousness will become as sharp and focused as a laser beam!

This technique can also be practiced with the photograph or a statue of an enlightened one, with a partner sitting opposite you, with your own image in a mirror, or, with darkness—in a completely darkened room. Practicing with a burning candle may make you fiery. If that is uncomfortable, practice in total darkness, which will have, a cooling effect instead.

Koki-Ho

As already mentioned elsewhere, we breathe in a mixture of gases, as well as energy. According to Koyama Sensei, this works best when the practitioner feels his breath as hot, internally.

Ogawa Sensei taught us how to do it in this manner: breathe in and pull the breath all the way down into your Tanden. Hold it there for a couple of seconds and then draw the power symbol with your tongue on the roof of your mouth. When you have drawn it, breathe out and breathe the symbol onto the body part to be treated. The out-breath is to be done very slowly and through tightly pursed lips. You will notice that the breath, even though hot internally becomes ice-cold. The body part to be treated should be 8-10 inches away from your mouth so that the recipient feels the breath on the body part to be treated.

I have had many strange experiences with this technique. Once, I treated a young boy who had fallen down a flight of stairs. He looked like a one-horned devil! He cried terribly and after three minutes of staring at his forehead, the horn was gone and he had fallen asleep peacefully on my lap. The mother was gratefully shocked … In this way, you can work on the physical body, in the aura, and with photographs, combining it with distant healing.

Precaution: this is an emergency method and to be done only for a few minutes. If you continue with this too long, you might get tired.

Instructions for the combined technique:

    1–Stare at the body part to be treated for two or three minutes.

2—Blow at the body part with slow breaths and tightly pursed lips.

3—If the skin is not ruptured, rub the body part lightly afterwards until the pain has eased. If it hurts again, rub some more. This is called "bushu" in Japanese.

靈氣運動

11. The Eleventh Technique: Reiki Undo, (Physical) Reiki Exercise

The Japanese word Undo means exercise/movement and it refers to letting the body move, unrestrictedly. Koyama Sensei introduced this exercise to the Usui Reiki Ryoho.

This technique is used all over the world and in many different cultures and traditions. In China, it is used as part of Qigong training. In Indonesia, it is part of the Subud practice, and in India, it is called Latihan. In Japan it was originally called Katsugen Undo and it was introduced by Haruchika Noguchi (see photo 90 on page 175). It was, and still is, taught by his association, the Noguchi Seitai.

The instructions for this exercise are very simple: Find a place in your house that is safe for you to be rolling around for twenty to thirty minutes undisturbed. Make sure that there are no sharp edges, no furniture that you could hurt yourself with. Start with Gassho and say in your mind "Reiki exercise start". Breathe in deeply, and when you breathe out, let go completely. If you are practicing with a partner, touch his/her shoulders from behind and allow your body to move, whichever way it wants to move. Breathe in deeply and let go as much as you can when you are breathing out. After a few deep breaths, your body will probably begin to move. If the movement doesn't come through you easily, be patient and don't create anything. Keep doing this exercise for at least three months on a daily basis. It may be difficult for you to let go completely and to allow your body to move by himself. You may be holding onto the idea that you're an adult who shouldn't act like a child. Let go of this concept for the next twenty minutes, and give yourself total freedom to be crazy, to be a child again.

You may feel too self-conscious, but now, no one is watching. Think of nothing and no one in particular, go on a little vacation from your adult self.

If sounds come out of your mouth, don't restrict yourself for the time being. If thoughts and feelings come up, acknowledge and feel them, don't hold back.

It is likely that you will start to yawn, you may burp and pass gas, and your eyes may start to tear. Sounds like fun, doesn't it! Don't hold anything

239

back for now and let the body cleanse itself. It knows what to do and how to do it. We just have a bad habit of restricting our own healing. Certain restrictions may be appropriate in our day-to-day interaction with others, but for now, let it all go …

In our seminars, we practice this exercise with the whole group, providing we have got a safe environment that allows us to all sit together in a "train". One group participant remarked after this experience that practicing Reiki Undo in a group was the closest feeling to what she had experienced at the Woodstock Rock Festival in 1969!

Katsugen Undo

The following, preliminary exercise is taught by the Noguchi Setai group. It is a wonderful way to get your autonomic nervous system going, to prime the pump, so to speak.

The Instructions

Make a light fist with both of your hands, putting your thumbs into it. Don't strain. Stretch both arms out straight in front of yourself. Now breathe in deeply through your nose. While rigorously breathing out through your mouth, pull both arms towards yourself and tighten all your muscles as tight as you can. When all the air has escaped your lungs and your arms are next to your body—the fists being somewhere near your shoulders—let go completely. Let your arms fall to your sides, and let your lungs fill with air, all by themselves.

Repeat the steps above three to five times and then proceed with the Reiki Undo. Your pump has been properly primed now!

Precaution

The Reiki Undo/Katsugen Undo/Latihan/Subud has been known to develop a life of its own if practiced for a long time. Therefore, it is important to keep one thing in mind while practicing: know that you hold the on/off switch in your hands. If at some point the movement should become uncomfortable, or the situation demands you to stop, you can stop at any desired time.

If you teach this to a group, it won't be possible for you to participate. As the teacher, your job is to make sure that no one gets hurt or hurts another. It has been my experience that some participants forget themselves completely: they forget the beautiful nose of the person sitting behind them, as

240

well as their own! So make sure that no one hurts themselves or others. In the Usui Reiki Ryoho, the Reiki Undo has been discontinued for this reason. If taught and practiced with awareness, this exercise is fantastic and will bring good results. I know a number of people who have cured themselves of serious illnesses doing this.

12. The Twelfth Technique: Hesso Chiryo, the Navel Healing Technique

The Japanese word hesso means navel. In this technique, the middle finger of either hand is used because it has the most powerful Reiki output. Make sure that you always include the middle finger when working point by point. This technique is one of my personal favorites, because its results are stunning. The Hesso Chiryo is used in the treatment of cancer, fungal infections (internal as well as external candida for example), viral infections and fever. It can be used on a client or on yourself. You always work until the byosen is gone, however long that may take.

I have had countless experiences with this technique over the years, mostly when treating fever. Our children never had to take medication, even if they had a high fever due to teething. When treating fever with the Hesso Chiryo, the temperature goes down to an acceptable level within three to five minutes—even if it is very high. The body produces fever for a good reason: it tries to detoxify the system with temperature. But if the fever goes higher than 102 or more degrees Farenheit, it becomes dangerous. With the Hesso Chiryo, you will bring it down quickly. If it rises up again some time later, you use the technique again.

The Instructions:

Place the middle finger of either hand into your navel and apply a little pressure until you feel a slight pulse. This pulse is very fast, comparable to the heartbeat of a child inside his mother's womb. Don't look for the pulse of the abdominal aorta deep inside the belly, but the energetic pulse that is felt when you touch your navel with very gentle pressure. The pressure you apply is as much as it takes to make a tiny dent in your cheek with one finger. The pulse in the navel is subtle. If you don't feel it the first time, just keep your finger in the navel for a few minutes. Next time, you will feel it for sure.

When you have found the pulse, you are ready to start this exercise: Let the Reiki energy flow out of your middle finger into your navel until you feel that your pulse and the energy are in harmony. In case of treating a fever, wait until it has gone down.

The hesso chiryo works beautifully with distant Reiki as well.

Precaution: The navel is a vulnerable and sensitive area. Therefore, the pressure that you apply must be minimal. You can either place your finger upon the skin, or on top of the clothing.

Contraindication: Some of us don't like their navel being touched. If this is the case with you or your client, do the hesso chiryo distantly. In my experience, a "navel phobia" points towards a birth trauma. Once that is solved, the navel can be touched …

邪気切り浄化法

13. The Thirteenth Technique: Jacki-kiri Joka-Ho, Transforming negative energy

The Japanese word jacki means negative energy, and the word kiri (from the verb kiru) means to cut. You may have heard the word "Hara-Kiri", meaning "cutting the Hara"-killing yourself! The word Joka means purification. This technique teaches us how to transform negative energy attached to any object. Personally, I don't like the wording "negative energy" because there is no place for that in my world. Energy is simply energy—and the secret is to transform it from base metal to gold.

However, there may be an incompatibility between "your" energy field and that of an object. Let's say you have separated from a partner and you now live with someone new. You have brought some furniture from your previous marriage into the new household, but now it doesn't fit in energetically. To adjust the energy of the objects to your current situation, you can use this technique.

However, this technique is restricted to be used on inanimate objects only: do not ever use it on a living being. For helping living beings transform their energy field, we have been given other techniques for purification. In that case, please use either Kenyoku, Joshin Kokyuu Ho, Hanshin Koketsu Ho, or Ketsueki Kokan.

We all know that any object may take on energy. Some objects, like crystals, gemstones and metals take on energy more readily than others. You

242

may have experienced the occasional "eeeek!—what is this" after you had either bought something at an antique store or inherited an item from a distant—or not so distant, relative! Perhaps your dislike may point to the energy of the person who wore or used the object, or the energy of the place where the object was kept. If the person was a saint or the place a holy spot, the object may have become an article of worship. But, if the energy attached to the object feels "bad" or uncomfortable, this is the technique to use. I set the word bad in quotation marks because energy is never bad, it is either incompatible or unsuitable. A friend of mine uses this technique on his massage table after each treatment. A hotel bed, too, would be a grateful object of practice.

The Instructions

Hold the object to be purified in your non-dominant hand and cut horizontally through the air with your dominant hand about 2 or 3 inches above the object three times. After the third time, stop the movement abruptly. While cutting over the object, remain centered in your Tanden and hold your breath. After you have purified the object, give Reiki to it for a few minutes—and—don't forget to breathe! If the object does not fit in your hand, place it on the floor in front of you. If it is too big to work on for you—a house, for example—do it via distant healing or with a photograph of the object.

解熱法 14. The Fourteenth Technique: Genetsu-Ho, the technique to bring down a fever

This Japanese word "netsu" means fever, and the word "ge" means to bring down. Treat the forehead, the temples, the back of the head, the neck, the throat, on top of the head, the stomach, and intestines, in this sequence.

This is the standard treatment Usui Sensei devised to treat any disease of the head, to tune in and work on the origin of a disease, and to bring down a fever. Ogawa Sensei suggests leaving the hands on the head positions for about thirty minutes. I would treat the stomach and intestines for ten to fifteen minutes, allowing the byosen to decide the exact treatment plan in each particular case. You may want to add an extra fifteen minutes of treating the kidneys to help the body get rid of the excess temperature.

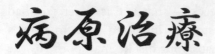

15. The Fifteenth Technique: Byogen Chiryo, Treatment of the Origin of a Disease

The Japanese word "byo" means disease, and the word "gen" means origin or root. The treatment prescribed by Usui Sensei is the same as the Genetsu-Ho treatment and the treatment of diseases of the head. By treating the head intensively, you are likely to get a complete picture of the physical and mental condition of your client.

We all know that what we refer to as a disease is often only a symptom. And, treating a symptom will often, but not always, only have a superficial or temporary result.

When someone complains of a headache, the actual problem may be in the neck, the spine or due to dehydration. When you work with the Reiji-Ho technique described above, it is possible that you may pick up the root cause of a disease. In this case, you learn to listen to your intuition/perception rather than to the description from the client!

16. The Sixteenth Technique: Hanshin Chiryo, Half the Body Treatment

The Japanese word Han means half, and the word shin means body. Rub the spinal column on both sides from the buttocks to the medulla oblongata (moving upward in direction).

This technique is used to help a client relax. It is very soothing to have both sides of the spinal column gently rubbed. I wish I could to it to myself sometimes! In Usui Sensei's handbook, this technique is prescribed for disorders of the nerves, and disorders of the metabolism and the blood.

17. The Seventeenth Technique: Hanshin Koketsu-Ho, The Blood Exchange Technique for Half the Body

The Japanese word hanshin means half the body, and koketsu can be translated as cross-blood, or exchanging, mixing-blood.

This technique is used to bring a client back to planet Earth after a treatment. It is also useful when working with a mentally disturbed client.

Caution: Clients with back pains have reported that their pains disappeared after the Hanshin Koketsu-Ho has been done to them!

The Instructions

Ask your client to stand in front of you, with his back towards you, with slightly bent knees. Place your non-dominant hand on his shoulder to steady him. Gently stroke down the client's spinal column ten to fifteen times with your dominant hand. Start at the seventh cervical vertebrae (C7), and stroke downward towards the right hip. Then repeat the same sweeping movement from C7, this time stroking towards the left hip. After you have completed the ten to fifteen strokes, put your index finger on the left side of the spine, the middle finger on the right side of the spine, and stroke straight down towards the buttocks. When you reach the point below the fifth lumbar vertebrae, apply a little pressure with both fingers and hold it there for a second or two.

18. The Eighteenth Technique: Tanden Chiryo, Tanden Treatment

The Japanese word Tanden describes the spot which is two to three fingers width below our navel that has been described in detail above. The Tanden is seen as the seat of your life force, and the home of Reiki in the body. Therefore, it is an important point in each and every treatment.

The Instructions

Place one hand on your Tanden (if you are treating yourself) or on the Tanden of your client. The other hand is placed on the back of the body behind the Tanden. Leave your hands here until they lift off by themselves. According to Koyama Sensei, the Tanden Chiryo is divided into five aspects. When treating the following symptoms/ailments, please proceed in this way, from the left side of your body or the client's body, to the right:

1—When treating the bowels or a problem with bowel movement, you touch the left side of your Tanden near the groin.

2—For urinary tract/bladder, you touch the area a little bit on the right of the above.

3—For something to do with perspiration, you touch the area to the right of the above—under the Tanden.

4—When working on something to do with infection/puss, you work on the right side of the Tanden.

5—For rashes, you treat the right side of your Tanden next to the groin.

The detoxifying process takes place where the hands are held. The Tanden Chiryo should bring a good result within three consecutive days of treatment.

This technique is used as a general power-up technique for yourself or others. It also strengthens your will power—or that of your client. I suggest you treat yourself in this way while you are traveling or watching TV, when falling asleep or upon awakening.

19. The Nineteenth Technique: Gedoku-Ho, The Detoxification Technique

The Japanese word doku means poison or toxin. The word "ge" means to bring down. This technique is used to detoxify a client or yourself. It can work miracles when treating someone who takes, or had to take, strong medication. It is used on drug addicts, and after chemotherapy or the like. Also, remember this as the perfect technique to deal with stomachaches, constipation, diarrhea and food poisoning. I will spare you my own experience with this technique when I had food poisoning—believe me, it works miracles!

The Instructions

Place one hand on the Tanden and the other behind it on the lower back, and leave your hands there for thirteen minutes. While doing so, imagine all the toxins leaving the body of the receiver. It helps, but is not necessary, to ask the receiver to imagine the same.

I, personally, imagine the toxins leaving the receiver through their intestinal tract, the blood and lymph vessels, and the sweat glands.

20. The Twentieth Technique: Ketsueki Kokan-Ho, the Blood Exchange Technique

At the end of each and every treatment, Chiyoko Sensei performed this technique that she learned from Hayashi Sensei. Ketsueki means blood or blood-flow, and Kokan means exchange. The toxins that were dissolved in the preceding Reiki treatment will be eliminated more effectively with the

246

help of this technique. In this way, a healing crisis can either be diminished or avoided all together. Because the term Ketsueki Kokan is so long, it is usually referred to as Kekko in Japan. It takes between four and five minutes to execute this technique after each treatment. Your clients will love it!

Chiyoko Sensei also suggested doing this if there is not enough time for a proper Reiki treatment. It is indicated for stroke victims, for diseases of the metabolism, and children who can't get going in the morning due to low blood pressure. You can repeat the Kekko, in these cases, twice.

If your client's physical condition does not allow some of the movements, leave them out. If the client can't lie on his stomach, it can be done sitting up.

The Instructions

1–Push the byosen symbol into the neck at C2 (the second cervical vertebrae) with the thumb and index finger of your dominant hand. If you have not learned it, use the power symbol.

2–Check the location of the client's spine with your fingers.

3–Rub both sides of the spine slowly and carefully two or three times with your index and middle fingers from the first thoracic vertebrae to the lumbar vertebrae.

4–Once familiar with the client's spine, rub it downwards vigorously 20 times, using your index and middle fingers.

5–Push the power symbol into the lumbar area, around L3 with the thumb and index finger of your dominant hand.

6–Divide the upper part of the body into five parts. First, rub from the spine sideways to the shoulders and down to the upper arms.

7–Second, rub from behind the heart down to the sides.

8–Third, rub from the spine behind the solar plexus down to the lower ribs.

9–Fourth, rub from the lower back to the sides.

10–Fifth, rub from the buttocks to the hips.

11–Do all of this three to five times

12–Now, rub ten times across the small of the back with the palm of your dominant hand, while steadying the client with the other hand.

13–Steady the client with one hand and rub with the other on the outside of his right leg from the hip to the ankles and beyond three to five times.

14–Repeat the same with the client's left leg.

15–Steady the client with one hand and rub with the other on the backside of his right leg from the hip to the ankles and beyond three to five times.

16–Steady the client with one hand and rub with the other on the inside of his right leg from the hip to the ankles and beyond three to five times.

17–Repeat the same with the client's left leg.

18–Now, push the root of the client's right thigh with your left hand, while you stretch the leg at the ankle with your right hand.

19–Repeat the same with the client's left leg.

20–To end the treatment, pat the whole backside of the body with your cupped hands. Begin with patting across the back, from the shoulders down behind the ribs to the lower back and the buttocks. Do this three to five times.

21–Pat on the outside of the client's right leg, from the hip all the way down to the outside of the small toe. Do this three to five times.

22–Repeat the same with the client's left leg.

23–Pat on the backside of the client's right leg, from the upper thigh all the way down past the soles of the feet to the tips of the toes. Do this three to five times.

24–Pat on the inside of the client's right leg, from the hip all the way down to the outside of the big toe. Do this three to five times.

25–Repeat the same with the client's left leg.

26–Done!

Give your client a few minutes to return to reality.

A Little Food for Thought

Please remember the beginning of this chapter: the best technique is the one that you don't need anymore. Techniques are, after all, tools to be used and not to be confused with the real thing. And, the real thing is YOU. You are the moon, and not the finger that is pointing to it.

Go beyond your thoughts and emotions, your body and soul. Transcend good and bad, health and disease. Rise above all your concepts, your dreams and aspirations. You are it! Always ask yourself who the experiencer is. At the end of the day, only one question remains, and that is "Who Am I? And when that question is answered, you can be sure that you have fallen asleep again: Wake up!

Afterword

Now, it is time to say goodbye. I hope that you have enjoyed reading this book, that you have found inspiration, and the Reiki Fire has been lit. It has been Usui Sensei's wish that we carry the light of Reiki into the world, and I trust that you are the right person to do it. It would be a pleasure to meet you some day in a workshop or for a cup of tea, or perhaps on the beach in Lesvos Island, Greece, where we live and love. What has been written above can only really be conveyed from heart to heart—in person: this is Reiki.

With love and gratitude,

Frank Arjava Petter

your friend Frank Arjava Petter

Appendices

From Koyama Sensei's Teaching Handbook.

(My comments are set in parentheses)[8]

The Five Objects of the Usui Reiki Ryoho

According to Koyama Sensei the five objects of the Reiki Ryoho are:

1. *Tai* (body)—*Ken* (health) (体—健)
The body is the temple of God. Because we know this, we should take care of it well and serve God within the body. You can only survive the event of enlightenment in a healthy body. We can strengthen the body with Reiki, Meditation, a healthy diet ... and with laughter.

2. *En* (Relation, connection, fate, love, karma)—*Bi* (beauty) (縁—美)
Beauty and Love go hand in hand. If you see the beauty in each sentient and insentient being, you will live a peaceful and contented life.

3. *Kokoro* (unity of heart and mind)—*Makoto* (sincerity, authenticity) (心—真)
Kokoro, the unity of heart and mind, is achieved by living your authentic self.

4. *Sai* (Talent)—*Chikara* (power) (才—力)
Talent and Power go together. If you live according to your talents, the result is irresistible power. There is no need to be afraid of your own talents.

5. Tsutome (Duty)—*Do* (work) (務—道)
It is your duty to work upon yourself. Always give your utmost, whatever you do. Never hold back what you could give to another, including yourself.

About the Gokai (the Five Reiki Principles), Koyama Sensei says:

[8] *Ogawa Sensei gave me a copy of this handbook in 1997. Koyama Sensei published it for the 50th anniversary of the Usui Reiki Ryoho Gakkai in 1972. Among other treasures, the Japanese Reiki Techniques from the last chapter are described in this document. The Handbook was given only to the teachers of the Usui Reiki Ryoho Gakkai. Akiko Sato and myself did the translation.*

"The Gokai are the basis of the Reiki Ryoho as given to us by Usui Sensei and I would like to suggest to you that you integrate them into your life. In them, you find (clear) instructions for life and for living a healthy life. By practicing Reiki, you live the Gokai and vice versa. I have thought about them deeply in my long Reiki Practice (more than sixty years)."

1. Ikaru-na. This does not mean to suppress your anger. What is meant is to stay cool and tell the other exactly what you think and feel.

2. Shinpai suna. When you rely upon Reiki, your worries are cut in half automatically.

3. Kansha shite. It is important to feel gratitude in your heart and to live it.

4. Gyo o hage me. It does not make sense to force anything. The point is to bring your talents to the surface with Reiki.

5. Hito ni shinsetsu ni. When you do work that has been given to you (by God/divine/existence) it is possible to be kind to others.

Koyama Sensei taught that the practice of Reiki is based upon three basic principles, Gassho, Reiji-Ho and Chiryo (meditation, diagnosis and treatment). These three should be worked upon and perfected daily. In the headquarters of the Usui Reiki Ryoho Gakkai in Tokyo, four meetings per month were held. They were called Reiju-Kai. She said that it was important for the members to participate in those meetings, to practice Reiki together, and to receive Reiju. The Reiju-Kai had the following curriculum:

The Reiju-Kai

1. A poem of the Meiji Emperor is read out loud. The president gives a lecture on Reiki illustrated with case histories. (In Hayashi Sensei's association, four poems of the Meiji emperor were read aloud and explained).

2. The Kenyoku technique is practiced. The significance of this technique is to purify body and mind. This is done as if, or instead of, taking a shower. (See the last chapter on the Japanese Reiki Techniques for all the techniques mentioned in this chapter).

3. The Joshin Kokyu-Ho breathing exercise is practiced. You breathe into your belly and imagine that you receive Reiki from heaven and

earth through your crown chakra. Let your whole body be filled and then breathe out through your hands and feet.

4. The Gassho Meditation. You fold your hands in Gassho and concentrate on the point where the middle fingers meet. Forget everything else!

5. Each participant receives Reiju from the Shihans and Shihan Kakus that are present. The teachers give the participants Reiju through the crown chakra so that the energy flows through the fingers of the students, just as Usui sensei has taught us. When the energy of the students has increased, they will feel an electric tingle in their hands as soon as they do gassho. If you open your eyes slowly and slightly, you may see the energy playing around your fingers. It is possible that the student sees a beautiful energy ball with closed eyes, when the Shihan/Shihan Kaku comes close to him during the Reiju. This sensation disappears again as the teacher walks away.

6. The Reiji Ho technique is practiced. Reiji Ho means that your hands are pulled to the body part that needs the Reiki the most. The Shihan will help you with this.

7. The byosen is explained and practiced. Byosen is the, possibly, uncomfortable perception you feel when positive Reiki flows into a negatively charged (tense or sick) body part. This perception may move up to your shoulders. The byosen has many different aspects of perception. When you keep your hands on the body of the client for a long time in the same position, this perception traces back down (from the shoulder) to your fingertips. (Only, then, you go on to the next position).

8. Questions of the members concerning their daily life are answered. They share their success stories of their private practice. Besides that, techniques (the Japanese Reiki Techniques from the previous chapter) are explained and practiced together.

9. The gokai are chanted together three times in succession. They were given to us by Usui Sensei as an ethical basis and are important.

10. The Reiki Mawashi is practiced. When practicing, all the members hold hands, including the Shihan. All the participants receive the Reiki from the right and pass it on to their left. If performed once a week

for at least ten minutes, the participants get healthy and stay healthy. (In the Hayashi Reiki Institute this technique was called Reiki Okuri (sending Reiki through the circle of practitioners).

My Health Methodology and the Reiki Ryoho, by Gizo Tomabechi

Let us now study an excerpt of Gizo Tomabechi's book titled "Kaiko Roku" (My Memoires) that was announced on page 65 (above photo 33).[13]

"Gizo Tomabechi was Minister of Traffic in 1947 before he became the Speaker of the House of Representatives. He was one of five Japanese politicians to sign the international peace treaty in San Francisco on October 8, 1951.

If one knows Gizo Tomabechi only as a politician, one would be surprised to find out that he also is a Shihan of the Usui Reiki Ryoho. If one knows him as the inventor of a certain fertilizer, one may laugh and find it hard to believe that he would be practicing such an unscientific method as Reiki.

Personally he always entertained a great interest for health. In his younger days as a student, when he could not afford medication due to his serious illness, he even wrote a book titled "The Theory of the Public Hospital".

Photo 94:
Gizo Tomabechi

Time and again he was ready to experiment upon himself with his gratuitous health methodologies, like change of diet and breathing (deeply) into the belly. Especially after he lost both of his children, his interest in health, life, and religious issues got sparked. He was interested in the esoteric arts like phrenology, (Japanese) astrology, the science of sleep, and the numerology of one's own name. He admitted that he had deep knowledge in these subjects.

After all his research in this respect, he engaged in the Usui Reiki Ryoho. Just as he was beginning to learn (Reiki), he heard that the wife of a colleague, Mr. Amami, was not able to stand up due to a health problem with her hip. He asked Usui Sensei to treat her. After Usui Sensei had treated her for about 20-30 minutes, he told her to stand up.

For a year, she had not been able even to turn around in bed by herself, and it had been impossible for her to stand up. However, she tried to stand up and managed it. As soon as she was standing, she screamed with joy. Usui

[13] *Printed in the year of Showa 26 (1951) on February 20th. Published on February 20th of the same year. Price: Yen 350. Publisher Asada Shoten*

Sensei watched her and told her to walk. She began to walk in a small room aided by her husband.

If there are miracles in this world, Tomabechi thought to himself, this is one. Meanwhile, Usui was watching the scene with a smile on his face.

Husband and wife, as well as Tomabechi, were left speechless due to this surprise. After the experience, Mr. Tomabechi learned Reiki with great conviction and received the Shihan certificate from Usui Sensei.

He wanted to help his fellow men with Reiki. At this time in his life, he was made director of the Kansai branch of the (area around Osaka) Dai Nippon Fertilizer Institute. After having moved to the new location to accede the new job, he lived alone in his apartment for a while without his family. This apartment was used for giving Reiki treatments. He hired several assistants and gave treatments free of charge.

Mr. Tomabechi reports: "After the great Kanto Earthquake in the twelfth year of the Taisho Era (1923), I spent a considerable amount of time with Usui Sensei, and I watched him giving treatments to the injured. I saw that the Reiki Ryoho heals physical, as well as, psychological illnesses very effectively. With great conviction, I learned Reiki and was given the Shihan certificate. I gave treatments to others and treated myself, as well. Since then, my health condition has improved astonishingly, and I weighed more than sixty kilograms. For the first time since my school days, I felt really healthy."

The Essence of the Reiki Ryoho

It is not easy to describe the concrete method of Reiki Ryoho in writing. In short, an illness is a physical condition that has been brought out of balance by a virus or something foreign. In this way, it grows and increases within the body. If the healthy parts of the body systems fight and struggle against it successfully, the illness can be overcome.

While the body battles against it (the intrusion), one experiences fever and pain. When the healthy body systems are supported by another healthy person who administers Reiki, you have increased strength to combat the illness. Thanks to Reiki, one can then conquer the illness.

When receiving Reiki, one should have a quiet and peaceful soul. If that is not possible, one should at least remain impartial. By no means, one ought to be on the side of the illness.

Personally, I don't find the Reiki of the Reiki Ryoho mysterious at all. Every human has this energy (the rhythmical cell movement) in his cells. Everybody's body is a conglomeration of these active cells.

When one is healthy, all the activities of the (bodily) functions work well. This is governed by clear principles and discipline. When changes occur in these disciplined systems, the result is illness. That means that these systems must be returned to their original order, to be healthy again. In order to achieve this, the sick body regions must once again receive a strong and healthy dynamic. In a nutshell, this is how Reiki heals.

Everyone has plenty of inherent Reiki—the life force—within himself. Most people are not aware of that, and therefore, cannot use this (life force) effectively. But, you should not become dependent upon Reiki exclusively, this would be too extreme. One should accept the conventional medical treatment as the basis for healing.

It happens so easily that one thinks in terms of black and white. If you hear that a certain method is supposedly good, you may not want to see a doctor anymore. Reiki Ryoho is a home remedy, and it should, therefore, be used as support. I must stress that we do have inherent healing abilities and are able to mentally use those for healing. If you receive help from the outside, you have to use your own power effectively at the same time.

Be Aware and (Act) from Inner Tranquility.

What I am about to say now, does not directly have to do with illness. But if you deal with your own life honestly and correctly, you are bound to rest in tranquility and are not likely to be pessimistic when you get ill. This is not a healing method, but it is an important aspect of healing. I would like to suggest several methods of (retaining) health to you.

1. Chant the Gokai in the morning and in the evening and incorporate them (in your life).
2. Thought and action shall be executed in tranquility and without force.
3. Allow your shoulders to relax and breathe quietly and deeply into your belly.
4. Keep an upright posture and a tranquil mind.
5. Sleep adequately.
6. Take care of stomach and intestines. Neither eat too much nor not enough.

If your (life) situation allows it, sit once a day quietly and rub your belly from the left to the right lightly.

Mr. Tomabechi, now aged 71, is still active in politics. His health methodology is described above. He propels that one does not grow old if one holds the tone of life and keeps the desire to develop (spiritually) further.

The last pages of this book include two interviews; one with Ogawa Sensei, and one with Chiyoko Sensei. Neither interview has been published previously. Some of the questions asked were personal and inquisitive, and both Senseis were asked not to feel offended and to say "No" when called for. In Japanese culture, personal affairs are kept within the family, and I knew that I stepped across some lines, but it was done out of love and with utmost respect. Both of them knew that and responded to my questions with an open heart.

Interview with Fumio Ogawa

This interview with Fumio Ogawa took place between May 17-21, 1997, in Shizuoka City. Shizuko Akimoto asked him the questions I had faxed her the day before, and let me know his answers upon her return.

Ogawa Sensei was pragmatic and focused on practical matters. He had collected his Reiki-memoirs in a manuscript that he titled "Everyone Can Do Reiki". In his book, he relates that one of his students worked with Reiki on silkworms. Another student used it at a water purification plant with great results. I offered Ogawa Sensei to get his book published, but he did not want it. He was content just giving it to those he met on the path. Please bear in mind that at the time of the interview, none of what is written in this book was known outside of Japan. Some of my questions have not been included here, because his previous answers made them unnecessary. Now, let's hear what he has to say:

Question: Where, why and when did you learn Reiki?
Answer: I learned Reiki from my father, Kozo Ogawa during World War Two between September 1942 and November 1943.

Question: Who was your father's teacher?
Answer: Usui Sensei

Question: Please tell me the lineage as far back as you know.
Answer: Usui—Ogawa (Kozo)—Ogawa (Fumio)

Question: Since there seem to be many different Reiki schools in Japan, do you think your's is the "original" one? Are you in contact with the other groups? Does rivalry between the groups exist?
Answer: The Usui Reiki Ryoho Gakkai was founded by Usui Sensei and is still active to this day. Therefore, this is the original school. I am in contact

with a few Japanese who learned Reiki abroad or from foreign teachers. (These are Mieko Mitsui from the Radiance Technique©, Toshitaka Mochizuki from Vortex, and Shizuko Akimoto who is interviewing him).

Question: Was your father part of the Usui Shiki Ryoho? If so, please indicate his position in the organization.
Answer: My father was a Shihan in the Usui Reiki Ryoho Gakkai, and so am I. I have never heard the term "Usui Shiki Ryoho".

Questions about Usui Sensei

Question: Is Usui Sensei part of your lineage?
Answer: Obviously, Reiki begins with him.

Question: How do you see him? Is he your idol, your teacher, your spiritual master?
Answer: Usui Sensei is the best example for what (practicing) Reiki does for a person.

Question: Do you know anything about him, his life, and his family?
Answer: The answer to this question is part of the text on page 30. His report is in accordance with what Koyama Sensei and Chiyoko Sensei say about Usui Sensei's life.

Question: Where did Usui Sensei learn Reiki?
Answer: He, himself, states in his handbook that he was given it by the Universe and did not learn it from anyone. (Author's note: Later on, Ogawa Sensei presented me with a copy of the Hikkei handbook).

Question: What are the origins of Reiki? Is it part of Qigong? Was it taught in China, India, and Tibet?
Answer: (Has already been answered above).

Question: Do you think he wanted to start a new religion, a movement?
Answer: No, otherwise he would have done so.

Question: What were his aims in your opinion?
Answer: In the interview with Usui Sensei (that we give to our members in the organization), he states that the person becomes God or Buddha-like when the mind is healed. In this way, the person becomes happy and this happiness spreads to those around him.

Question: Was Usui Sensei a Christian? Was he a religious person?
Answer: On his memorial, it is said that he was interested in the world religions. He was a Buddhist.

Question: How did society react to Usui Sensei? Was he well known? Did he have friends and enemies?
Answer: He became well known rather quickly after the great Kanto earthquake in 1923. For his humanitarian aid, he later received a medal from the Tenno (Emperor). (Author's note: Later on, I researched this with the Imperial offices. I was told that thousands of people received medals from the Tenno and it was only recorded in very special cases).

Question: Did Usui Sensei become rich by teaching Reiki? Was he interested in money, fame or power? What was charged for learning Reiki?
Answer: The Reiki education, up to Okuden, cost about 50 Yen back then. Author or Interviewer's note: (This is equivalent to about US $4,000. You notice that Ogawa Sensei does not answer all my questions. I had asked him previously not to mind my impolite questions. They were simply asked for clarity's sake. Money, power and fame were obvious issues in the West at that time. In Japan, Reiki was meant to be a path for transformation.)

Question: How many years did he teach Reiki?
Answer: He taught from April 1922 until his death on March 9, 1926.

Question: Did he teach Reiki only?
Answer: He had a colorful career, but in the last four years he only taught Reiki.

Question: Did Usui Sensei travel abroad? If so, where did he go, when and for how long? Did he find what he was looking for?
Answer: He traveled abroad on political missions with Shinpei Goto. This had nothing to do with Reiki.

Question: Are there any written documents by Usui Sensei? What about photographs?
Answer: There is a handbook that Usui Sensei gave to his students; we continue this tradition. It is called Reiki Hikkei no Shiori. Oishi-San has a beautiful photo of Usui Sensei (see photo 32). The Usui Reiki Ryoho Gakkai was suspected to be involved with the peace movement during World War Two and had to work in secret. They moved several times during the war, and once, their headquarters in Tokyo were bombed during an air raid.

Whatever had been saved until then was lost forever. Author's note: (As far as I know, the most Reiki documents/treasures are in possession of the Yamaguchi Family).

Question: Are there any living relatives? Do you know anything about them?
Answer: No.

Question: Are they connected to Reiki in any way?
Answer: As far as I know, they have nothing to do with Reiki.

Questions about Hayashi Sensei

Question: Hayashi Sensei, we were told, was the successor of Usui Sensei. Do you know anything about him?
Answer: Hayashi is a very common name, but I don't remember any Shihan by that name in the Association. Usui Sensei's successor was Ushida Sensei (the second president of the Association). Author's/Interviewer's note: (Ogawa Sensei did not know Hayashi Sensei because he became a member long after Hayashi Sensei had founded his own institute. Later on, he checked his records once more and found Hayashi Sensei as one of the 20 Shihans given the Teacher's permission by Usui Sensei. See the chapter on the associations presidents and other important teachers, page 72).

Question: Was he part of your lineage? Do you know anything about him—about his life and his position in the Association? If so, where did he live, what did he do for a living? Did he learn from Usui Sensei? Did he have a struggle /conflict or disagreement with Usui Sensei or his successor?
Answer: (All the answers to these questions were later on provided by Koyama Sensei, and both Chiyoko and Tadao Sensei).

Question: Was there a title "Reiki Master" and "Reiki Grand Master"?
Answer: The teachers are called Shihan. The president of the association is called Kaicho. The present Kaicho is Koyama Sensei.

Questions about Takata Sensei:

Question: Have you ever heard of Takata Sensei? Is she part of your lineage?
Answer: No, I have never heard about her. Author's note: (In the context of the Usui Reiki Ryoho Gakkai. Later on, we found out that Takata Sensei learned from Hayashi Sensei in the lineage of the Hayashi Reiki Kenkyukai.

She was given the Shihan status by Hayashi Sensei, not by the Usui Reiki Ryoho Gakkai).

Question: Were you aware of the fact that she reportedly said that she was the only remaining Reiki Teacher in the world after the war?
Answer: I heard about this more than ten years ago from Mitsui Sensei but I cannot comprehend that. (This statement seems to contradict what he answered to the previous question, namely that he never heard about her.)

Practical Questions:

Question: Is your Reiki system divided into different degrees?
Answer: We divide it into Shoden, Okuden and Shinpiden.

Question: If there are different degrees, how many are there and what is taught in each one?
Answer: In Shoden, you learn how to treat yourself and others. You learn about the byosen. In Okuden, you learn how to work with psycho/emotional issues and you are instructed how to perform distant treatments. In Shinpiden, you learn how to give Reiju and how to teach others Reiki.

Question: Can anyone learn all the degrees?
Answer: In theory, yes. If you develop your skills well after you have learned Shoden, and you perceive and understand the byosen, you can learn Okuden. Shinpiden is not for everyone. At the moment, we are only six Shihans from about 500 members.

Question: Who decides who will become a Shihan?
Answer: The Kaicho (the president, in this case, Koyama Sensei) alone decides in all cases.

Question: Is there a set regulation about the time span between the different degrees? How long did it take to learn the whole system? Were there any other requirements like age, education, wealth, religion etc?
Answer: It solely depends upon your development, in a practical way.

Question: How much do you pay for instruction? Is money involved in Reiki at all? What do you think the relationship between Reiki and money is? Are you aware of the fact that Reiki is a very good business in the West? The teacher degree goes for about $10,000 US dollars, one million yen.

Answer: The membership in the Association costs 10.000 Yen per month (about $100 US dollars) and enables the member to take part in the Reiju Kai.

Question: What about initiations? Were the students initiated? If yes, by whom and how often? Were only some students initiated or all of them? In case no initiation was given, how did the student learn?

Answer: Each and every Reiki student receives Reiju. This is the only way to transmit Reiki to the student. We follow Usui Sensei's instructions. In Usui Sensei's time, he asked his prospective students to sit in front of him with their hands folded in gassho. He then walked through the rows and touched their hands, measuring their energy. Those with a high-energy output were permitted to receive Reiju right away. The others had to practice some preliminary exercises (Hatsurei-Ho).

Question: Do you use twelve or fifteen hand positions that correspond to the chakras or the endocrine glands, as we do in our Western Reiki tradition? How long do you keep your hands on or above the particular position? Do you keep your fingers together? Do you use both hands? This is how we learned to do it.

Answer: We let the byosen guide us and don't use a standard treatment. Once you learn to listen to the byosen, there is no need for a system. The most important point is to treat the head. Sometimes, it is best to stay in one position for an hour or so, for example, when treating the Tanden.

Question: Do you do multiple-hands-on sessions?
Answer: Yes, we call it Shu Chu Reiki.

Question: How long is one of your Reiki treatments? On how many consecutive days do you work on a client? Do you treat pain directly by touching the body part that hurts? Do you touch the body or do you work in the Aura?
Answer: The body of the client decides how long and how often a treatment is done. When the byosen has disappeared, the problem has vanished. In the case of pain, you treat the body part that hurts until the pain is gone. If you cannot touch the body part directly, you can hold your hands above it.

Question: How many symbols do you use? What do they look like and where do they originate?
Answer: The first symbol comes from Shintoism, and the second is a bonji (Sanskrit seed syllable). The third is a shortened conglomeration of five Kanji, a Jumon (magic formula) (author/interviewer's note: I had asked Shizuko

to show him the symbols that are commonly used abroad, and he agreed with them, more or less.)

Question: What about the Master Symbol? (Shizuko writes it and shows it to him)
Answer: I have never seen that before.

Question: What is seen as secret in your tradition? Are there any secrets that are kept within the Association, or are secrets only kept from outsiders?
Answer: The student is shown certain symbols and techniques, depending on the skills he has acquired. In this sense, they are not secret—they are given to someone who is ready for it. The symbols are to be kept absolutely secret.

General questions:

Question: What is Reiki in your opinion?
Answer: The secret art of inviting happiness, the spiritual medicine for all ailments.

Question: Is Reiki something for the chosen few, or can the masses benefit from it?
Answer: Everyone can do Reiki.

Question: Do you need any special qualification like a university diploma, or a certain age to be able to practice Reiki? Do you need to be especially spiritually evolved?
Answer: No.

Question: How many people are practicing Reiki in Japan, or abroad, approximately? Do you believe in a right and wrong Reiki way? If so, why. If not, why not?
Answer: I only know that our Association has about 500 members. Reiki that comes from the West is getting more and more known, but I have no idea about numbers. There is only one Reiki. (Author/Interviewer's note: Remember the meaning of the Reiki Kanji. Everyone I interacted with from Japanese Reiki circles says the same: Reiki is your birthright!)

Question: What is healing? Does healing start with the body or with the mind/ emotions? Are mind/body and emotion one? How does Reiki affect someone's health?

Answer: You begin with the mind. Reiki means inner purification, working on your character. I am 90 years old …

Question: Are you aware of what is going on in the West in the name of Reiki, at the moment? Did you know that one of the major associations has patented the words Reiki, Usui, Usui Shiki Ryoho?
Answer: I can't believe it.

Question: Have you been contacted by foreign Reiki teachers before?
Answer: Yes, in 1984, I was visited by (Mieko) Mitsui-San, a teacher of the Radiance Technique® from New York.

Question: I have heard that you have written a manuscript with the title "Everyone Can Do Reiki". My publisher would certainly be interested in publishing it.
Answer: Thank you for your kind offer, but I don't want to publish this.

Interview with Chiyoko Yamaguchi:

After I had met Chiyoko Sensei in the year 2000, her son Tadao, and myself, planned a book project together. Part of this project was an interview with Chiyoko Sensei that took place later in the year 2000. The two of them sat together with a cup of tea and recorded her answers with a tape recorder. The book project never materialized in that form, and recently I asked Tadao Sensei if I could use it for this book. He readily agreed, and I don't want to withhold it from you any longer. The information on Hayashi Sensei is incomplete, and Tadao Sensei perfected it in later years with great love and diligence (see page 264).

Question: When and where were you born?
Answer: In Kyoto, on December 18, 1921.

Question: What are the names of your parents?
Answer: My father's name is Torasaku Iwamoto, my mother's name is Toki Iwamoto.

Question: How many siblings do you have? What are their names and when were they born?
Answer: We are seven. My eldest brother is called Masanobu, and my eldest sister is Katsue. After that comes Noboru, Yoshio, myself, Hisako and Tokijiro. The first two were born in Osaka Sakai; the others were born in Kyoto.

Question: Did you grow up with your extended family, with your aunts and uncles, and so on? Or did you grow up with your grandparents?
Answer: I grew up under the great love of my grandmother.

Question: What did your father do for work?
Answer: He had a grocery store in Kyoto.

Question: What about your mother?
Answer: She was a housewife.

Question: Where did you go to school?
Answer: During the first year of elementary school, I was in Kyoto. From the second to the third year, I lived in Osaka with Wasaburo Sugano and the family of my mother. I went to the Tezukayama Gakkuen school. In the fourth year, I moved to Daishoji Kinjyo Shogaku in Ishikawa Prefecture, and lived there until I got married. After elementary school, I went to the Daishoji high school. I grew up in the Ushio family. The name of my grandmother was Missu Ushio.

Question: What kind of child were you?
Answer: Thinking about it now, I was a simple, open-minded child with a strong character. Even though I had to change school so often, I immediately found friends.

Question: How old were you when you graduated from High school?
Answer: I graduated from the Daishoji Jyogakko Koko (Girl-school) when I was seventeen.

Question: What did you do after graduation?
Answer: My grandmother was conservative, yet it was important to her that her female grandchildren received a good education. (This was unusual in those days). For two years after I left school, I learned traditional tailoring for kimonos, and then I learned tea ceremony and Ikebana (flower arrangement). Every day.

Question: How and when did you hear of Reiki for the first time?
Answer: I heard from my foster father and uncle, Sugano, that he had learned Reiki in Osaka, and it touched me immediately (author/interviewer's note: Wasaburo Sugano had learned Shoden and Okuden in 1928, in Osaka, from Hayashi Sensei).

Question: How many of your relatives practiced Reiki?

Answer: Both my foster parents, and two of my siblings (Katsue and Yoshio) learned Reiki. Also, several cousins and their partners, as well as some of the neighbors, did the Reiki training.

Question: And how many of them practiced Reiki seriously?
Answer: My foster parents were successful business people, while my siblings and myself were still unmarried (and had time to practice). One of my cousins and his/her partner had a textile factory in the countryside. Including my siblings and the cousins with their partners, we were seven or eight people who practiced Reiki earnestly.

Question: Where did you live during the war?
Answer: In Manchuria.

Question: What happened to you after the war?
Answer: After the war, we first moved to Suo Machi Daishoji where we stayed with the family of my husband.

Question: What is the name of your husband, and when did you get married?
Answer: My husband's name is Shosuke Yamaguchi. We married in February of Showa 17 (1942) before leaving for Manchuria. I stayed there until the end of the war.

Question: What did your husband do for a living?
Answer: He worked for a large company called Okura Yoshi.

Question: Did he practice Reiki too?
Answer: Yes, he did. He had learned Shoden from Mrs. Sugano. That was just before we got married. He learned from his aunt (both Chiyoko Sensei and her husband were related to the Suganos), in a private setting and knew only the basics. He never got as much involved in the work as I did.

What Effect Did Reiki Have Upon Your Personal Life?

Question: How did Reiki affect your attitude towards life? How do you see yourself and others?
Answer: I have learned from my clients during my entire life, and I still do.

Question: Did Reiki make you happy, and did it give you more depth and self-confidence?

Answer: I always give my utmost, and those who received Reiki from me, were happy about that. In turn, this made me happy—I am grateful that I was able to learn Reiki and to practice it for so long.

Question: Do you treat yourself with Reiki, and if yes, how long?
Answer: Ever since I learned Reiki I treat myself daily, whenever I have time. Since I grew old and have more spare time, I always give myself Reiki when I am resting. If I can't sleep, for example, I treat myself for a couple of hours or so. The older I get, the more I treat myself. But it works better when you treat another person.

Question: How did Reiki influence your personal relationship with your husband?
Answer: I treated my husband every day. He was heavily seriously injured in the war, and thanks to Reiki, we could take care of him well. It worked out without serious complications. I am telling you that it helps a lot if you don't have to go to the hospital all the time, and you can take care of it yourself. By word of mouth, the people in the neighborhood heard about what I do, and I treated others every day of my life. My husband supported me in this.

Question: How did Reiki influence your family life?
Answer: I am grateful that I learned Reiki. I managed to rear my (four) children with Reiki and inner tranquility. I always felt supported and taken care of by Reiki.

Question: What about your grandchildren?
Answer: My grandchildren, too, appreciate Reiki, and they come to me when they need a treatment. (All of them were initiated into Reiki by Chiyoko Sensei)

How Did Reiki Influence Your Professional Life?

Question: Did you practice Reiki your whole life long?
Answer: I practiced for more than sixty years now, in the course of time, the Reiki has become stronger and stronger. Even in old age, Reiki becomes stronger and my clients and myself profit benefit from it. Every time someone heard of me by word of mouth, I have treated him.

Question: Was Reiki your main business? How much time did you spend with Reiki treatments per week?

Answer: I did not turn Reiki into a business, but I treated someone daily. Looking back at my life, I see that a lot of it was spent doing Reiki. If someone from the neighborhood came with a burn, for example, I treated him daily for weeks, until he was healed.

Question: How often did you treat your clients?
Answer: Serious burns, for example, heal completely, providing you treat the person daily for at least an hour for two weeks. With not so serious burns, it may take only one week, in my experience. I arranged the treatments with my work schedule (author/interviewer's note: Chiyoko Sensei had a stationery store and treated her clients during the store hours. When a customer came in she interrupted the treatment for a moment, only to continue later on).

I had clients that came five to six times per week. Others came once a week only, or once a month. There is no rule for the amount of treatments needed; it depends upon the individual case. In any case, you treat the client until the byosen is gone; therefore, the treatment length and duration must be adjusted to what is needed. It also depends upon the illness. When the client feels good again, you can stop. My clients kept coming to me until I told them one day that there was no need to continue anymore.

Questions about Hayashi Sensei (more information on page 83)

Question: What do you know about Hayashi Sensei's family background?
Answer: I, personally, knew his wife, Chie Sensei, and I know that they had children. But that's all.

Question: Do you know which religion he belonged to? (This question is about which Buddhist School he belonged to)
Answer: No

Question: Do you know where he was born, what his parents' names were, and where he went to School/ University?
Answer: No, I don't know, but we are in the process of finding this information. (See the chapter on Hayashi Sensei on page 83). Hayashi Sensei was from Niigata Prefecture.

Question: Why was your uncle interested in Reiki, in the first place?
Answer: I guess he was curious and was interested in spirituality.

Question: How did he hear about Hayashi Sensei?
Answer: I don't know.

Question: How did he help Hayashi Sensei?
Answer: He was convinced of the power of Reiki, and he spread it with many people in the countryside who were interested.

Question: When, and how, did you first meet Hayashi Sensei?
Answer: I met him in Daishoji. He came to hold a workshop that my uncle had organized for him.

Question: When did you learn Reiki from him?
Answer: I participated in Hayashi Sensei's Reiju Kai in April of the year Showa 13 (1938).

Question: Please tell us about the workshops with Hayashi Sensei that you took part in.
Answer: My first impression of Hayashi Sensei was that he was tall and well-dressed. He was cultured and was a (ex) Naval officer. I admired him. He repeated again, and again, that the human being was the crown of existence and should behave and live according to this.

Question: How many students took part in the training?
Answer: We were about ten people.

Question: How long did the training take?
Answer: The workshop took five days. In the mornings, we worked from 10:00-12:00 PM. Then, we took a lunch break and continued until around 2:00 PM. We finished around 5:00 PM. I was there for five days and learned Shoden and Okuden.

Question: What was the price of the workshop?
Answer: Shoden and Okuden cost 50 Yen.

Question: What would that be in today's value?
Answer: In those days, a teacher received 30 Yen per month. By today's standards, that would be about 400,000-500,000 Yen (about $4,000-$5,000 US Dollars). It was very expensive. You also had to take five whole days off work, and that was impossible for most people. Therefore, his students came from a certain social class. Moreover, one could only take part in the training if one had been properly introduced to Hayashi Sensei or Sugano

Sensei by someone who already knew him or her well. The person who had introduced you was of extreme importance.

Question: Was anyone able to learn Shoden and Okuden together right away, or did some people have to wait in between the degrees?
Answer: It was not easy to get accepted.

Question: Was it possible for anyone to become a Shihan?
Answer: At that time, there were only two of them. Hayashi Sensei and my uncle.

Question: What were the prerequisites, and was there some sort of test?
Answer: My uncle was Hayashi Sensei's organizer (author/interviewer's note: Later on, I found out that someone who wanted to become a Shihan was expected to spread Reiki and to organize workshops for his teacher. There was no formal Teacher's training—it was done in private).

Question: How much did the Shihan Training cost?
Answer: I am sure that it did cost something, but I don't know how much.

Question: Was the Shihan permitted to begin teaching right after his graduation?
Answer: The Shihans had to assist Hayashi Sensei before they were permitted to work on their own.

Question: Where did Hayashi Sensei hold his workshops?
Answer: Sometimes, the workshops took place at the house of one of my relatives. At other times, we did it at our house. It required quite a bit of space, and, therefore, the workshops were always held in the spacious homes of the wealthy.

Question: What was the workshop schedule like? How many days and how many hours did you work?
Answer: Five days, 50 Yen, about six hours per day.

Question: How often did you meet Hayashi Sensei?
Answer: About 15-20 times.

Question: What kind of person was he? Was he friendly, strict, humorous, philosophical, serious or playful?
Answer: He was a good person. He was dignified and trustworthy. He was one who was above the clouds. (This is a Japanese term describing someone

who is spiritually evolved, close to the gods who live above the clouds). He was tall and good looking, sophisticated and genuine.

Question: What kind of person was his wife, Chie?
Answer: She was loving and kind. She was a good woman.

Question: Do you remember any conversation you had with one of them, no matter how superficial it may have been? Please tell us.
Answer: I was still in school back then, and too shy to speak with them!

Question: Do you know how many Shihans Hayashi Sensei taught? We have heard that it was thirteen in 1938. This is what it says on Takata Sensei's certificate. Do you remember their names?
Answer: If I remember correctly, there were four in our group. Two of them were my aunt and uncle, but I don't remember the names of the others.

Question: Was there a clear hierarchy between students who held either Shoden, Okuden and those who were Shihans?
Answer: There was no such thing in Ishikawa. Reiki has nothing to do with Shukyo (sectarianism, cult).

Question: Did Hayashi Sensei work by himself, or did he have assistants?
Answer: He came twice a year, once in the spring and then again in the autumn. After his death, his wife Chie continued to come to us. He always traveled alone, but he had local assistants—those who organized the workshops for him.

Question: Did Hayashi Sensei travel a lot? Do you know where else he taught?
Answer: He was on the road a lot, but I don't know where else he taught (author's note: later on, Tadao Sensei found out that he taught in many other prefectures).

Question: Did Hayashi Sensei perform the Reiju by himself, or was it done the same way it is done nowadays, with several Shihans?
Answer: They always gave Reiju with the two of them, Hayashi Sensei and my uncle, who was the organizer. They must have practiced that.

Question: When did Hayashi Sensei break away from the Usui Reiki Ryoho Gakkai?
Answer: I only know that we learned Usui Reiki Ryoho from him …

Question: What sort of people were his students? From which social group did they come from?

Answer: The participants in Daishoji were wealthy. They were business people, housewives (from wealthy families) and midwives. I don't know anything about the other parts of the country that Hayashi Sensei taught in.

Question: Were there any well-known personalities?

Answer: Not in Ishikawa.

Question: Where did Hayashi Sensei work?

Answer: He came to Ishikawa from Tokyo, that's all I know.

Question: Did he practice Western medicine?

Answer: He was not against medical science and also endorsed thermal therapy.

Question: Did he practice Reiki exclusively after his retirement from the navy?

Answer: As far as I know, he did nothing but Reiki.

Question: Do you know why he took his own life?

Answer: He worked for the good of humanity. He healed his fellowman, and in the war, he would have had to kill. For an officer, there was no other way, except taking his own life.

Question: There are rumors that Hayashi Sensei may have had an affair with Takata Sensei. Do you know anything about that?

Answer: This is not appropriate for a Naval Officer. I find this highly unlikely.

Question: Who took over the Hayashi Reiki Kenkyukai after Hayashi Sensei's death?

Answer: After his death, his wife Chie took over the leadership of the Institute. This is another indication that there was nothing personal between him and Takata Sensei. Chie Sensei never said anything in this respect (author's note: if an affair between Hayashi Sensei and Takata Sensei had been the reason for his suicide, Chie Sensei would never have taken over the Association).

Question: What happened to the Institute after his death?

Answer: Chie Sensei took over the presidency, but I don't know much about it, because we lived in Manchuria then.

Question: Are there any others alive today who learned from Hayashi Sensei and his wife, or from the other Shihans?
Answer: Not that I know. But, those who had become Shihans back then, must be using Reiki as a home remedy in their families, for sure. I am not aware of any of them teaching in public.

Practical Questions

Question: How long were the workshops with Hayashi Sensei? How many days and how many hours per day did he work?
Answer: Five days, six or seven hours per day.

Question: How many participants were usually present?
Answer: All together, there were 15-20 people. Those who had learned before came again to repeat. Additionally, Hayashi Sensei held meetings for the members of the group only (Reiki Share Group).

Question: Did he always teach Shoden and Okuden together in one block?
Answer: When he came to Ishikawa, this is how it was done. Whether he did this differently elsewhere, I don't know (author/interviewer's note: later on, we found out that he taught Shoden and Okuden together when away from home. He did this because he did not want to make his students wait until his return the next year. When teaching at the Institute headquarters in Tokyo, he taught Shoden and Okuden separately).

Question: In which degree were the symbols taught?
Answer: One symbol was taught in Shoden, two in Okuden.

Question: When was the distant healing taught?
Answer: On the final day of the workshop.

Question: Did Hayashi Sensei advertise for his workshops? If so, how? Or, was it all done by word of mouth?
Answer: You had to be properly introduced by someone from the group. This created mutual trust, and that enabled you to participate in the workshop. All of this happened by word of mouth.

Question: Did Hayashi Sensei give public lectures on Reiki and, perhaps, other subjects?
Answer: He gave Reiki treatments, but I don't think that he gave public lectures.

End of the interview

List of References

All the photographs in this book that are not mentioned below were taken by Frank Arjava Petter. The calligraphies of the Reiki Kanji on the pages 10-15 are also done by him.

The gorgeous Japanese calligraphies of the Kanjis for Love, Soul, Truth, Gratitude, Transformation and Devotion on the pages 4, 24, 29, 117, 151 and 177 were done by Hiroko Arakawa.

Photo 7: Utako Shimoda, *public domain, Internet*
Photo 17: Count Shinpei Goto, *public domain, Internet*
Photo 23: The Meiji-Emperor, *Windpferd Oberstdorf, from the archives of Frank Arjava Petter*
Photo 24: After the great Kanto Earthquake, *postcards from the archives of Frank Arjava Petter*
Photo 25: Ushida Sensei, *with the kind permission of Tadao Yamaguchi*
Photo 32: Usui Sensei in Shizuoka, *with the kind permission of T. Oishi*
Photo 33: Signing of the International Peace Treaty in San Francisco, *with the kind permission of the McArthur Memorial Archives, Norfolk, VA*
Photo 34: Usui Sensei and his Shihans, a few weeks before his death in 1926, *with the kind permission of Tadao Yamaguchi*
Photo 35: *Hayashi Sensei, with* the kind permission of Tadao Yamaguchi
Photo 37: Calligraphy of the Gokai by Ushida Sensei, *with the kind permission of T. Oishi*
Photo 38: Watanabe Sensei, *with the kind permission of the University of Toyama Faculty of Economics*
Photo 39: Wanami Sensei, *with the kind permission of the Wanami Family*
Photo 40: Chiyoko Yamaguchi with Hayashi Sensei in 1938, *with the kind permission of Tadao Yamaguchi*
Photo 41: Hayashi Sensei in Hawaii, *with the kind permission of Tadao Yamaguchi*
Photo 42: Ogawa Sensei, *with the kind permission of F. Ogawa*
Photo 43: Ogawa Sensei's certificates, *with the kind permission of F. Ogawa*
Photo 87: Nao Deguchi, *public domain, Internet*
Photo 88: Onisaburo Deguchi, *public domain, Internet*
Photo 89: Mokichi Okada, *public domain, Internet*
Photo 90: Haruchika Noguchi, *public domain, Internet*
Photo 94: Gizo Tomabechi, *public domain, Internet*

Photo: Elvira Willsch

About the Author

Author, Frank Arjava Petter, has been actively involved in the area of self-development and Reiki internationally for many years. He is acknowledged worldwide as a pioneer in the revival movement of the original Japanese Reiki tradition. Having lived in Japan for twelve years, he knows the language and culture well, and he draws from those close contacts, but above all, from his own wealth of experience in the practice and teaching of Reiki, which has always been sourced by his tireless, inquiring mind and enormous dedication to the possibilities of Reiki. Arjava travels extensively and conducts public lectures and workshops worldwide. His best selling books have been translated into sixteen languages so far.

Arjava lives on beautiful Lesvos Island in Greece, with his wife, Georgia Bhakti, and their two children, Christina Amrita and Alexis.

His previous titles available from Lotus Press Publications, Twin Lakes. WI, are "Reiki Fire", "Reiki—the Legacy of Dr. Usui", "The Original Reiki Handbook of Dr. Mikao Usui", "The Spirit of Reiki", "Reiki—Best Practices" and "The Hayashi Reiki Manual".

You can contact Arjava directly through his website at www.ReikiDharma.com and subscribe to his online newsletter free of charge.

By Dr. Mikao Usui and Frank A. Petter

By Frank Arjava Petter

The Original Reiki Handbook
For the first time available outside of Japan:
The Traditional Usui Reiki Ryoho Treatment Positions and Numerous Reiki Techniques for Health and Well-Being

This book will show you the original hand positions from Dr. Usui's handbook. It has been illustrated with 100 colored photos to make it easier to understand. The hand positions for a great variety of health complaints have been listed in detail, making it a valuable reference work for anyone who practices Reiki. Now that the original book has been translated into English, Dr. Usui's hand positions and healing techniques can be studied directly for the first time. Whether you are an initiate or a master, if you practice Reiki you can expand your knowledge dramatically as you follow in the footsteps of a great healer.

80 pages, 100 photos, $14.95
ISBN: 978-0-9149-5557-3

Reiki–The Legacy of Dr. Usui
Rediscovered documents on the origins and developments of the Reiki system, as well as new aspects of the Reiki Energy

A great deal has been written and said to date about the history of Reiki and his founder. Now Frank Ajarva Petter a Reiki-Master, who lives in Japan has come across documents that quote Mikao Usui's original words. Questions that his students asked and he answered throw light upon Usui's very personal view of the teachings. Materials meant as the basis for his student's studies round off the entire work. A family tree of the Reiki successors is also included here. In a number of essays, Frank Arjava Petter also discusses topics related to Reiki and the viewpoints of an independent Reiki teacher.

128 pages, $12.95
ISBN: 978-0-9149-5556-6

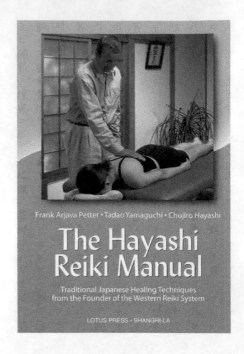

By Frank Ajarva Petter

Reiki Fire
New Information about the Origins of the Reiki Power – A Complete Manual

The origin of Reiki has come to be surrounded by many stories and myths. The author, an independent Reiki Master practices in Japan, immerses it in a new light as he traces Usui-san's path back through time with openness and devotion. He meets Usui's descendants and climbs th holy mountain of his enlightenment. Reiki, shaped by Shintoism, is a Buddhist expression of Qigong, whereby Qigong depicts the teaching of life energy in its original sense. An excellent textbook, fresh and rousing in its spiritual perspective, this is an absolutely practical Reiki guide. The heart, the body, the mind, and the esoteric background are all covered here.

128 pages, $12.95
ISBN:978-0-9149-5550-4

By Frank Arjava Petter, Tadao Yamaguchi and Chujiro Hayashi

The Hayashi Reiki Manual
Traditional Japanese Healing Techniques from the Founder of thc Western Reiki System

Dr. Chujiro Hayashi is the highly renowned student of Reiki Founder, Dr. Mikao Usui. Dr. Hayashi developed his own style of Reiki and became the teacher of Hawayo Takata, who introduced Reiki to the West.
However Dr. Hayashi also taught Reiki to Japanese students such as young Chiyoko Yamaguchi, born in 1920. Frank Arjava Petter was allowed to become her student and learn the original Hayashi Reiki system from her.
The manual presents the story of Dr. Hayashi, newly researched and sensationally illustrated with previously unpublished archive photos, Reiki techniques never taught in the West before, and specific documents such as the original certificated of Dr. Hayashi.

full color, 112 pages, $19.95
ISBN: 978-9149-5575-7